Effective Conflict Management

CEDR

Published by
ICSA Information & Training Ltd
16 Park Crescent
London W1B 1AH

© ICSA Information & Training Ltd, 2013

The right of CEDR to be identified as author of this Work has been asserted by them in accordance with sections 77 and 78 of the Copyright, Designs and Patents Act 1988.

All rights reserved. No part of this publication may be reproduced, stored in a retrieval system, or transmitted, in any form, or by any means, electronic, mechanical, photocopying, recording or otherwise, without prior permission, in writing, from the publisher.

Typeset by Hands Fotoset, Woodthorpe, Nottingham

Printed by Hobbs the Printers Ltd, Totton, Hampshire

British Cataloguing in Publication Data
A catalogue record for this book is available from the British Library.

ISBN 978-1-86072-541-8

Contents

Foreword v
Introduction vii
Contributors x
Acronyms and abbreviations xvi
Acknowledgements xvii

1 Common sense and sensibility – conflicting priorities for the company secretary
Graham Massie 1

A universal condition 1
The cost of conflict 2
Is there any good news? 4
Advice for company secretaries 5
Conclusion 10

2 The company secretary and board involvement in organisational conflict and employment disputes
Fiona Colquhoun 14

The key role of the company secretary 14
Board involvement in employment and workplace disputes 15
When disputes become personal 18
Disputes on pay and remuneration 20
What conflict management skills and models are most useful to a company secretary? 22

Using conflict management skills – key models 24
Dealing with crisis situations arising from conflict and disputes 26
Case study: building broken trust among trustees 28

3 Avoiding boardroom warfare – remedying board disputes
James South 35

Boardrooms: an incubator of conflict 35
Why might you get warfare in the boardroom? 37
Boardroom warfare: common causes 38
Tools for resolving board disputes 39
Case study: the family boardroom fallout 48

4 Managing emotional turbulence – the psychology of organisational conflict
Dr Karl Mackie CBE and Tracey Fox 58

'Who is the company secretary?' 58
The company secretary's role in managing emotions 59
The brain in conflict situations 60
Reconciling science and society 64
Global opportunities, high stakes 66
What can a company secretary do to manage turbulent emotions? 68

The practice – how can a good company secretary respond?   72
Case study: handling high emotions   74

5 Working with powerful people in a dispute context
Eileen Carroll QC (Hon) and Ranse Howell   **83**

Case study: managing a CEO's exit   83
Working with the past – preparation   90
Dealing with the present – managing emotions   94
A closer look at Fisher and Shapiro   94
Considering the future – breakdown and rebuilding of trust   97
Conclusion   100

6 Projected success – how not to let conflict undermine critical projects
Andy Grossman   **103**

Introduction   103
Adapting to a changing world   103
Model clauses   105
Creating an 'ADR culture'   108
Building mediation into projects   111
Case study: nipping conflict in the bud with a contract clause   115

7 The world outside – managing conflict with external stakeholders and clients
Gregory Hunt and Andy Rogers   **121**

Introduction   121
Reputation, reputation, reputation   121
Two approaches to stakeholder conflict   122
Handling conflict   123
Who are my audiences?   123
Preventing stakeholder conflict   124
Working in a vacuum?   125
Business communication scenarios   126
Dynamics affecting communication with stakeholders   127
Handling conflict with stakeholders   132

8 The potential for conflict over ownership – who is in control?
Andy Rogers and Gemma Oke   **150**

Introduction   150
Owners: managing the managers or relinquishing responsibility?   152
Two levels of dialogue   153
Essential information   153
Tone and openness   154
Types of shareholders and examples of disputes   154
Summary   169

Appendices   171
Bibliography   173
Web directory   176
Index   177

Foreword – Realisation and preparation

There is no walk of life that is free from conflict. This is usually regarded with resignation – something that will inevitably sap energy, enthusiasm, time and resources. But it need not be so. If conflict is anticipated, properly prepared for and appropriately dealt with, it can have a positive outcome while minimising any negatives. In business, this can be a considerable competitive advantage. In all undertakings, it can increase efficiency.

It is with large-scale disputes that the business case for good conflict management practices is clearest. Some conflict at some stage is inevitable. So it makes sense to plan for it rather than simply react when it happens. This requires an appropriate organisational culture and embedding conflict management into the organisation's risk structure. It should embrace conflicts arising at all levels in the organisation – and particularly those potentially long-running disputes which gravitate to board level.

The Centre for Effective Dispute Resolution (CEDR) was founded in 1990 with support from the Confederation of British Industry (CBI). At the time, alternative dispute resolution existed in UK business only in the imported textbooks produced by American business scholars and theorists – and like so many 'good ideas', the concept of alternative dispute resolution was dismissed by some as incompatible with the needs and pace of the business world. I hope that after 23 years of cutting and polishing, CEDR's time has come to shine as a jewel in the City's economic and business crown. Its evolution from a hotline in Deputy CEO Eileen Carroll's work office to Europe's largest independent ADR body eloquently testifies to its business, and indeed human, utility. At its inception, CEDR was an idea ahead of its time. Now, it is the embodiment of it – the simple message that good can come of well-managed conflict.

This book is as necessary as it is timely, as our 'Good Conflict Management' survey carried out in conjunction with the Institute of Chartered Secretaries and Administrators (ICSA) highlights with clear detail. Over half of the people CEDR and ICSA surveyed say that they have seen conflicts increase in their working lives over the past 12–18 months, and a staggering 91% of people surveyed agreed to varying extents that workplace conflicts are costing UK businesses. This represents a sad loss of productivity and potential, made all the more poignant for the fact that with ways to manage conflict effectively, these figures need not be half as high as they are.

I hope that this book will become an essential text for management in a wide range of private and public undertakings and that it will find a place in every boardroom.

Sir Peter Middleton GCB, Chairman of CEDR (2004–2011)

Sir Peter Middleton is UK Chairman of Marsh & McLennan Companies, Chairman of Marsh Ltd, Chairman of Mercer Ltd, and former Chairman of the Centre for Effective Dispute Resolution. He was Chairman of Camelot Group plc from 2004 to 2010; a Director, Chairman and Deputy Chairman of United Utilities from 1994–2007; and a Board member of OJSC Mobile Telesystems from 2005–2007, Bass plc from 1992–2001 and General Accident (later CGU) from 1992–1995.

Sir Peter became Group Chairman of Barclays Bank plc in April 1999 and retired in August 2004. He joined Barclays in 1991 as Group Deputy Chairman and Executive Chairman of BZW, became Chairman of Barclays Capital following the reorganisation of BZW in October 1997 and was Group Chief Executive from November 1998 until October 1999. He was also President of the British Bankers' Association from 2004–2006 and a member of the National Institute for Economic Research from 1996–2007. Sir Peter spent nearly 30 years at HM Treasury, working closely with nine Chancellors, and was Permanent Secretary from 1983 to 1991. He also chaired a review of the British Film Industry for the Thatcher Government and a review of Civil Justice for the Blair Government.

Introduction

'…all the good-to-great companies had a penchant for intense dialogue. Phrases like "loud debate", "heated discussions" and "healthy conflict" peppered the articles and interview transcripts from all the companies'.

– Jim Collins, *Good to Great*

'Hard times arouse an instinctive desire for authenticity.'

– Coco Chanel

Mme Chanel may not have foreseen a time in which her luxury designs are the stuff of counterfeit proliferation, but I feel that for our current business climate, her comment here is absolutely accurate. We have in the past decade run a full gamut of boom and bust, and in the wake of the Great Recession, the certainties of the past are not so solid. Now is a time of great opportunity and change – we have a chance to reclaim honesty, truthfulness and imagination for business as we reassess the how, when and why of our corporate lives.

Grasping this opportunity fully means that we will be forced to look again at difficult or uncomfortable issues such as how we handle conflicts and disputes. Most people will have experienced conflict situations in business, perhaps at a board meeting or with shareholders, and in many of those situations conflict has been seen as something bad – something that saps energy, enthusiasm, time and resources. This does not have to be the case. As necessity is the mother of invention, so conflict can be the crucible for innovation and transformation: if it is anticipated, acknowledged, and appropriately administered to. The case studies accompanying each chapter will testify to this – drawn from real-life events, each study proves that the company secretary is perfectly placed to make a real difference to how organisational conflicts are managed in real time and in the future.

I believe you cannot be in business without experiencing conflicts and having disputes – this is true in the Boardroom, the AGM hall and on the 'shop floor'. I notice a wry sense of democracy surrounding the conflict experience, even in the more 'David and Goliath' situations: everyone's heart races, everyone wants to be heard, and everyone feels they are in the right. Chapter 4 explores the psychology of conflict in more detail, looking at how we all share the same biological, and many of the psychological, responses to conflict.

With larger-scale disputes too, there is a clear business case for good conflict management as a risk manager and minimiser. If we acknowledge that conflict of some kind will inevitably befall our businesses; we can take steps to plan for it. This shift from reaction to anticipation should also include a shift in focus from individuals and personalities to processes: as Chapter 6 shows, having the right processes in place can make the difference between the success or failure of a business or large-scale project. My suggestion may appear strange – after all, conflict is very much about people – but some disputes can engulf entire companies and projects for years after the original incident, and have escalated merely because of the absence of an early effective handling process. It is not unusual for disputes involving external stakeholders, for example, to be bequeathed like family silverware from board to board and CEO to CEO. While an individual, or set of individuals, may be particularly adept at managing an ongoing conflict or dispute, the overall effect is detrimental to the business if and when it is no longer able to access these skills and talents. Introducing appropriate systems for conflict management, and nudging organisational culture change towards favouring vigilance and early intervention, is a stronger way of ensuring 'albatross disputes' can be handled successfully and intelligently at board level. Good corporate governance demands effective conflict governance.

All board members share fiduciary responsibility, but the company secretary perhaps more so. The company secretary role often requires a broad knowledge and experience base, as well as finely tuned antennae for factors that could jeopardise the business' operational capability, moral standing and its ability to pull together. It makes sense, therefore, that the company secretary is the person in a business serving on a board who thinks about a long-term conflict management strategy. Chapters 2 and 3 explore these responsibilities and qualities, and their applications, in more detail, and give a clear set of tools for organisations and individuals to handle conflict successfully.

Certainly, the evidence of experience suggests that the costs of poorly managed conflicts, and ensuing disputes, are far greater than one's initial comprehension or expectation. A public dispute with an external stakeholder might depress a company's share price; it will also be hideously expensive to finance ensuing litigation because any specific financial provision for this might be interpreted as a sign of guilt. Landing in court over an exiting board member's compensation package could take you years, and runs the risk of your former colleague revealing facts and 'home truths' you might prefer to keep private rather than have aired in a very public forum. A court judgement may fall in your favour, but this may not assuage hurt feelings or point to a pathway for you to work together in the future. Chapters 5 and 7 deal particularly with these issues, exploring the significance of reputation and trust for individuals and organisations in the public eye.

There are of course many reasons to be cheerful about good conflict management and its many benefits, and I hope that after reading this book you will be as convinced of them as I am. Good conflict management reduces instances of conflict and limits conflict contagion: this creates immediate improvements to morale and colleague relationships. Time and energy not spent on pursuing conflict can instead be redeployed to exciting, constructive, innovative activities that add measurable value for colleagues and customers alike. Clear conflict management policies rooted in the board's work practices also indicate a dedication to social and economic responsibility, two factors that are becoming increasingly important to business reputation and employee retention. And, of course, proactive effective conflict management results in lower costs – a benefit that everyone, particularly the business owner groups discussed in Chapter 8, can appreciate.

Conflict is inevitable in business and among your board members; the kind of conflict that unfolds is not. 'Strife-sense', added to common sense, can be a powerful organisational competence. The power to change is in your hands, through holding this book and through what you choose to do with the information herein. A product of collaboration and cooperation itself, I hope that this book will form part of your 'essential texts' shelf for many years to come, and a springboard to effective action by corporate leaders.

Dr Karl Mackie CBE, CEDR Chief Executive

Contributors

Eileen Carroll QC (Hon) is CEDR's founder and one of the world's most experienced and successful commercial mediators, as well as the organisation's Deputy CEO. A litigation lawyer by background, she became a partner in a major London law firm in 1987 where she served on the management committee and acted as an international strategy partner. In over 20 years of legal practice, she has worked with multinational corporations in Europe, the Far East, India and the United States in a wide range of areas, including engineering, insurance and reinsurance, shipping, aviation, copyright, IT, libel, acquisitions and a range of negligence and other commercial claims. She spent ten years working intensively with an American client, spending time with a US firm in San Francisco. She was also one of the first European accredited mediators, and has mediated thousands of cases covering a full spectrum of clients and claim values. Eileen was recently appointed Vice Chair of the International Mediation Institute's Independent Standards Commission. She is a member of various international panels including the Council of Distinguished Advisors of the Straus Institute for Dispute Resolution at Pepperdine University, California, and the CPR mediator panel in New York. Eileen has been invited to give addresses and speak at many international events, including the World Bank, Harvard Business School, and the Organisation for Economic Co-operation and Development (OECD); and has made various guest appearances on national broadcasts. Recent publications include *International Mediation – the Art of Business Diplomacy*, co-written with Karl Mackie CBE.

In 2013, Eileen was made an Honorary QC, an award conferred on individuals who have made notable contributions to the legal system outside of advocacy in the courts.

Fiona Colquhoun is a Director of CEDR and has been a CEDR Solve Panel Mediator since 2004. She has an excellent reputation for a wide range of commercial, employment and workplace mediations, facilitations, independent reviews, investigations, and other neutral interventions. Clients have praised her versatility and unique mixture of business, corporate, ADR and coaching credentials describing her as their 'first choice', 'very impressive' and 'an exemplary mediator'. Fiona also coaches individuals through challenging organisational change and difficult interpersonal situations.

Fiona has a strong business background, having previously worked at plc board level in the Telecommunications and IT sector for almost 20 years. Previously, Fiona held senior positions in the public sector, as a Director and Non-Executive Director within the National Health Service (NHS).

Fiona's clients are from varied sectors including global and top FTSE companies, the public sector including central government and the NHS, professional partnerships and many others. Her industry experience has given her invaluable expertise in general business projects, mergers and acquisitions, disposals, partnerships, complex employment, change management and pension issues.

Fiona is also a Henley Business School coach, an ACAS arbitrator, a Harvard Business School alumna, and a CEDR Employment and Workplace Lead Faculty.

Tracey Fox joined CEDR in 2002 and is a Consultant, Mediator and Trainer within the Skills team. A psychologist by training, Tracey worked in various clinical and neurobiological rehabilitation positions before combining her interests in people and organisational behaviour in her work with CEDR. With a BSc Psychology (Hons) and an MSc in Occupational and Organisational Psychology, Tracey has particular expertise in the areas of change management, organisational development and performance management. She is qualified to deliver and interpret Level A and B psychometric instruments (personality and ability) including the Myers-Briggs Type Indicator, the Hogan Development Survey, Belbin and the Thomas-Kilmann Instrument. Tracey has designed and delivered courses on the Psychological Underpinnings of Mediation, Conflict Management and Employment and Mediation Skills, both in the UK and internationally. Additionally, she has responsibility for conflict coaching, was a contributor to and project manager of the *CEDR Mediation Handbook* (4th Edition) and has been a judge on the International Negotiation Competition. Tracey is a member of the British Psychological Society, the Association of Business Psychologists, a Conciliator for the Funeral Arbitration Service and an elected member to the Special Group in Coaching Psychology.

Dr Andrzej (Andy) Grossman has been a senior director of CEDR since he joined in 1999. An architect by original qualification, Andy spent the early part of his career with an international structural and civil engineering consultancy based in London. He then joined a niche architectural practice as a project architect specialising in nuclear medicine installations before establishing his own firm. His experience covers work with private, commercial and public sector clients on residential, hospital, airport and urban development projects. As one of CEDR's senior trainers, he has trained hundreds of mediators around the world and has worked with international agencies including the Council of Europe, the International Finance Corporation and the United Nations High Commissioner for Refugees. His development work at CEDR has involved production of a number of CEDR publications including its ADR Guide for Public Authorities, ADR Guide for Local Authorities in Public Private Partnerships and Dispute Resolution Procedure for PFI and Long Term Contracts. Andy is a member of the International Association for Contract and Commercial Management and a member of the Civil Mediation Council (UK). He holds a Doctorate of Professional Studies in Commercial Mediation Development.

Ranse Howell is Head of CEDR's Negotiation Academy and has been instrumental in the design of the CEDR Certificate in Advanced Negotiation, which is a six-day reflective learning course designed to develop and enhance an individual's negotiation strategy. Ranse has assisted clients in developing a broad range of mediation and negotiation skills in the UK, USA, Singapore, Pakistan, China, Bulgaria, Romania, Croatia, Finland, Norway, Georgia, Moldova, Luxembourg, Poland and Greece.

Ranse has had the opportunity to present 'Master Class' and conference presentations both nationally and internationally and has written extensively on ADR, and these have included: 'Debriefing the debrief', *Rethinking Negotiation Series*, DRI Press Vol. 4, 2013; 'Managing Conflict Effectively in Asset Management', *Rail Technology Magazine*, 2011; *Emotional Intelligence and Projects*, N. Clarke and R. Howell, Project Management Institute Press, 2010; 'Two to Tango', *Venturing Beyond the Classroom*, 2010; 'Railway Strategy Comes at a Price', *Railway Strategies*, September 2009; 'Prepared for Conflict', *The Growing Business Handbook*, Kogan Press 2009; 'We Came, We Trained', *Rethinking Negotiation Teaching*, DRI Press, 2009.

Ranse trained as a mediator in New York and California, and received his CEDR accreditation, in the UK in 2006, and is also a member of the CEDR mediation skills training faculty.

Ranse received his Juris Doctor (JD) from the City University of New York, NY and is continuing his doctoral studies in business administration (DBA) at CalSouthern, CA. He received his Master of Law (LLM) from the Straus Institute at Pepperdine University, CA. Ranse also holds a Master of Social Work (MSW) and a Bachelor's degree (BFA) from Temple University, PA.

Gregory Hunt is a member of the CEDR Executive Team, and leads CEDR's Business Development Unit – a new team supporting and coordinating all business development, sales, marketing and client relations activities across the organisation.

Most of Gregory's time is spent supporting the development and promotion of CEDR's core business units – CEDR Solve, CEDR Skills and IDRS Ltd – in the UK and Ireland, whilst also overseeing development of the business across the rest of Europe and working with colleagues on initiatives in other jurisdictions such as Hong Kong, Dubai, Dohar and Singapore. He also works closely with the CEDR Foundation, promoting CEDR's charitable mission.

Before CEDR, Gregory held several senior positions at the CIArb and specialised in developing bespoke ADR arrangements with businesses across many sectors. He was the UK government representative at the EC on consumer ADR and has developed more than 100 consumer and commercial ADR schemes – saving industry millions of pounds in legal fees and lost management time by providing parties in dispute with cost-effective, time-saving alternatives to litigation.

Gregory is a CEDR Accredited mediator and member of CEDR's Mediator Panels in the UK and Ireland.

Dr Karl Mackie CBE is the Chief Executive of CEDR and recognized as one of the leading mediators in Europe an expert on mediation, conflict and negotiation. He has undertaken some of CEDR Solve's most difficult cases including cases pioneering the use of mediation in new sectors. These have included mediations and mini-trials of disputes up to £1 billion in value. Sectors include international, commercial and construction disputes and claims in financial services, information technology, engineering and energy, partnerships and family businesses, education, national and local government, employment, insurance, telecommunications and media, company law and corporate acquisitions, and industry association conflicts. Parties to these disputes have included multinational and FTSE 100 companies, national governments and others.

In addition to involvement with CEDR's services, he has been a mediator/arbitrator for ACAS (the Advisory Conciliation and Arbitration Service – the UK statutory employment relations agency) since 1980. He is a Fellow of the Chartered Institute of Arbitrators, a barrister and psychologist by training and a former partner in a business strategy consultancy drawn from several UK business schools. He is Chief Adjudicator of the Ofsted Independent Complaints Adjudication Service and an Ombudsman in Euronext Liffe financial services disputes. He is on the Advisory Council for the All-Party Parliamentary Group on Conflict, a former Vice Chairman of the Civil Mediation Council and has been Special Professor in ADR at the Universities of Westminster and Birmingham.

Karl was made a Commander of the British Empire (CBE) in the Queen's Birthday Honours in 2010, for services to mediation.

Graham Massie is one of the most experienced accountant mediators in the UK. He is regularly approached by businesses and the public sector to act as independent chair for strategic discussions and deal-making negotiations. After qualifying as a Chartered Accountant, he spent ten years with KPMG in London where he ran a professional services department responsible for a broad cross-section of clients ranging from major plcs to small owner-managed businesses before joining CEDR in 1996. His current client portfolio includes working with a range of leading corporates, public sector bodies and international financial institutions to develop their in-house negotiation skills and conflict management systems. He also leads CEDR's research projects on 'Cutting the Cost of Conflict'; the role of Collaboration in Tax Disputes with HM Revenue & Customs; and Benchmarking of Organisational Conflict Management Performance. Graham is author of 'The Mediation Audits', a biennial survey of the UK commercial mediation profession; a co-editor of *The EU Mediation Atlas*, a survey of practice and regulation within each member state of the EU (published by Lexis Nexis); and has regularly contributed a chapter on conflict management to *Managing Business Risk*, a practical guide to protecting businesses from risk, published annually by Kogan Page. He is also a regular trainer and speaker on negotiation and conflict management issues.

In addition to his client and project work, Graham is currently CEDR's Chief Operating Officer, responsible for overseeing key financial, operational and client projects, and is its Company Secretary.

Gemma Oke joined CEDR in 2012 and is part of CEDR's central Business Development team, specialising in communications. Her work largely centres on helping the Business Development team manage CEDR's media output and presence through print and online press outlets, with particular emphasis on content creation and digital media. Before joining CEDR, Gemma worked as a freelance and staff journalist, with particular experience in consumer finance reporting, alongside wider financial, economic and political reporting and commentary interests. She has written for an influential consumer finance website, and has been quoted widely in national print media. She graduated from Trinity College, Cambridge in 2011 with a BA (Hons) in English, and has acted as CEDR's in-house editor and project manager for this publication.

Andy Rogers is CEDR's Director of PR and Communications. He is a CEDR Accredited Mediator and has experience of mediation in contract, employment, property and probate disputes, with cases ranging from disputes between private individual parties through to large multinational organisations.

Andy represents CEDR on the Board of the Civil Mediation Council, the recognised authority in the country for all matters related to civil, commercial, workplace and other non-family mediation.

Prior to joining CEDR, from 1998 to 2005, Andy was a Senior Communications Account Director in two leading public relations consultancies, where he headed business units, advising private corporations and government bodies on managing their reputations. In this time he led numerous strategic campaigns for clients such as 3i plc, 3M plc, BIS (the Department for Trade and Industry), BTG plc, the Consumers' Association (*Which?*), Fujitsu plc, Motorola plc and RS Components and Electrocomponents plc. He has worked on and led projects in Canada, France, Germany, Ireland, Italy, Spain and the UK.

After graduating in 1990 from Wolverhampton, Andy became a broadcast journalist working for LBC Radio in London, before going on to work for IRN (Independent Radio News), the BBC and various Channel 4 production companies. In his career, Andy has authored numerous articles for publications ranging from *The Lawyer* to *FHM*.

Swapping the world of journalism for the business of communications, Andy spent two years with travel company Cosmos plc before spending four years in the telecoms and entertainment field as the PR Manager for Cable & Wireless Communications plc.

Andy is a Member of the Chartered Institute of Public Relations and has won two prestigious *PR Week Awards* for the Hero At Work campaign in 2004 and the Post-It Art for Schools Exhibition and Auction in 2000, which also won the global *IPRA Golden Award* for creativity.

James South is a Barrister and Solicitor of the High Court of New Zealand. He has over ten years' experience as mediator in a wide range of disputes in different contexts and jurisdictions; the first four years spent as a government-employed mediator for the New Zealand Ministry of Justice, during which time he mediated over 500 disputes. In 2000, James became a full-time CEDR employee and accredited mediator, and he now mediates regularly.

As CEDR's Director of Training and lead trainer of the CEDR training faculty, James has extensive experience in the training of mediators, lawyers, judges and other business professionals both in the UK and many other jurisdictions. Recent assignments include project Technical Director for the establishment of a court-based mediation pilot in Karachi, Pakistan, funded by the International Finance Corporation/World Bank 2006; Project Director for development of court-based mediation pilot in the Commercial Court of Zagreb, Croatia 2005/2006; design and delivery of a series of ADR awareness workshops for judges and lawyers in Macedonia, Bosnia and Herzegovina and Croatia 2004–2005; and Consultant trainer for a scoping visit to discuss the introduction of ADR into Zanzibar Civil Justice with Chief Justice, President of the Law Society and Attorney-General 2004.

He holds a Masters in Law (Distinction) in Dispute Prevention and Resolution from the University of Westminster, London and is currently a lecturer on the International Commercial Mediation module of the Masters programme at the University of Westminster. He wrote and lectured on the Negotiation/Mediation Course for undergraduates at the University of Westminster and has taught ADR at Birbeck College, University of London, Southbank University, Straus Institute for Dispute Resolution, Pepperdine University, Los Angeles, and the University of San Francisco.

Acronyms and abbreviations

ADR	alternative dispute resolution
BATNA	best alternative to a negotiated agreement
CDR	collaborative dispute resolution
CEDR	Centre for Effective Dispute Resolution
CEO	chief executive officer
CIPR	Chartered Institute of Public Relations
C-level	the highest corporate executive level
COO	chief operating officer
DIC	Dubai International Capital
EWHC	High Court of Justice
HMRC	Her Majesty's Revenue and Customs
HDS	Hogan Development Scale
REAL	Renewable Energy Assurance Ltd
SME	small and medium enterprise
SWOT	Strengths, Weaknesses, Opportunities and Threats
TEIQ	Thomas-Kilmann Emotional Intelligence Questionnaire
VC	venture capitalist
WATNA	worst alternative to a negotiated agreement

Acknowledgements

The seeds of inspiration for this book were first planted some 18 months ago, when Fiona Colquhoun and Tracey Fox – working with ICSA – began a conversation about producing a book on conflict management. Proving that talking really can get things done, the end result of that conversation is this publication of *Effective Conflict Management*.

Sir Peter Middleton's tenure as CEDR's Chairman was marked by dedication to the ADR cause, and we appreciate his generosity in contributing a Foreword.

CEDR's work with the International Finance Corporation on conflict in corporate governance has been useful in compiling the book, and we are grateful to have worked with them internationally on such a vital project in developing nations.

From the CEDR team, particular thanks goes to Gemma Oke for her work as in-house editor and project manager – her knowledge, skill and dedication have been invaluable.

CEDR is in the business of 'people', and its people are one of its great strengths. This book on *Effective Conflict Management* would not have been realised without the help, knowledge and support of so many people at CEDR, across the entire business. We would like to thank them for their contributions, their efforts and their care which have helped turn an idea into exciting reality.

The publishers would like to thank the following organisations:

Chapter 3: 'What Skills are needed for CG Dispute Resolution', module 1 of volume 3 of the 'Resolving Corporate Governance Disputes Toolkit'. Reproduced with the kind permission of Global Corporate Governance Forum/IFC.

Chapter 3: Toolkit 4: Resolving Corporate Governance Disputes, 'Volume 1: Rationale'. Reproduced with the kind permission of Global Corporate Governance Forum/IFC.

Chapter 4: Extracts and diagram from *Beyond Reason: Using Emotions As You Negotiate* by Roger Fisher and Daniel Shapiro, published by Random House Business Books. Reprinted by permission of The Random House Group Limited.

Chapter 5: Five core concerns diagram from *Beyond Reason: Using Emotions As You Negotiate* by Roger Fisher and Daniel Shapiro, published by Random House Business Books. Reproduced with the kind permission of Random House, London.

Chapter 7: Merrill-Reid Model of social styles. Reproduced with the kind permission of CRC press, London.

1
Common sense and sensibility – conflicting priorities for the company secretary

Graham Massie

The quality of canapés offered at law firm receptions has increased significantly in recent years. And so has the quality of conversation – at least to the extent that I don't have to explain my job and what the Centre for Effective Dispute Resolution (CEDR) is quite as often as I used to. But what hasn't changed, particularly when I'm talking to businesspeople – to company secretaries, finance directors, chief executives and chairmen, rather than simply to litigation lawyers – is what happens when I move into sales mode:

> 'So, tell me about your business – do you get involved in many disputes yourself?'
>
> 'Oh no, we don't really have disputes. It's not really my area as our lawyers deal with that sort of thing.'
>
> 'Really? So do you have any conflict in your organisation?'
>
> 'Oh yes, conflict – we have lots of that.'

And nine times out of ten, the non-verbal answer is even clearer – a thin smile and a resigned look as I see the guy recall an argument, a difficult colleague, or most often a simple reality of business life.

So what's going on here? When Sun Tzu's *Art of War* is required reading at all of the leading business schools, why is it that business managers shy away from the word 'dispute'? It's certainly not because they don't have any – or because it doesn't have any impact on their business.

A universal condition

Conflict is a fact of life even in the best-run organisation. It goes under many names – disagreement, disharmony, dispute, difficulty or difference – but the results of mismanaged conflict are the same: at best, unwelcome distraction from a heavy workload; at worst, damage that may threaten the very future of the organisation.

Managers meet conflicts and disputes in many different ways in organisational life – failures of suppliers to provide or customers to pay, employee grievances or non-performance, inter-departmental territorial arguments, breaches of intellectual or physical property rights, disagreements over corporate policy or practice either internally or with joint venture and alliance partners, disputes over allocation of risk and reward in projects, personality clashes, divergence of expectations and understandings.

Within an international business context, managers also have to deal with differences in cultural expectations and standards, problems of communication, divergence of decision-making, mismatched business goals, economic or business upheavals.

The cost of conflict

Poorly managed conflict costs money, creates uncertainty and degrades decision quality.

Furthermore, it pervades through an organisation's activities; its effect can be significant but is usually unmeasured; and no one is really designated to deal with it.

A 2005 research project by CEDR and law firm CMS Cameron McKenna gathered data from lawyers and business people involved in over 300 separate business disputes. We identified nine possible adverse consequences of business disputes and surveyed the extent to which each may have been significant. Remarkably, this revealed that in 80% of the disputes surveyed, at least one (but frequently more) of these consequences were described as being 'significant' or 'very significant' to the business.

Possible consequences of business disputes:

- Effects on company reputation
- Exposure in the public domain
- Effects on company morale
- Effects on personal reputation
- Damaged business relationships
- Lost customers
- Increased staff turnover
- Failure to meet targets
- Missed opportunities

I'm not sure I agree with the late business guru, Peter Drucker, who coined the phrase that 'you can't manage what you can't measure', but what I would say is that if you aren't trying to measure something, it's a pretty good indicator that you aren't even trying to manage it.

But one of the problems with corporate conflict is that the majority of the costs fall through the cracks of management responsibility. The company secretary or in-house lawyer may be accountable for the legal costs of disputes, but even here financial management leaves a lot to be desired – the 2005 Fulbright & Jaworski Litigation Trends Survey reported that 43% of corporate lawyers are unable to budget adequately for litigation costs.

And yet, the costs of conflict are huge. A 2006 study by CEDR revealed that conflict costs British business some £33 billion a year – and of that amount, less than a fifth relates to legal fees whilst the vast proportion can be categorised into three broad categories:

- Damaged relationships
- Tarnished reputations
- Lost productivity

Damaged relationships

Because of the way that most of us behave in conflict situations, disputes cause damaged business relationships, which in turn can lead to breakdowns in previously fruitful customer or supplier relationships, or to increased staff turnover.

And even where conflict does not result in a parting of the ways, its effect on day-to-day business efficiency can be debilitating. One of the universal symptoms of conflict (and, generally, one of its most common causes) is a breakdown in communications – just as spouses who are having a row tend not to talk to each other, managers and business colleagues fail to communicate well when there is tension or conflict in the relationship. And this behaviour can lead to failures to communicate vital information, possibly leading to missed opportunities and/or some key inputs to a decision being either suppressed or ignored.

Tarnished reputations

Evidence of our historical love of conflict as a spectator sport can be found in the ruins of the Coliseum, but today's corporate combat can be tracked from the comfort of your armchair, courtesy of the media.

However, you don't have to read too many news reports of corporate disputes to conclude that they really are 'a plague' on both 'houses', with even the winner's reputation often tarnished by what is revealed during the course of the battle. Whether it's the publicity about a harassment or discrimination case which harms both employer and claimant equally, or a professional negligence claim which reveals shortcomings on both sides, exposure in the public domain is frequently damaging to both personal and corporate reputations – damage that is usually described in the language of the brand or public relations consultants, but is often most visible in reductions in stock market value.

Have you ever heard of an organisation whose public reputation was enhanced by reports of its involvement in a significant dispute?

EFFECTIVE CONFLICT MANAGEMENT

Lost productivity

In their *Commercial Disputes Survey 2003*, accountants BDO Stoy Hayward identified the personal impact of disputes on senior management, with 46% admitting that their stress levels increased, many (24%) losing sleep over a dispute, and almost one in five even suffering from decreased motivation towards their own business.

Other forms of lost productivity are also commonplace in business conflict – CEDR's research shows that a typical £1 million value dispute will burn up over three years of line managers' time in trying to sort it out – that's time that takes them away from their real jobs, creating a cost of conflict which far outweighs the legal fees involved.

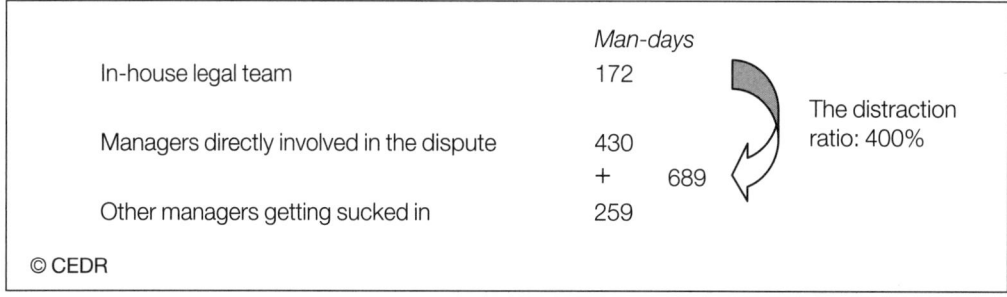

Figure 1.1: Time spent on a typical £1 million+ dispute

This distraction cost is one of the key hidden costs of corporate conflict. As our research shows, managers spend four times as much time as in-house counsel involved in a dispute, meaning that 80% of the cost of conflict comes out of management unit budgets. And since engagement in conflict isn't a line item in most managers' budgets, this means that the cost comes through in the form of reduced time available for other priorities.

Is there any good news?

There might be. Well-managed conflict can be productive, with a healthy disagreement often fuelling the cauldron of debate from which new ideas and innovation emerge. Conflicting views can lead to debate and refinement of solutions, or can act as an impetus for further information gathering, leading to more informed decisions. In fact, some of the healthiest companies have some of the most intense discussions.

> '…all the good-to-great companies had a penchant for intense dialogue. Phrases like "loud debate", "heated discussions" and "healthy conflict" peppered the articles and interview transcripts from all the companies.'
>
> Jim Collins, *Good to Great*

'It ain't what you do (it's the way that you do it).'

Sy Oliver and James 'Trummy' Young

Research[1] of top management teams has found that the more productive ones were able to manage conflicts without getting involved in personality conflict, treating conflicts as opportunities for collaboration to achieve the best solution for the organisation as a whole.

Conversely, when a separate research team[2] studied a group of business failures arising from highly unsuccessful strategic decisions, they found a remarkably consistent pattern of stifled debate, with negative opinions or adverse information discounted as unhelpful.

So the challenge for management is to realise the benefits of creative tension without straining relationships to breaking point. From an unhappy customer to a disgruntled director, business can experience the challenge of conflict from any direction – and just as with all other aspects of risk management, the goal is to maximise the benefits whilst minimising the downside and avoiding, or at least surviving, the catastrophic.

Advice for company secretaries

The wide-ranging remit of the modern company secretary should mean that all of the above issues are within your area of interest. You may not be designated as the senior executive responsible for managing the cost of conflict – but then who is? You are, however, well placed, both as a technical adviser and as a respected influencer, to ensure that your organisation does something about improving the way it handles conflict.

Probably the first problem you'll encounter – maybe even within yourself – is what seems to be a natural human reluctance to confront conflict situations. Many of us are avoiders – a Roffey Park[3] survey found that '…57% of respondents reported that "inaction" was their organisation's main method of conflict resolution…and cited "avoidance and pretending it is not there" as a regular course of action.'

The cocktail party conversation also seems to suggest that businesspeople are not doing much beyond resigning themselves to the inevitability of it all. And perhaps the reason for this is that they aren't very comfortable in dealing with conflict in their day-to-day roles. This isn't so surprising when we consider the limited training most have had in this area – a recent CEDR survey of over 600 business people revealed that only 37% regarded themselves as being adequately trained to cope with business conflict.

Furthermore – or, more likely, because of this lack of training – managers also revealed themselves to be significantly conflict-averse. Over a third of managers (35%) would rather parachute jump for the first time than address a performance problem with their work colleagues, whilst just under a third (27%) would rather shave their head for charity – and some (8%) would rather live on 'bush tucker' bugs for a week!

Later chapters of this book contain a variety of subject-specific recommendations, but there are some relatively simple things that can be done to help your organisation make a start on improved conflict management across the board:

- Make use of third-party neutrals
- Design systems rather than respond (often in a knee-jerk way) to situations
- Focus on conflict management, not just dispute resolution
- Create options and build capabilities
- Don't get trapped by the language and protocols of disputes

Make use of third-party neutrals

The idea of compromise, often facilitated by a neutral third party, is nothing new. Mahatma Gandhi is quoted as saying: 'a large part of my time during the twenty years of my practice as a lawyer was occupied in bringing about private compromises of hundreds of cases', and many cultures have the tradition of a respected elder or community member interceding into a dispute, often using a combination of personal stature and social pressure to encourage parties towards settlement.

What is new, however, is that in recent years mediation by a third-party professional has become firmly embedded in the litigation landscape, not only in England and Wales, but also in many other jurisdictions. Following the Civil Procedure Reforms of 1999, mediation has become an established feature of commercial litigation. It may not be mandatory, but the system now has a strong presumption in favour of parties and their advisers trying mediation before troubling the judge; and mediation is taking place in virtually every type of case passing through the commercial court system.

Mediation is also taking off around the world. UK mediation alone produces aggregate savings for clients in excess of £1 billion a year by avoiding wasted management time, damaged relationships, lost productivity and legal fees. Other jurisdictions in which commercial mediation is firmly established include the United States, Canada and Australia; whilst within Europe, mediation is now available in every single member state; and the EU itself has issued a Directive promoting its use across the entire spectrum of cross-border civil and commercial disputes. This requires member states not only to encourage the take-up of mediation but also, where necessary, to modify their legal frameworks so as to provide an effective climate in which mediation might take place. Other international agencies are also espousing mediation – in its Guidelines for Multinational Enterprises, the Organisation for Economic Co-operation and Development (OECD) encourages the use of facilitated dialogue through processes such as mediation in conflicts relating to areas of corporate social responsibility; and the World Bank has financed mediation projects throughout the world.

Clearly, then, any company secretary involved in commercial litigation needs to be familiar with mediation, and to appreciate that this is likely to be a sensible step to go through before getting to court. Indeed, Jan Eijsbouts, the former General Counsel of Akzo Nobel, the Dutch chemicals and pharmaceuticals multinational, has been quoted as saying:

> 'Mediation allows you to keep control of a dispute and to aim at commercial solution rather than legal remedies. It can turn a dispute from a business threat into a business opportunity. ADR is a first option – arbitration and litigation are alternatives'.

The key features of mediation are encapsulated in the formal definition set out below but, in effect, mediation is simply assisted negotiation. It is a private dispute resolution process in which a trained professional mediator works with parties to assist them to conclude negotiations in those situations in which they have previously been unable to achieve agreement.

> 'Mediation is a flexible process, conducted confidentially, in which a neutral person actively assists parties in working towards a negotiated agreement of a dispute or difference, with the parties in ultimate control of the decision to settle and the terms of resolution'.

Where negotiations break down or parties are unable to agree a common solution, a mediator can often provide a new dimension to the negotiation process by:

- Restarting negotiations that have stalled with little or no progress and when trust and confidence between the parties may also be at a low.
- Bringing a fresh, neutral set of eyes to an old problem – conflict, by its very nature, tends to narrow a party's focus and entrench positions.
- Taking a broader perspective on the problem and helping the parties to explore creative solutions, even in disputes where money is the only issue for resolution.
- Exploring and challenging the strengths and weaknesses of each party's case in the safety of private meetings and helping to move parties toward a realistic negotiated settlement.

One critical difference between face-to-face negotiations and mediation is the use of private meetings that provide a confidential and safe environment to explore settlement options.

So why would business benefit from using professional mediation? Quite simply, because it works. Last year, the commercial cases handled by CEDR's mediators in the UK involved disputes with an average of £1.5 million at issue. Many of those mediations took place only a few weeks after the parties first approached us for assistance (in fact, a mediation can be set up in just a matter of days); and the average duration of each mediation was slightly over one day. And yet, in spite of such a brief intervention by a mediator, over 75% of those cases reached an agreed settlement by the end of that single day, with another 10–15% settling shortly thereafter.

It is hardly surprising, therefore, that in a recent survey by leading international law firm CMS Cameron McKenna, over 77% of companies that have used mediation said it was quicker than litigation, over 78% said it was more effective and almost 80% said it had reduced their anticipated legal costs.

And savings go far beyond reducing the fees paid to outside counsel. From a business perspective, mediation can be a risk management tool in that it provides a route to avoid many of the potentially adverse consequences of litigation through the courts: because it is quick, businesses avoid wasted time and management distraction; because its outcome is a negotiated settlement rather than an imposed decision, businesses can manage their risk; and because it is a private process, businesses can avoid the reputational damage and adverse publicity of trial in a public forum.

Design systems rather than respond to situations

Mediation offers a new business tool for managing relations precisely at the point where relationships are vulnerable and at their most difficult. There is, however, a reactive tradition of 'let's hand it over to the lawyers' when problems arise, and it can be difficult to move a dispute into mediation at this stage. Hence, we recommend a proactive strategy, namely that businesses should adopt mediation by way of incorporating it into standard contracts or as corporate policy. Realisation of its benefits as a policy of good practice led the UK government to adopt a 'pledge' to use mediation in its own contracts and disputes in March 2001, and we recommend that all businesses make use of this approach.

At its simplest, a contract clause for dispute resolution might simply specify that: 'If any dispute arises in connection with this agreement, the parties will attempt to settle it by mediation in accordance with the CEDR Model Mediation Procedure'. More sophisticated versions might define a multi-tiered process, possibly starting with negotiation at senior executive level, escalating to mediation if that process fails, and then to adversarial arbitration or litigation only when all methods of consensual resolution have been exhausted.

Remember also that mediation might be deployed in other dispute contexts even if formal court processes are not an option. For example, many leading organisations incorporate workplace mediation approaches in their staff handbooks.

Focus on conflict management, not just dispute resolution

Mediation as a formal process has often been triggered for lawyers or managers only when a business faces the prospect of litigation or of further litigation cost. This is when a business dispute has become sufficiently serious to be taken out of the control of the managers negotiating directly. However, mediation also has significant potential for dispute avoidance and for conflict management by managers rather than lawyers. The key is to recognise that the process of introducing a skilled, independent third-party alters the dynamic of any negotiation – it adds discipline, communication value and problem-solving capacity whenever there is a difficult or sensitive negotiation or discussion required. And even in cases that might ultimately have gone to litigation, early use of mediation usually ensures optimal cost-saving and relationship maintenance.

Managers should therefore consider using mediation as a core management technique which can be adopted in situations where there are likely to be communication difficulties or 'sensitivities', even if not necessarily classified (yet) as a formal dispute. For example:

- handling employee or customer grievances (grievance mediation)
- intervening in cross-department or team rivalries or helping with restructuring of business units (organisational mediation)
- negotiating complex contracts (deal mediation)
- providing conflict prevention/management for the duration of a complex project, joint venture or strategic alliance or in setting up such a project (project or alliance mediation).

Create options and build capabilities

In their book *International Mediation – The Art of Business Diplomacy*, two of my colleagues, Eileen Carroll QC (Hon) and Dr Karl Mackie CBE, both experienced international mediators, comment that in their experience:

> 'resolution of complex commercial problems requires not only a better approach to conflict management, but also many layers of understanding and approach. The more complex the problem, the greater the need for a broader and flexible approach to solutions'.

It is important that a conflict management system provides options for all types of problems for all people within the organisation, and a 'one size fits all' strategy is unlikely to be workable beyond a very narrowly defined area of conflict. Generally, therefore, a comprehensive system will provide for a range of entry points and a variety of options, both rights-based and interest-based, for addressing conflict.

Training for managers themselves in the principles and techniques of mediation can not only improve the personal competencies of managers to use the process informally, but also help them to identify conflict earlier and to manage sensitive negotiations in more positive ways so as to make wise agreements with better results for the organisation.

However, as with any change management project in an organisational setting, implementation of a conflict management programme requires activity at a variety of levels. It's not enough simply to build protocols and provide training; leadership needs to come from the top such that open communication and effective conflict management become embedded in the culture of the organisation.

Don't get trapped by the language and protocols of disputes

It is worth remembering that organisational conflict can go much deeper than open warfare – a lot of conflict occurs on an informal and sometimes covert level. It's important also to remember that conflict isn't necessarily bad.

Secondly, a lot of conflict arises – or escalates – as a consequence of how people behave in difficult situations. Life experience causes all of us to acquire preferences and habits of how to respond to conflict, and we tend to use these over and over again. Individuals and organisations can have different conflict styles, each depending on the extent to which they place emphasis on two key areas: their own needs/agenda (the outcome); and the relationship with the other person.

For both of these reasons, language can become very important. As our earlier cocktail party conversation reveals, many of us perceive a difference between a dispute and mere conflict, but this is often a function of our unwillingness to articulate a truth or concede a failing rather than reflecting any substantive difference. Because of this, a company secretary may encounter situations in which more nuanced language can be helpful. We are probably all familiar with the re-labelling of a dispute as a 'difficulty', 'problem' or 'situation', but the role of the mediator can also be nuanced – why not talk about the idea of bringing in 'a neutral chair' to run a particular meeting or to assist in a 'difficult conversation'? Not only is this a perfectly accurate description of what the individual will do, it is potentially less threatening in that it seems like a small step forward rather than a major escalation of process. And the term also emphasises the wider range of situations in which the third-party neutral can be of assistance.

Conclusion

Conflict is part of working life, but it is how we deal with it that is important. Effective management of conflict can reduce the amount of time and money spent trying to sort out a problem, reduce the damage it could cause to those involved and enable decision makers to make smarter choices earlier on. There aren't any silver bullets, but a lot can be done, and company secretaries can play an important role in alerting their organisations to the time wastage that lack of proper conflict management causes. We can't make conflict go away, but we can help organisations manage conflict more efficiently and effectively – cutting the cost of conflict.

Case study: the 2012 CEDR and ICSA 'Good Conflict Management' survey

In preparation for this book, CEDR and the Institute of Chartered Secretaries and Administrators (ICSA) carried out a survey to determine the landscape of conflicts and disputes at board level. The survey ran between October and December 2012, and asked participants 22 questions about their attitudes to conflict and conflict management, and their experiences of these in their working lives. The survey was completed by 106 people, of which nearly two-thirds (64%) self-identified as company secretaries, and a further 20% described themselves as holding board-level positions.

What did we find?

Our findings were fascinating – they managed to confirm many of our own professional experiences of workplace conflicts and disputes, but also revealed unexpected details about how conflicts play out at a senior level.

Astonishingly, 19% of respondents reported that their company 'occasionally' or 'never' keeps records of disputes, with a further 12% saying that they were 'unsure' whether records of this kind are kept. This finding has implications on a number of levels. Firstly, a lack of consistency when recording disputes could have a knock-on effect when compiling company reports, annual returns, or even presenting evidence should the company be involved in legal proceedings. Employment disputes are the obvious candidates for this grey area – if a board member instigates legal action for unfair dismissal or benefits not honoured, it is immeasurably helpful to have a clear, detailed record of events from the beginning of the dispute charting what happened, who is involved and, perhaps, educated guesses as to motivations and interests at each stage.

Secondly, the relatively high figure (31%) for 'unsure' combined with the number of respondents who said that their company keeps dispute records 'occasionally' or 'never' suggests that internal reporting and information-sharing structures may not be effective in keeping directors in the loop about organisational disputes. While it might not be sensible for each director to be aware of every individual dispute that occurs in a complex transnational company, it is sensible for directors to be aware of company procedures and policies for handling conflicts and disputes at each organisational and stakeholder level. Effective systems for information sharing are key, and can positively enhance the board's understanding of how the company 'looks' to colleagues at different organisational levels – thus helping them to serve the company more comprehensively.

Handling the conflict 'hot potato'

The survey revealed that while over four-fifths of respondents said they understood how to handle boardroom conflict, only two-thirds of respondents felt comfortable doing so. This divide is interesting but not unexpected, and could be caused by a number of factors. The most obvious cause is a gap between knowing what *could* be done and having the confidence and opportunity to put those ideas into *practice*. We might know intellectually how to place a person in the recovery position, but have less confidence in doing so when faced with an ill person, if indeed someone else has not already come to the person's aid. We might equally assume that we *do* know this aspect of first aid, but find that when it comes to it, we are more limited than we had first thought; it would be easy for a company secretary to make similar assumptions about their conflict management skillset.

Other findings from the survey bear out these two theories. When we asked the same questions about attitudes to conflict in a more general workplace environment, we saw similar responses: 84% of respondents said they knew how to deal with conflict, while 73% said they felt comfortable dealing with it. This indicates that more generally, there is a discrepancy between understanding and practice surrounding workplace conflict. Similarly, theory and practice do not occur in tandem where methods for dealing with conflict are concerned. While respondents maintained that the involvement of an external neutral would be desirable for conflict resolution, only 6% of cases saw this in practice. According to one respondent, 'an adviser would be the best but [my company] won't employ one'. This is particularly telling about the value, or lack thereof, that companies place upon resolving conflict, in spite of the fact that over 90% of respondents agree that conflict does cost UK business.

Who do boards fight with, and why?

When asked 'Who do your boardroom disputes typically involve?', over half of the responses we collected identified 'disputes between board members' as their typical experience. In some ways, this is not surprising, but when paired with comparatively low identification figures of board conflict with shareholders (17%) and external third-party stakeholders (11%), we see a picture of 'infighting' emerging. Intra-board disputes left to fester, as we will see in Chapter 3 of this book, can be crippling to individuals and businesses – with so much at stake so close to home (so to speak), it is a matter of no small importance to have systems in place to deal with disputes as they arise. Additionally, it was interesting to see that all respondents nominated at least one group that boards have disputes with: this suggests that, as in our experience, conflict forms part of the everyday backdrop to boardroom life. As Chapter 7 explains, it can be very beneficial to consider implementing a number of dispute resolution methods and processes appropriate to different disputes – maybe a boardroom agreement to mediate disputes before litigating, and encouraging managers to set up a consumer redress scheme for customers with complaints.

It was also fascinating to see the range of responses we received detailing the reasons for conflict in workplaces and in boardrooms. Individuals reported that in the last 18 months, they had personally encountered conflict involving 'employment issues', 'working conditions', and 'long-term strategy'. However, when asked about the most common cause of board conflict, individuals identified 'long-term strategy' (45.83%) as the most common cause, followed by 'crisis management' (39.58%) and 'short-term strategy' (38.54%).

These findings indicate that boards tend to encounter conflict when dealing with responses and planning. Thinking in the short term, long term, and 'what if?' term causes particular problems. Issues surrounding vision and execution are typical at board level, and it is perhaps to be expected that the board is a hothouse of conflict for this reason. The board's custodial role makes encountering these issues inevitable, and consequently makes learning how to handle conflict effectively a significant issue. In light of this, it is perhaps surprising that only 16% of respondents agree entirely that their company shareholders care about board-level conflict. This is striking when compared to the 43.42% of respondents who agree that shareholders care about conflict that will affect profits. Conflict that is detrimental to *profit* is viewed as a more concerning issue than conflict that is detrimental to *people*. While this is not an unexpected result – of course, shareholders are primarily concerned with profits – it must be remembered that it is the board that is the driving force behind profits. A board riddled with conflict and inconsistency sets the tone

> for the rest of the company. If conflict at board level is not addressed, productivity within the rest of the company is inhibited and, consequently, profits will be affected.
>
> When we asked for the respondents' opinion on the most common cause of conflict for their board, 'difference of opinion' and 'lack of communication' were tied in first place, each gaining almost 23% of total responses. This is worth dwelling on, not least because the two options polled equally. It is interesting to observe that differing opinions in themselves do not necessarily have to be attritional. In fact, the following chapters will show that when properly managed, conflict can, paradoxically, be a force for good in an organisation. It is clear that a lack of communication is not only a primary cause of conflict but it also inhibits its effective resolution, as one of the most vital tools for managing conflict is clear communication. Where 'lack of communication' is the root of the problem in the first place, a vicious cycle will develop. In order to break this cycle, measures must be taken as early as possible to prevent further problems arising. These measures might include, for example, simple training in dealing with difficult conversations, the avoidance of which would otherwise hinder clear channels of communication.

The Conflict Management Survey revealed that conflicts and disputes are woven into the fabric of business and like dropped stitches or tangled threads, we sometimes need special tools to unpick them. While special tools and strategies can make a big difference, they are also only as effective as the skills of the person wielding them – practice makes perfect, and beyond the strong business case for conflict management, the big incentive to implement the ideas provided in this book is that they get better the more you use them. Although the majority of respondents claimed to understand how to deal with conflict, a high proportion of them felt uncomfortable with this in practice. This finding is supported by the fact that there is clearly a high volume of conflicts occurring, primarily between board members, and less commonly between the board and external agents like shareholders and communities. It is not unexpected that the board itself is an incubator of conflict and the ensuing stress that proves to be an all-too-common by-product. 'Difference of opinion' and 'lack of communication' are symbiotic factors in board disputes, but can be managed effectively with alternative dispute resolution training and tactics, as we will see generally throughout this book and specifically in the next chapter.

Notes

1. Eisenhart, KM, Jean L Kahwajy, & Bourgeois, LJ (1997) *How management teams can have a good fight*, Harvard Business Review.
2. Finkelstein, S (2003) *Why smart executives fail*.
3. Roffey Park 'Management Agenda 2004'.

2
The company secretary and board involvement in organisational conflict and employment disputes

Fiona Colquhoun

The key role of the company secretary

Sometimes the most troubling and difficult disputes are between senior individuals in positions of power and authority. This chapter will examine how, if left unmanaged, power struggles and disputes between senior individuals can derail an entire organisation, affecting its performance, reputation and culture. Invariably, a company secretary is in the unique position of not only being the 'custodian' of good corporate governance and practice, but also the sensor on the dynamics and relationships between chairmen and chief executives, non-executive and executive directors, as well as, in some organisations and charities, between and amongst trustees.

The way in which a company secretary contributes to an organisation's equilibrium and manages any emerging conflicts can make a sustainable difference to any board's effectiveness. In small and medium business enterprises, the company secretary may sometimes be an amalgam of the Finance, Legal and Human Resources functions. In other and larger organisations, the company secretary's support will often be invaluable to senior functionaries, as they will often be an important thread or the glue in holding members of the board together and a trusted confidant of many individual directors and senior executives. Company secretaries have a wide range and spectrum of roles throughout organisations. The traditional image of the company secretary to the plc or in a commercial limited company board is different to the company secretary's role and statutory responsibilities in the public or voluntary sectors or organisations where there are no shareholders. In any situation, however, a company secretary can expect to deal with tensions and disputes of all types, and is well placed to intervene and help to resolve or adjudicate matters proactively.

An organisation's corporate diplomat

As with any profession, there is a spectrum of ways in which company secretaries can undertake their roles. Some company secretaries come from other professions, particularly the legal and finance areas, and are qualified lawyers, chartered accountants, or HR managers; others are career chartered company secretaries. Their respective backgrounds and experiences will influence how they perform their roles within organisations.

There are some generalisations that apply to all company secretaries. Frequently, they will know more about an organisation than anyone else and be the recipient of many types of sensitive information connected with the organisation and those in it. In their position as the primary board contact, the company secretary will often know more about the concerns and propensities of board directors than anyone else, and the relationships they have, particularly with the chairman and non-executives, can be very influential.

In type, there are at least three company secretaries and probably more working throughout UK plc's boardrooms, and these types are not exclusive to each other:

- First, there are the transactional company secretaries, whose strengths are in planning, corporate governance and effectively running the business of the board, including all its meetings and records.
- Second, there are those company secretaries whose strengths lie in their relationship skills and who perform most effectively working with different board executives.
- Third, there are those with a combination of such skills and experience who are familiar and comfortable in navigating through the corridors of power and are wise, proactive and diplomatic. These individuals will be an organisation's 'corporate diplomats', and will add the most value to an organisation.

It is interesting, however, that a great deal of a company secretary's role or work will not be visible and will only be known to a few in an organisation. This is because they handle so much sensitive and confidential information and some of their most prominent and important actions will only take place behind closed doors. This makes it particularly important, therefore, that they practise and perform their roles with integrity, confidentiality and the trust of those with whom they work most closely. The skills that make a successful company secretary are remarkably close to those of a mediator, and one could go as far as saying that company secretaries would all benefit from mediation awareness training, and learning about its tools and techniques. As in other professions, this would complement their existing capabilities and a number have already embarked on this path of professional development.

Board involvement in employment and workplace disputes

Early stage intervention will always save costs

Employment and workplace disputes, like boards themselves, come in all shapes and types, and clearly a one-size solution will not fit all. Such 'disputes', or on a broader basis, tensions and conflicts between people in organisations, do have common features. Any employment dispute will cost money in terms of time and resources and will invariably have a negative impact on the relationship between any individuals involved. Consequently, the earlier that tensions, however small, are dealt with, the more chance there will be of saving costs and achieving reconciliation without protracted and litigious disputes. This fact, whilst proven, is sometimes difficult to illustrate: when matters are resolved early, the adverse impact of a dispute does not materialise and is not evident, and costs are limited or have not even begun to accumulate. The company secretary has a valuable role in ensuring that pragmatic and cost-effective ways of resolution are available at as early a stage as possible.

Types of disputes and conflict

The 'typical' board level dispute does not exist as they all have their own features, but the most usual often involve 'fall outs' and 'breakdowns of relationships' between the board members themselves. In this respect, such disputes are similar to those at any other level of an organisation's hierarchy. For example, the dispute may be a difference of opinion in the context of responsibilities, structure, respective roles and business strategy. Sometimes board level differences arise because people have different approaches to work, opposing and non-complementary management and leadership styles, and very different values or beliefs, meaning that they do not share the same priorities, likes or dislikes.

Furthermore, the top level of any business or organisation is often populated by strong-minded individuals, who have built up their careers over periods of time, so the 'stakes' in any conflict can be very high. Even in some normally constructive business environments, healthy competition can sometimes be destroyed by jealousy and interpersonal power struggles. Sometimes it is the comparatively simple phenomenon of individuals not liking each other and being unable to collaborate or accept team or cabinet responsibility. In other instances, it is about egos, pride and prejudices, and environments where each individual acts in their own interest, everyone wants to be seen to win or there is a 'dog eat dog' mentality.

At board level, the context in which people operate is often tense and issues are not always verbalised, so there is sometimes a fair amount of conflict and disharmony under the surface. The company secretary will invariably have more knowledge and understanding of what is happening than any other individual. They may well be asked for their opinions on matters, but it is important that they always act with objectivity in the interests of the company, and that any of their interventions are both appropriate and professional. This becomes an even greater priority if directors are entangled in a tense conflict situation, which can divert their attention from their role as company custodians. If directors are pursuing intra-board conflict at the expense of working for the good of the company, it becomes increasingly important that the company secretary is vigilant and acts to protect shareholders and ensure the company, as far as possible, stays on track.

The sorts of situations the company secretary may find themselves involved in are varied. Most commonly, however, they may be called upon to deal with difficulties between directors, including the sometimes extremely challenging relationship between the chairman and the chief executive. There may also be differences between the chairman and the non-executives, which either directly or indirectly involve the company secretary. The other major area where there may be both significant tensions and difficulties is in relationships with shareholders: this may be particularly pertinent in times of change, when business is tight or during periods of mergers and acquisitions when there is a great deal of negotiated activity.

Some very senior and otherwise able people are neither confident nor equipped to deal well with conflict or disputes. Sometimes they revert to taking positions on matters too quickly and can make matters worse, rather than aim for a more consensual resolution. A company secretary who has the skills to support chairmen and directors to manage tensions and prevent matters escalating unnecessarily will always be of value to a board.

The custodian of corporate ethics

Company secretaries are much like 'ministers without portfolio' – while they may have no one specific area of responsibility, their breadth of knowledge and understanding places them naturally as an organisation's wise counsel. Sometimes this position can be very uncomfortable and can bring company secretaries themselves into conflict with directors, the chairman or the chief executive officer (CEO). These situations can arise when an individual board member places their own personal reputation or desires above those of the organisation: a director anxious about maintaining a strong industry reputation, for example, may approach the company secretary and ask that information about his work for the organisation be presented more favourably in the company's annual report than it actually is.

Here, the company secretary faces a difficult choice over how best to proceed. The director's wishes are in conflict with action that is best for the organisation, raising numerous questions about corporate ethics in practice. While the company secretary has a responsibility to iterate that they work for the good of the company rather than for particular board members, this must be done in such a way that does not alienate the individual, or overstate any accusation of misconduct. There are also more individual questions for the company secretary to consider – should a request of this nature be made known to the CEO or chairman? If the director's wishes would actually benefit the company's reputation, should the company secretary agree to carry them out?

This chapter does not discuss in detail the ethics of the company secretary's role, nor does it advise on what is or is not acceptable conduct. What this sort of situation does highlight, however, is how skilled a diplomat a company secretary must be in handling numerous conflicting pressures. There is a delicate balance to achieve, encompassing professionalism and discretion, and also quiet firmness and assertiveness. Furthermore, the company secretary also needs to be a good judge of situations – depending on the context, there might be a need to receive and handle information in such a way that protects confidentiality or commercial sensitivity. In delicate circumstances, the company secretary must have confidence in their own confidence – that is to say, they have to be personally comfortable with their own conduct.

When disputes become personal

At board level, these sorts of interpersonal disputes between individuals are accentuated and can be detrimental to the whole of the organisation. Decision-making falters, a board becomes dysfunctional and often positions become polarised very quickly. Managers and employees take on the mantle of their senior leaders and the effects of board-level employment disputes and differences permeate rapidly through the organisation. People imitate their leaders and there is little doubt that morale and motivation can be adversely affected.

Market impact

In these sorts of situations, what has perhaps started as a difference about a business issue can become not only positional, but intensely personal. The mixture of business and personal differences can often become a 'lethal cocktail' and impact on other relationships with other stakeholders so that the dispute affects the well-being and success of the whole organisation. One of the most extreme examples is when chairs and chief executives fall out and disagree. Often this places the organisation in the public domain and at reputational risk, and 'corporate war zones' develop between the two parties, sometimes dividing executives and non-executives into camps resulting in boardroom splits and factions, and public or shareholder votes of no confidence. This not only affects the share price of the company where the market loses faith in the organisation's leadership, on a human level it can also destroy careers and lives.

The company secretary as the trusted and neutral adviser

Even in organisations where there is a competent and experienced human resources or legal function, the company secretary has a key role to play in these matters, either working with their colleagues or on occasion being the person to help individuals in dispute work positively and responsibly through the issues causing conflict. In such instances, the company secretary at board level needs to be equipped with a range of sophisticated skills in order that they can both contribute to and advise on these issues.

Navigation in these areas and in the corridors of power is often challenging and the ability to stand back and be neutral and objective, as well as impartial, is very important. Understanding the legal and statutory implications arising from conflict or disputes is also a core area where the company secretary can add immense value to the board. The alternative dispute resolution (ADR) skillset or the skills of a mediator, with the knowledge of where to find external expertise and support, will always stand the company secretary in good stead, giving them the confidence to intervene and make a positive difference on such issues.

There are a range of other types of employment or organisational disputes which boards and company secretaries will be involved in, and in today's world they absolutely need to have the adaptability and capabilities to deal with such situations.

Disputes on performance, disciplinary and grievance matters

In many organisations, particularly those with hierarchical employment policies and procedures, a workplace or employment dispute may well culminate in some shape or form at board level or with the chair or chief executive. For example, this may be as a final appeal hearing against a management decision made during a disciplinary or grievance process.

With the company secretary's closeness to the board or its senior officers, they will often be engaged in managing the handling process of these matters. This can mean a great deal of detailed work and meticulously arranged procedural arrangements to ensure the scrupulously fair management of this process. In some situations, the company secretary may be put in the position of 'deal maker' or one of the negotiators inside the organisation. This can occur if one of the executive directors is involved in disciplinary or performance procedures and a 'managed exit' results.

For example, a chief executive determines that an executive director is not performing well and has lost the confidence of his colleagues. The human resources director and the company secretary work on the exit arrangements together to compromise the individual out of the organisation. The company secretary is particularly involved as the individual has some complex stock and pension arrangements as part of his package. The company secretary needs to work with the chairs of the board of the non-executive directors and of the remuneration committee to support the agreement and thereby ensure the deal can take place. An effective company secretary who has the skills to do this is often invaluable as an influencer, peacemaker and deal maker.

Procedures that can perpetuate disputes

Grievance and disciplinary procedures and policies can, however, encourage boards to be judgemental and uphold management decisions that have been a key component of the dispute rather than seek to resolve the matters and avoid lengthy litigation. Procedures can be unnecessarily bureaucratic rather than pragmatic. Often the company secretary is the 'first on the case' for these types of issues, and it is important for them to deal with such situations personally and know how to prevent escalation of the conflict.

In such situations, a company secretary who can deal with matters impartially without being emotional, and who has the techniques and aptitudes of a good mediator, such as being able to deal with entrenched personal positions and personalities, is invaluable to any organisation.

With their skills and organisational position, the company secretary is a natural negotiator. They can be a strong and supportive employer representative, but can also excel in deal making because they are recognised for their professional position, and as a trusted and empathetic confidante to individual members of a board.

The company secretary, with their quasi-legal role that incorporates governance matters, is in this respect often the most neutral person in the top level of an organisation. They are *de facto* without a personal agenda and can be both a trusted, reasoned and objective advisor at the top level of the organisation. There are a number of instances where the company secretary can be instrumental in resolving long-winded employment or workplace disputes.

Interventions by company secretaries

Examples include an organisation where a long-standing complaint against the conduct of a senior member of staff had become completely disproportionate to the original incident. The matter had become tangled during investigations and reviews by the chief executive without the problem being resolved in the first instance. The company secretary and the chairman worked together to halt what had become an incredible drain on resources and effectively and successfully concluded matters in the organisation's interests.

A more typical example is that of an individual in a medium-sized organisation who had appealed against redundancy and whose case was proceeding to an employment tribunal. The claimant was alleging sex and race discrimination and the company secretary supported the chief executive throughout, and negotiated the settlement as they had the appropriate skills to do so. This intervention saved the organisation a six-figure sum in costs.

So the company secretary, by their proximity to the board and senior management, can often make a difference, and through their own initiative and capabilities rescue an organisation from a complex resource-intensive dispute.

Disputes on pay and remuneration

Boards may also be involved in collective employment disputes or differences about pay. Annual pay negotiations between management and unions in the commercial sector with negotiated agreements, for example, may still require board approval. In many instances, individual performance pay arrangements have replaced the need for annual pay negotiations and collective bargaining, although boards have general involvement in the affordability of pay increases and managing this consistently across their organisations.

The company secretary's role in board-level remuneration issues can be complex and challenging. This is an area where diplomatic skills coupled with detailed knowledge and the ability to focus and work with a great deal of detail need to be carefully developed. In plc environments, negotiations on the chairman's salary and particularly on other very important parts of a director's package, not least of all stock options, bonuses and pensions, fall into this area. Treading a path between acceptability to shareholders, the market, and most particularly in recent years, a potentially antagonistic media, is seldom easy. The company secretary plays a big role in bringing any director, whether executive or non-executive, into a company and it is important that they establish trust in their relationship with each director and their role as a primary contact and source of advice as early as possible. If matters do not go well at this stage, the implications can be very damaging later.

The company secretary who works with their chairman to bring in a new chief executive often faces this issue. If this is an external appointment, invariably the chairman will want a speedy appointment which does not require their involvement in the minutiae of the process. However, in large plcs, the appointment of a new chief executive is often a multi-million pound transfer; with such high financial, personal and reputational costs, keeping a cool head is essential. Until the new chief executive is 'signed up', everything is tense and the other board members inevitably lack direction. The stakes are also very high as the chairman/chief executive relationship is probably the most important in any organisation, so early negotiations and rapport between those two people are essential to avoid later misunderstandings and problems.

It is not only the remuneration arrangements which need to be negotiated between chairmen and incoming chief executives. It is no less important that roles and responsibilities between these key leaders are properly understood and that they do not intrude on or compete with each other. The demarcation between non-executive and executive roles is important in this respect, but so too are the personalities of the individuals. Working with a chairman and chief executive who neither like nor respect each other, or who have genuinely different visions or agendas for the organisation, is unsustainable, and places a competent company secretary in a position of navigating and managing many quandaries.

Remuneration committees

Supporting a remuneration committee and applying good principles of corporate governance, as well as setting the tone for public statements including those for the company annual report, will often require considerable tact, careful direction and precision to satisfy all stakeholders. Demonstrable qualities of calmness and patience will be essential in what can be the most sophisticated of negotiations.

The company secretary as a negotiator

The company secretary can often be in a tremendously important position as a negotiator. While so much of what a company secretary does is a negotiation and takes place naturally throughout their work, there will be many occasions where the company secretary is the most suitable organisational negotiator. There is undoubtedly a key role in terms of contracts and remuneration including stock and entry and exit packages, whether or not this is done in collaboration with other executives such as HR, legal or finance directors. Having experience in these sorts of advanced negotiations, as suggested above, can often require considerable experience and sophistication.

The company secretary may be asked to play a part in a variety of 'internal' and 'external' negotiations. For example, they may hold a neutral position between individuals, or between director factions who have adopted different positions on an issue. They may be in the best position, by design or default, to engage with individuals or groups who are experiencing conflict. These are relatively informal positions for a company secretary to hold, even though bringing these situations to a successful conclusion may have important commercial implications. There are also, of course, more commercial or business-oriented negotiations with a more formal company secretarial role, which can include shareholders and other stakeholders in more complex ways.

This may particularly be the case in merger and acquisition discussions and negotiations where the company secretary is involved in the initial board-level negotiations that can fundamentally shape the whole initiative. As well as the confidentiality the company secretary will enjoy at board level, they may well be in an equally important position in the regulation and distribution of stock and share arrangements, and may also negotiate or coordinate aspects of commercial transactions. The role of the company secretary varies according to each individual's credentials as well as the context and size of their organisation. However, the skills of negotiating and bargaining are core qualities that will serve any company secretary well.

What conflict management skills and models are most useful to a company secretary?

The eight key skills

Active listening

The most important skills to anyone in corporate or indeed public life is active listening and maintaining confidences, and this is where a company secretary needs to be an exemplary professional. Without this skill, trust will never fully be developed between individuals and the company secretary will be unable to do their job effectively. In any difference of opinion, or understanding the key points of any business dispute between directors, these skills are paramount.

Objectivity

The ability to stand back and review any situation knowledgably, fairly but also objectively is crucial to being an effective adviser and sounding board – a position that a company secretary will need to be in to ably assist the chairman and any other director. They must also do this without an agenda of their own, and act in the best interests of the company.

Questioning

The intellect to *ask questions* in a natural rather than an interrogative way so that issues can be explored and considered rather than decided upon hastily, or without knowing all the facts and issues.

Interpersonal rapport

The ability to relate to all levels of people but particularly to be able to develop rapport with the variety of characters on a board, and in that respect have the skills to deal with difficult people or individuals who have concerns and may be angry or emotional.

Negotiating

This is possibly the most important and all-encompassing skill of all, and whilst it may not be defined as such, it is the way in which a company secretary undertakes their role every moment of their working day. The negotiations can invariably be very complex.

THE COMPANY SECRETARY AND BOARD INVOLVEMENT 23

Conflict Management:
Eight Key Skills

1. ACTIVE LISTENING — Skill that must be cultivated
2. OBJECTIVITY
3. QUESTIONING
4. INTERPERSONAL RAPPORT
5. NEGOTIATING
6. NAVIGATION
7. PROBLEM SOLVING
8. SUMMARISING — Skill that a company secretary already has at a very sophisticated level

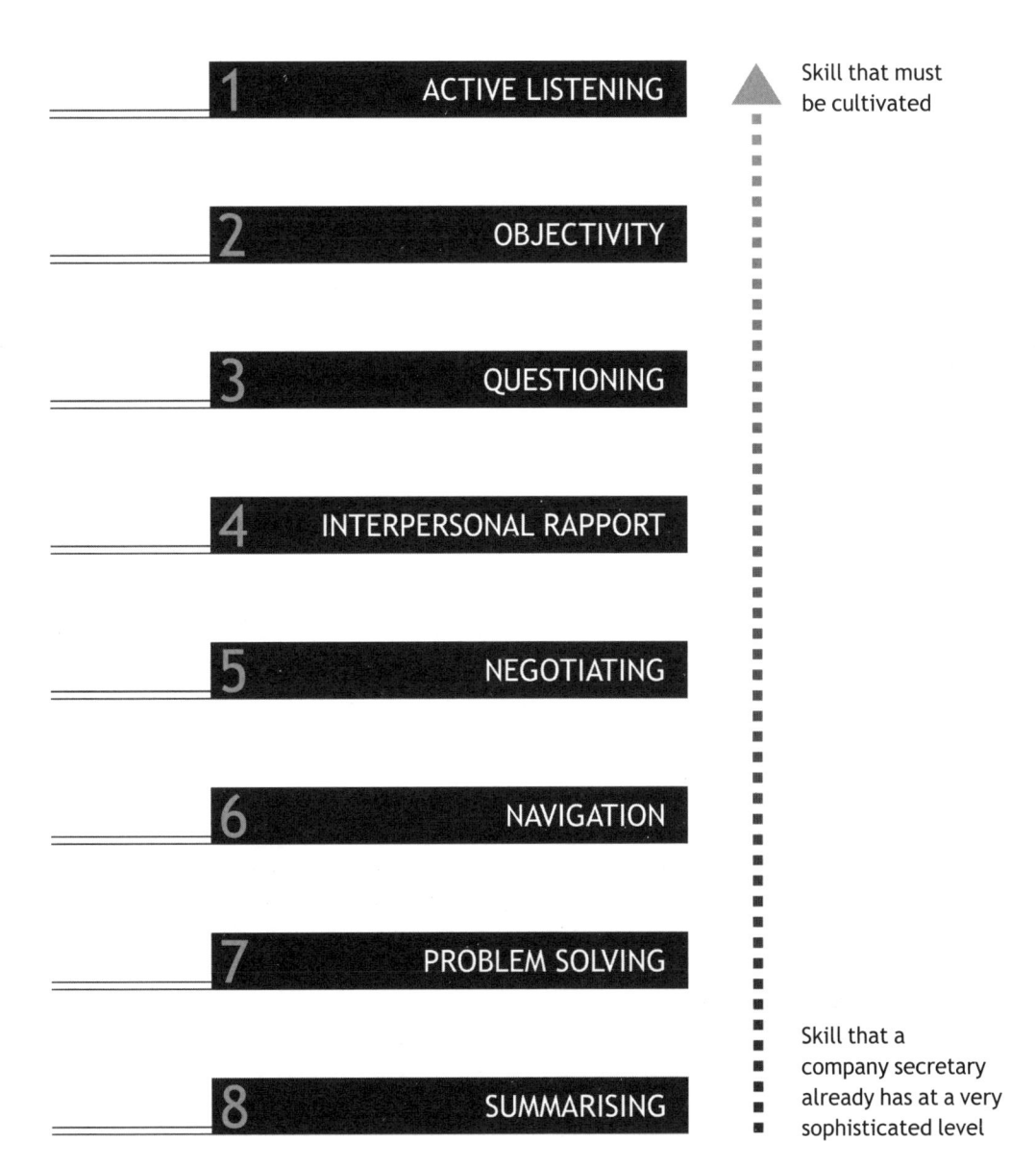

Figure 2.1: Eight Key Skills

Navigation

The instinctive ability to work with senior people using resilience and self-reliance to carry matters through, as often the context with aspects of confidentiality and sensitivity can make the company secretary's role somewhat lonely. In this respect, we can also consider the ability to manage and take directors through a supporting process or framework of corporate governance without necessarily directing them.

Problem solving

Whilst a company secretary must comply with regulations and has statutory responsibilities, problem solving and dealing with matters pragmatically will often prevent and deal with tensions.

Summarising

One of the great skills in dispute resolution, and one in which company secretaries are often well trained for through taking minutes and briefing chairmen on issues of governance. The ability to understand and note issues accurately – and then summarise them objectively – will always be helpful to a company secretary in performing their role.

Using conflict management skills – key models

In most organisations, there will be situations where experts in the field of conflict resolution may be needed, but these should be exceptional rather than the rule. As long there is recognition and understanding of when this is required, the company secretary who has the skills identified above is generally in the position of being able to deal with these issues.

Having difficult conversations

Company secretaries are usually naturally experienced in having difficult conversations – whether this is saying no to plc directors on matters of corporate governance or giving feedback on a situation which is not to a senior person's liking. This calls for finely crafted diplomatic skills as suggested above as well as wisdom and maturity. The model for having a difficult conversation is a proven and adaptable framework for dealing with all sorts of conflict issues and problems which emerge in the everyday work of board matters and the relationships between different directors. The first principles are curiosity and exploration, rather than advocacy or opinions, to enable objectivity. Next, it is important to prepare for the conversation and think through the issues involved both for the company secretary (as the conversation's instigator) and for the other individual involved.

Timing and confidentiality are key as well as establishing empathy and trust with the individual with whom the difficult conversation will take place. Identifying a time and place where individuals have the peace and security to be able to focus on the issue, rather than, for example, a rushed conversation added to a long day's agenda, is equally important.

Identifying and explaining the purpose of the conversation in order to stay on course and not being distracted by someone who either consciously or unconsciously is trying to avoid the issue or has not recognised its significance is very important both at the start and throughout the conversation.

Exploring the issues using the key skills of listening and questioning enables a full understanding of the core matter and its implications. It is essential to take all the issues into account before reaching a well-considered solution. Exploring options and including others' ideas is a skill in its own right which company secretaries will often put to use. Stamina, perseverance and patience will invariably stand a company secretary in good stead.

There are two other key features that work within this model which are easily adapted into other approaches. These are the company secretary's ability to:

- deal with strong opinions and emotions
- recognise the risks to the directors and the company in any difficult situation.

Dealing with emotions

Individuals in senior roles are only human, but must cope with very difficult business decisions, exceedingly busy schedules and have the responsibility of leadership through challenging times. Time is always a key commodity and, as with any group of people, boards can work together constructively, albeit with healthy differences of opinion and debate, or destructively. Often when boards break down or fall apart, this involves personal differences and relationship problems rather than solely business matters. These personal differences can destroy the business if they are not dealt with. So there are situations where chairmen and chief executives fall out on what appear to be business or strategic business issues. The situation can become very destructive when the matter turns to personal criticisms and dislikes.

In such situations, it is first very important for the company secretary to *recognise* the emotion in the first instance. In the corporate boardroom, this may manifest itself in many ways and not be as obvious or as tangible as in more operational parts of the organisation. There may be tensions that only the company secretary has the full measure of because of their role. Quiet anger can often develop into broader conflict, and the earlier those involved can be helped to manage it, before adapting rigid positions, the better. It is in these situations that the company secretary will be both a sounding board and a wise counsel, sharing confidences with directors and helping them to reflect on all the issues and the implications, including the risks and benefits, of different options.

Recognising the emotion and acknowledging it will enable the company secretary to then *reflect* on the best way of trying to deal with it. For example, should the company secretary initiate a difficult conversation between two individuals with conflicting views? Should the company secretary have a difficult conversation with a chairman – perhaps to advise them that they have lost the support of others or that their approach on some matters should be modified? If so, it is best that the company secretary prepare for such a conversation by exploring the issues with each individual before suggesting any form of joint meeting, which may or not be appropriate depending on the degree of emotions involved.

Having recognised the sensitivity and depth of any emotion, the company secretary will need to consider and prepare to deal with it. They will be able to handle this through a combination of their own skills and intuition, and be able to sense how far they can *respond* or deal with and resolve the problem. The more a company secretary is equipped and able to diffuse situations and deal with undercurrents of conflict, such as quiet anger, without giving the issues time to escalate or fester, the more effectively the board will be able to perform.

In many instances, the company secretary's contribution may neither be tangible nor visible and their actions may only rarely be commented upon or fully acknowledged. However, the ability and the confidence to navigate through the top levels of an organisation where human emotions can often be high and pressurised is what can make a good company secretary a great corporate diplomat.

Dealing with crisis situations arising from conflict and disputes

Every organisation will have conflict within it to some degree and only a few will escape the occasional crisis.

At board level, this may be a leadership crisis, a matter that is in the public domain where reputations are involved and the media exercises its own pressures on individuals and organisations. These sorts of situations are invariably very damaging to morale and productivity and organisations become similar to a 'jungle', losing direction and energy and often becoming corporate warzones with a great deal of politicking and infighting. The company secretary is often the only person who can bring a sense of normality and practicality to deal with such issues and behave in a calming and non-threatening way to all the stakeholders involved.

Just like in a zoo, the competing animals in any company organisation can collectively be an astonishing display of vibrancy, energy and excitement. Like a zookeeper, the company secretary understands that these different personalities can require skilful handling and management to keep them on track and performing together. Without this careful handling, the competing animals can clash rather than cohere, storing up problems for each individual and the wider business. The better prepared, trained and equipped the company secretary is to be the figure of calm, trust and consistency in such situations, the more easily the crisis will be diverted or dealt with effectively.

Proactive conflict management

Similarly, the company secretary, with knowledge of the business issues, strategies and performance of an organisation, is in a pivotal position to understand the organisation's risks and consequently the benefits of managing conflict proactively rather than reacting to it when it happens.

Therefore, a familiarisation with ADR and ideally some practical experience or ADR training, for example, as a mediator or in the mediation skillset will give any corporate executive additional management capabilities. The company secretary is no exception and the leaders of organisations do not like admitting that they may find dealing with conflict difficult or choose not to acknowledge that it exists. Having the mediator skillset will give a company secretary both a set of competencies and confidence to navigate through any corporate organisation's corridors of power.

By being able to practice ADR and influence the way in which matters are handled at board level, a company secretary's influence can permeate their organisation. This in turn will affect the culture of the organisation so that its board works collaboratively and constructively on conflict matters by listening, reflecting and resolving problems, rather than taking a positional or litigious approach. This will always save costs and make the organisation a more positive experience for all stakeholders. Inevitably in business there will be situations where litigation is necessary, but making it the exception rather than the norm is beneficial to any organisation.

Proactive conflict management in practice

A number of organisations now have dispute resolution systems and/or conflict management strategies and have implemented these from board level. If proactive conflict management is to work, the board has an important role to play in making sure that employees and managers are trained in issues such as conflict awareness and how to approach difficult situations. Equally, the board can help to change attitudes through leading by example. Setting the tone by resolution principles to board-level disputes, both internal and external, sends a clear message about the organisation's attitude and values.

Learning from problems and issues is particularly important in the corporate context, and at board level this can be facilitated by the company secretary. Having the equivalent of an early warning system, identifying and communicating on issues that need to be addressed, then encouraging and stimulating the earliest possible resolution of the problem is essential, but so too is having an action review to prevent the same issues arising in the future. The company secretary is also often the person in the best position to make resolutions as consistent and sustainable as possible.

Enhancing the company secretary role

The company secretary often fulfils the role of the corporate diplomat, either inadvertently or deliberately, with some company secretaries not always having their contribution in this area fully acknowledged. In many ways, being largely unnoticed in the way they deal with the tensions and difficult situations at board level is one of an effective company secretary's key attributes. It is the role of the trusted, objective confidant and listener – the man or woman without a personal agenda – who is the board's most natural mediator and navigator. It is an area for company secretaries to develop both their own experiences and skills.

Case study: building broken trust among trustees

This case study is based on a real-life situation in which a company secretary played an instrumental role in handling a conflict and facilitating a solution. It illustrates the positive influence an experienced company secretary can exert on conflict situations, and highlights the importance of approaching the situation with intelligence, integrity and professional discretion. In keeping with this, all names and certain details in this case study have been altered to preserve anonymity.

Background information

A well-established charity with local historical interests had a number of trustees drawn from the local community as well as those with interests in the sector.

There were 12 trustees, some of whom had only taken up their appointments in the last two years. Four of them were very long-standing trustees and one of them, Mr D, had been a trustee for many years and had previously been the board's chair. Mr D and his wife had also been active, well-known figures in the wider community: Mr D had, for example, been closely involved in local government. Mr D was in his early 70s and had right of tenure as a trustee of the charity – he was entitled to serve until he chose to retire or died.

The Trust had recently appointed a new chairman, and had also attracted a great variety of younger people to the charity's work and interests. The younger grass-roots supporters were more motivated to make governance changes, but were also much less steeped in the history and traditions of the Trust.

This was also true of the newer trustees.

The Trust's chief executive was also relatively new, having been appointed to his role on a part-time, three-days-a-week basis. He was assisted by B, a retired company secretary, who undertook all the company secretary duties on behalf of the company and the trustee board.

The dispute

The dispute arose because Mr D had spoken with his wife of over 50 years about a land management issue, which was being dealt with by the charity and more specifically the trustees. The land management issue was controversial for a number of groups in the local community, and the trustees' desire to keep their decision-making process private was a reflection of this. Furthermore, the trustees were not wholeheartedly united behind one course of action, and the decision the Trust was likely to forward was an acceptable compromise rather than a decision of conviction.

Mrs D had inadvertently spoken with a local news reporter and in response to a specific question she had indicated that the Trust might well be supportive of a particular plan. The local press had subsequently followed this up with the Trust and the company involved, who were very concerned that this information had been disclosed and discussed. The matter was traced back to D.

D was advised of this problem by the company secretary, B, and understood the ramifications of what had happened. Mrs D was both embarrassed and upset, and apologised unreservedly for her actions.

The matter may have rested there, but some of the trustees considered that Mr D should resign, arguing that he had broken the trust and confidence of his colleagues, and that he had behaved inappropriately by mentioning the matter to his wife. They were certainly also motivated by the thought of getting other, younger, trustees to join the board.

The chair of the trustee board picked up on the tensions and the possible reasons behind them, and felt that the only way out would be to reach an amicable agreement where Mr D volunteered to resign from the board. He guessed that D would be unwilling to leave the board, and that his right of tenure would make any attempt to forcibly encourage his exit difficult as it would leave the Trust open to criticism and possibly legal action. He also understood that other trustees saw Mr D as unprofessional for his slip-up, and as a barrier to progress for the future of the charity. Not wanting to jeopardise any future relationships, the chair asked the chief executive and the company secretary to handle the dispute.

Handling the dispute

It was clear that as uncomfortable as the situation was, it would not be possible to ignore the conflict and that handling the conflict and trying to find a solution would be the responsibility of the chief executive and the company secretary. This turn of events actually offered an ideal way forward, as the chief executive and the company secretary were well placed to handle matters intelligently. Company secretary B's involvement brought particular benefits:

- B's career as a company secretary working in the private sector had given him direct experience of handling similar conflicts between directors involving delicate topics. He was therefore in a prime position to advise the chief executive on how to handle the conflict, and to use his experience as a way of reassuring each side in the conflict that he was skilled enough to help achieve a solution.

- B's role as company secretary gave him a clear position as acting in the interests of the charity. As the guardian of the charity's 'corporate values', his perspective was different to that of the trustees in conflict, and his perception of each parties' interests was more measured. He was able to be the neutral face of the conflict, focusing everyone's energies on solutions rather than recriminations.
- B's experience and position within the charity made him the prime neutral figure in the dispute, and the Ds, the board of trustees, and the chairman had confidence in his ability to act fairly, professionally, and in the interests of the charity. This confidence gave B legitimacy to act: he could ask open, exploratory questions of each side, he could receive confidential and sensitive information, and in doing these things he could work as the dealmaker between the parties in conflict.

The chief executive and company secretary decided that it would be best if B acted as the lead peacemaker. This would avoid any suggestion of the chief executive acting partially and would let B apply his experience to the situation.

Issues to consider

Taking a broad overview of the dispute, the chief executive and B observed that besides the central tensions between Mr D and the board of trustees, four big issues were affecting the dynamic of the dispute:

Mr D's life tenure presented an immediate practical difficulty – violating the tenure by forcing Mr D out, for example, would invite negative publicity and possibly legal action against the Trust. However, there were also the very immediate facts that a) Mr D had indeed acted improperly in discussing the Trust's work with his wife, especially as the subject was a sensitive one, and b) this was causing considerable tension and upset among the other trustees. Reconciling the interests of both parties posed a significant challenge. The issue of Mr D's life tenure also developed as an issue in itself – raising delicate questions over whether what Mr D could contribute to the charity as a tenured trustee was still in line with the charity's aims and ambitions.

Mission drift – all companies have corporate values, whether these are openly espoused or implied; charities have an altogether more overt attachment to ethical standards and values. Most people would expect a charity to act with a high degree of ethical and moral sensitivity – 'encouraging' Mr D to resign his position may, to some, appear inconsistent with a charity's ethos. Additionally, the influx of new members and trustees with a looser connection to the Trust's history posed questions over possible mission drift. Mr D was seen by some as a stumbling block to progress, but it was not especially clear whether what those individuals hoped to achieve was truly consistent with the charity's stated aims and actions.

Political awareness – the chief executive of the Trust was in an especially difficult position: faced with the conflicting desires of the trustees and Mr D, acting in clear favour of either party would upset the other and create more intricate difficulties for himself and the charity. He had to consider the future implications of present actions: positioning the charity and Trust as unfriendly to newer, younger members, for example, carried the risk of the charity stagnating as an interest of older, established members. He also had to consider his own position, and how best to achieve a solution that wouldn't detrimentally impact his ability and authority to work with the board of trustees.

A wider audience – resolving the conflict between Mr D, the board of trustees and the chief executive would take place in a more public sphere than might otherwise have been desired by the parties in conflict. Mrs D's comments to the local news reporter had piqued the interest of the local press; as well as their interest in the land development issue, they were also engaged with the idea of a 'Trust in Crisis' story involving prominent local community figures. The younger followers of the charity were also interested in the outcome of the conflict, partly because they were now part of the charity's membership and partly because the conflict's outcome would have an effect on their potential roles in the charity's future.

Meeting with each side

In keeping with their earlier decision, the chief executive and company secretary B agreed that B should meet with both sides to hear their stories, then report back to the chief executive with what he had learned.

Meeting the Ds

B's first port of call was to meet with Mr and Mrs D: recognising that they were older, and felt nervous about the meeting, he agreed to meet with them at their house to make them feel more at ease with the discussion.

As expected, Mr and Mrs D expressed tremendous embarrassment and regret over Mrs D's comments to the local journalist. They both said that they understood why the board of trustees would be upset over a sensitive issue being commented on publicly, but emphasised that no ill intent was meant by the remarks. They said that openness was an important part of their marriage, and that Mr D had honestly not thought anything of mentioning the basic details of the issue to his wife in the privacy of their home.

On the subject of his life tenure, Mr D was very upset that the board of trustees seemed to want him to stand down from his position. He said that 'after all I've given the charity and could still give; it's a real insult that they want to get rid of me. They think that because I'm old, I'm stupid – that's not true or fair at all!' Mr D was also very upset that the chairman hadn't come out to support him, and took this as a personal slight.

Listening to Mr D talk through this, it seemed to B that:

- D was genuinely sorry for the impact of his wife's comments, and had not fully considered the implications of such remarks being made public.
- D was very attached to the charity, and aligned a large part of his identity with being a trustee. Accordingly, the other trustees' wish to see him step down was about ingratitude and disrespect as well as conduct.
- D was keen to save face in the conflict, and not be discounted as foolish, outdated or lacking judgement because of his age.

As the conversation continued, Mr D confided in B that he had recently found out that he had a chronic health condition, which could limit his ability to participate fully in the Trust's work. Mr and Mrs D both stressed that this was recent news, and that they had not yet decided how to inform family, friends and the trustees of D's condition. They explained that telling B was in the spirit of full disclosure, but that they did not wish for other people to learn the news yet.

Meeting the board of trustees

B's next meeting was with the board of trustees – to accommodate a larger group of people comfortably, the meeting took place at a local function room which provided a catered lunch for the group. This group was attended by the chairman as well as a good cross-section of trustees.

The delegates from the board of trustees all said that they were disappointed by the information leak – it was a sensitive issue and Mrs D's comments to the local reporter were very uncomfortable for the Trust. Although they understood that Mr D's intention may have been innocent, the delegates emphasised that he should not have disclosed the information to anyone, not even his wife. One delegate raised the question, 'If D thought nothing of telling his wife about this, what else has he said? And to whom?'

The delegates were less united on the question of what action they thought should be taken. A significant group thought that Mr D should be made to resign his position, and that his actions justified going against his life tenure. Others said that D had made a mistake, now recognised the total impact of his actions, and that the matter should naturally conclude there. The meeting became heated, people frustrated, and progress seemed to come to a standstill.

B saw that the meeting was becoming tense, and decided that a sidebar conversation with the chairman would be a good opportunity to hear his view clearly and give everyone else a chance to take a break.

Away from the other trustees, the chairman was able to confide in B that, in one sense, he was hoping that Mr D would leave the trust and let the 'new blood', as he called it, take greater control over the charity's direction. The chairman disclosed that the trust's revenues were falling as donations dried up and subscriptions were left to expire without renewal. He felt that a big part of this was due to the charity's image as a staid, old-fashioned organisation with no room for change or new ideas. He told B directly that this information was confidential, and that he especially didn't want Mr D to know about the problems.

Reporting back to the chief executive

After hearing everyone's views, B reported back to the chief executive with what he had heard.

As well as providing information, B also had to decide what information to withhold. He had been privy to confidential and sensitive information from both sides, and had been asked not to repeat some things he had heard. On the other hand, this information was significant enough to alter the dynamic of the dispute.

B decided that he could keep the information confidential while also ensuring that the dynamic-changing sentiments were still conveyed. He told the chief executive that he had heard sensitive information that he had been asked to keep quiet, but that he believed altered each side's incentive and ability to reach an agreement. He suggested that it was certainly in each side's interest to find a settlement, and that encouraging this would be a worthwhile use of time.

Acting in this way was in accordance with B's personal values and comfort zone; it also served a practical purpose. The conflict had begun on a chance remark to a local news reporter, and since then the local press had been following the activity of the trustees with more interest than they had ever done before. B was determined that there would be no further information leaks. Successive breaches of trust could potentially derail any budding willingness to negotiate, resulting in unsatisfactory outcomes for all concerned.

Deciding a way forward

The chief executive and company secretary decided that a group session facilitated by them would be a good way of getting the sides together and encouraging them to talk, listen and find a settlement. A neutral venue was found, and invitations made to the Ds, the chairman, and key representatives from the board of trustees.

The meeting opened with B setting out ground rules encouraging civility and staying 'on task'. He also took the opportunity to say that, having spoken with everyone, he believed that it was in everyone's interests to find a solution. From an interests point of view, settlement was not only desirable but very possible too.

B and the chief executive then opened the meeting to discussion. Each party was able to explain to the other their views and feelings, which carried additional force as it was face-to-face. Meeting in person also helped to strengthen each side's commitment to sorting the problem out; instead of an issue and adversary, each side saw the other as 'people just like them'.

B helped guide the discussions by asking the question, 'What is the ideal outcome for you today?', which revealed that, while the trustees were focused on reinvigorating their support base, and Mr D on continuing to serve as a trustee, each side wanted what was best for the Trust. This was a breakthrough, highlighting that the sides had common interests and that they could both look at the issue from a 'best for the Trust' perspective.

Looking at the issue this way led to a resolution where Mr D's life tenure as a trustee took on a more consultative aspect. This was a good outcome because:

- The trust did not have to violate Mr D's life tenure, but were free to focus on appealing to new, different audiences.
- Mr D was still able to be active within the Trust but on his own schedule, accommodating his health issues more comfortably.
- The Trust still had access to Mr D's experience, contacts, reassuring presence, etc.
- Mr D felt excited and reassured to still have an important role to play in the Trust's life.
- The discussion revealed that each side still valued the other and wanted to preserve a working relationship together. The new thoughts and boundaries established through the discussion meant that this relationship could still productively exist, along guidelines that met each side's needs.

3
Avoiding boardroom warfare – remedying board disputes

James South

Boardrooms: an incubator of conflict

In a private company, the board of directors is in charge of monitoring the company's performance, overseeing its affairs, and guiding the company towards success. The board is at the centre of a company's governance structure: by law, the board has ultimate responsibility for the company's affairs, hiring and giving direction to management, and representing shareholders' interests. As part of this remit, the board is usually informed of disputes or litigation that might affect the company's reputation, operations, and finances.

The board does not operate alone. Management, appointed by the board, are responsible for the day-to-day running of the company; shareholders are represented by the board. There are also any number of 'stakeholders' – people and groups with an interest in how the company operates. Stakeholders can include public bodies, financial institutions, suppliers and employees, and it is the interaction between the board, managers handling the day-to-day running of the organisation, and various stakeholders that generates conflict.

With so many parties invested in a company's fortunes, the potential for dispute is great. Commonly, disputes arise between:

- Shareholders and the company
- Shareholders and the board
- Board and the CEO
- Board and the company's senior management team
- Board and local communities
- Members of the board itself – between the chairman, the CEO, executive and non-executive directors.

For the purposes of this chapter, it is the last dispute scenario we will be looking at in more detail. When disputes arise between board members, important long-term issues such as the company's ethos and long-term vision come under particular scrutiny, exposing *subjects* at the core of the company's being.

36 EFFECTIVE CONFLICT MANAGEMENT

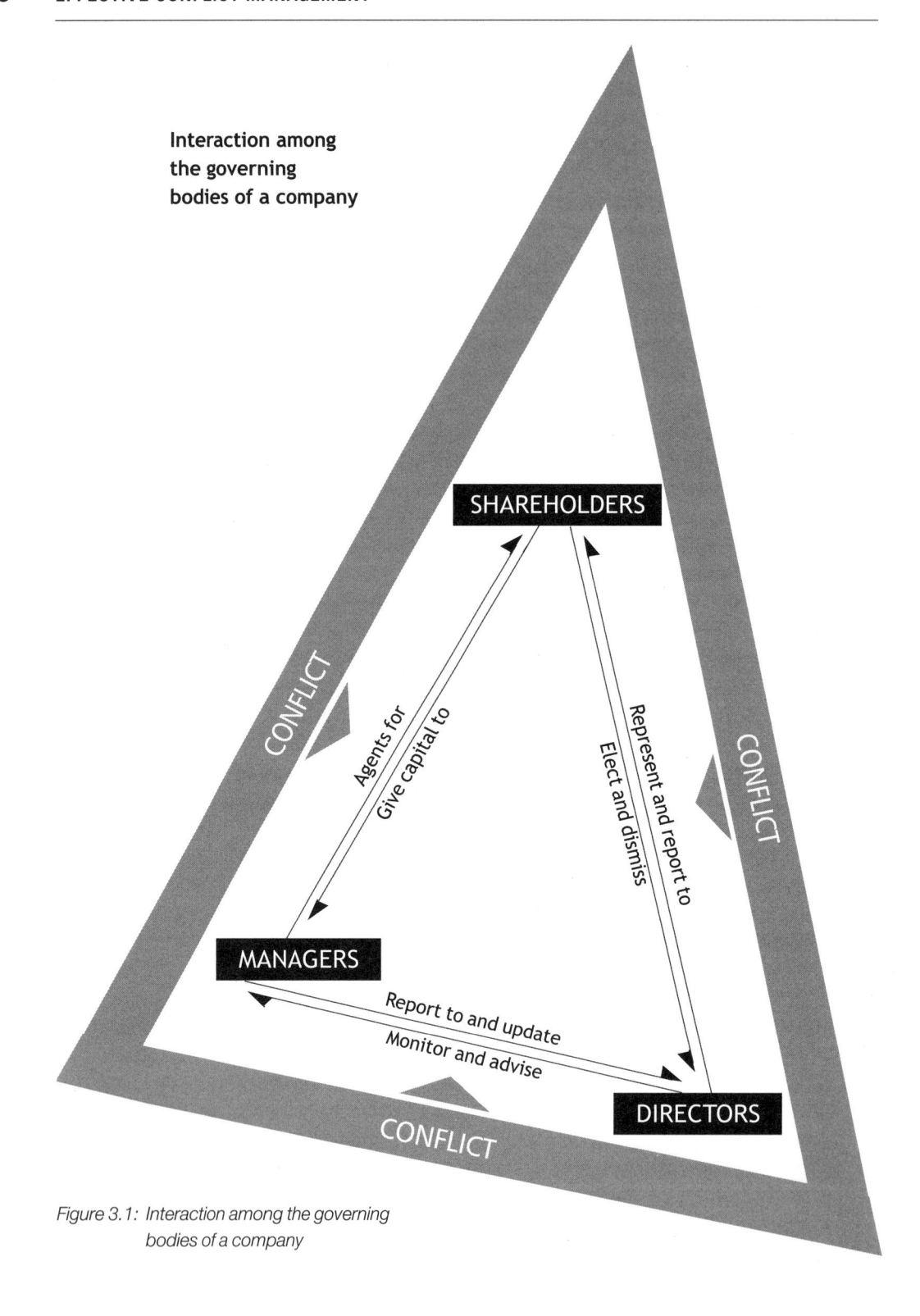

Interaction among the governing bodies of a company

Figure 3.1: Interaction among the governing bodies of a company

Why might you get warfare in the boardroom?

Boardroom disputes are of course unique to the company and the parties involved. However, there is a strong tendency in many conflicts for there to be two main factors at work which underpin a range of possible reactions: the people sitting on the board, and the processes the board uses to get its work done.

People

The composition of boards can provide fertile ground for conflict to arise: the typical board member is accomplished in their field, results-driven and confident in their skills as a professional. In many cases, this concentration of high achievers produces an exciting, invigorating working environment, but sometimes the voices compete with, rather than complement, each other. Directors may have different aims, but even when working towards a common goal they may differ on how best to achieve them. The opportunities for misunderstanding when welcoming new board members are countless, with glancing remarks and novel working methods taking on a new weight of significance through the magic mirror prism of first impressions.

Equally, sometimes there is no obvious reason for directors to find working together objectionable. It is fair to say that from time to time, two or more people simply find building a strong personal connection difficult. In these cases, problems occur when the people involved make little or no attempt to put personal differences aside for the sake of a smooth working environment. At board level especially, directors need to remember that how effectively they work has real implications for many other people connected with the business. Given this, directors have a particular responsibility – and interest in – concentrating on the *greater good* rather than wasting time and energy on perpetuating a dispute.

Process

The board is able to carry out its significant responsibilities because it has appropriate authority: it has the legal capacity to make and act on decisions. A full framework of access to financial resources, legal knowledge, goodwill and experience is available to directors to help implement its decisions. Furthermore, the board has a kind of moral authority based on how much confidence other invested parties have in its talents. The board's judgement is trusted to produce the best course of action for the business in any given case.

The question of how this authority can, and should, be used is at the heart of many boardroom disputes. The act of exercising these resources to decide control and direction is the underlying cause of conflict between board members. One or more directors may want to apply control for their own personal ends, or on behalf of shareholders they represent; and among directors, there may be clashes over the organisation's overall direction.

On a 'local' level, administrative processes may be found wanting, leaving directors without, for example, full information about a situation or enough opportunities to discuss issues. On a personal level, individual directors may feel unhappy about issues like the granting of compensation to themselves or the CEO. Casting wider, directors may develop objections to the company's long-term strategies for growth and development; responses to crises; and other fundamental shifts in the company's position.

In either case, it is imperative that boards find a way to harness the productivity of having different viewpoints while also embracing a united and fair decision-making process.

Boardroom warfare: common causes

The International Finance Corporation (IFC) and the Global Corporate Governance Forum (GCGF) have produced detailed work on corporate governance disputes, and the factors likely to instigate or magnify boardroom disputes. I summarise their excellent checklist below:[1]

- **Adopting new strategies**
- **Mergers and acquisitions**
- **Fundamental changes** such as those following a merger or significant deleveraging
- **Transformation to/from a not-for-profit organisation**
- **Crisis emerges/the post-crisis vacuum**
- **Change in board composition** – this is a very common cause of boardroom strife and has a number of impact strands which all involve issues of trust and accommodation. The good news is that much of the accelerant factor of a shifting board diminishes after time
- **Succession on the board and in management** which forces the board to confront seriously the question of where the organisation is, and might be headed
- **New CEO/chairman**
- **Directors nominated by dissident shareholders** – in practice, directors installed by a wave of dissident shareholders are likely to bring differing opinions about the company's direction and practices. This clash of vision is an immediate ground for disputes and conflict
- **Failure for board and management to respect one another's roles** – in a two-tier board structure, this would translate as the failure to respect the supervisory board's role versus the management board's role
- **Board-CEO difficulties** – the CEO typically has a dual role in practice, as manager and board member. The board depends on the CEO to both run the company and develop strategies that the board can review, amend and adopt. In this situation, there are lots of opportunities for disagreement and dispute between a company's board and CEO
- **CEO-chairman difficulties** – major conflicts can occur in companies where the positions of chairman and CEO are separated or in a two-tier board structure.
- **Dissatisfaction with content and conduct of board meetings** – even the meeting itself can be a source of malcontent for some directors. In this scenario, the most common problem is a procedure that prevents issues being discussed satisfactorily
- **One/a group of poorly performing directors**
- **Conflict of interests**
- **Personality clashes** – in some cases, the dislike between two or more directors is so powerful it poisons the atmosphere of the entire board

- **Confrontational directors** – in this scenario, it is important to determine the reasons behind the maverick's actions. Independent thought that adds to the board's perspective, for example, can be a real asset to the group
- **Adverse regulatory finding** – although management deals with the day-to-day aspects of the organisation, the board's role as reputational guardian can mean that an issue which is not originally under its remit eventually becomes one
- **Executive misconduct**, or the accusation of it, can make for a toxic boardroom atmosphere.

Tools for resolving board disputes

So now we have diagnosed some of the potential for disputes to occur within boards, let's look at some of the tools – both organisational and personal – that can be used by company secretaries serving on boards to help resolve such conflict.

Organisational tools for resolving boardroom conflict

In an ideal world, incidences of boardroom conflict would be few and far between. In the real world, boardroom conflict is both common and – happily – often preventable. The five-step plan below outlines steps organisations can take to anticipate and handle boardroom conflict successfully.

1. Embrace the idea of dispute resolution

This might seem like an overwhelming step, but the good news is that adopting a dispute resolution strategy will pay dividends in the future. It is well worth taking the time to have a critical look at your organisation: decide what works as it is, what could be better and what behaviours and procedures inhibit your ability to work together as an effective team.

In your thinking, playing the 'what if' game can be very effective in making sure you have all bases covered and discovering important factors that you may not have even considered. It can be applied to big and small matters; for example, to how board meetings are timetabled, or to a policy of delivering the last meeting's minutes in the morning of the next scheduled meeting. Some examples of corporate governance dispute resolution strategies at an organisational level include:

- Encourage effective board culture that stimulates discussion and debate but manages conflict
- Clarify roles of board vs management
- Establish orderly board processes
- Ensure proper flow of information
- Allow time for discussion, debate and deliberation
- Improve communication between board members.[2]

Once you have a comprehensive idea of how your organisation is currently working, you can implement policies that fully meet the organisation's needs and that encourage positive behaviours.

2. Be aware of your peacemakers

In charge of preventing and resolving disputes before they escalate into litigation or arbitration, the peacemaker has an important role in corporate dispute resolution. This person can be internal – such as the company secretary or an independent board director – or external, such as a third-party institution, firm or individual. When deciding on a peacemaker, boards should consider things like who is best suited to leading discussions or intervening in disputes; what additional training a peacemaker might need to be effective; and under what circumstances an external peacemaker should be involved.

There are advantages and drawbacks associated with both internal and external peacemakers, and deciding on which to use will depend on individual circumstances. While an internal peacemaker may have the advantage of insider knowledge of a dispute, for example, an external peacemaker might bring a fresh perspective through actively listening to each party in the dispute. Equally, developing internal peacemakers might form part of your organisation's training and professional development programme. Equipping people with the skills and confidence to deal with conflict effectively is not only personally empowering, the skills gain is also beneficial to the capacity and capabilities of your business.

3. Introduce a formal corporate governance disputes policy

Just like other organisational issues, a dispute resolution policy will be more effective when codified: writing down policy and procedure arms boards with the ability to react quickly when disputes arise. A written policy shows that the board is united and serious about corporate dispute resolution, and provides a helpful 'go to' information point for internal and external stakeholders.

Deciding where to include these policies in company documents will depend on the nature of the company and existing codes and laws governing how the company is organised. For example, including a dispute resolution policy statement in articles of incorporation can only be done with shareholder agreement, which can for various reasons be difficult to achieve. A public policy statement carries less logistical problems, but in the event of the policy changing, the board would need to be very careful in explaining the change to the wider public. Board committee charters offer a third option for signalling intent and outlining procedures.

Internal corporate governance dispute policies might include:

- Planning for board and board committee executive sessions
- Recommending dispute resolution training for directors and senior executives
- Scheduling board retreats and committee self-assessment meetings
- Ensuring that all directors have the opportunity to speak freely at executive sessions and retreats
- Using a third-party facilitator for assessments, retreats, and other board matters
- Including alternative dispute resolution (ADR) skills among the qualifications for board membership
- Identifying certain directors and corporate staff to play peacemaker roles
- Improving board procedures.

4. Monitor successes and areas for development

Qualitative and quantitative measures can be used to determine how effective a dispute resolution strategy is, providing helpful feedback and information. In terms of external disputes, or for information given to external stakeholders, it may be useful and appropriate to use performance metrics that clearly outline targets and strategies.

For internal purposes, however, the success of dispute resolution procedures is less formal. Are there fewer cases of intimidating disputes? Can board members give their views and air differences publicly? Have mechanisms been put into place to keep debates and disagreements on the right side of dispute and conflict? Does the work of the board feel easier, more straightforward, better at accomplishing goals? The answers to these questions won't be found in a graph or annual report, but can be revealed by candid conversations. Indeed, the ability to have honest discussions about these issues is an inherently good measure of the policies' impact.

5. Have faith in ADR processes and techniques

Introducing ADR techniques into the boardroom may at first feel strange, especially if most directors have only previously experienced litigious ways of settling disputes. Some directors may feel that because there is not the same kind of formal legal authority behind it, they can't fully trust that when enacted, dispute resolution processes will work. These people should be encouraged to take a leap of faith and 'go with' ADR: it offers many benefits with comparatively few downsides. At the Centre for Effective Dispute Resolution (CEDR) alone, we record that around 80% of mediated cases settle on the day of mediation, with many more citing the process as instrumental in achieving settlement at a later date. Following ADR processes will not revoke your legal entitlements, so in the event that does require litigation, no party has disadvantaged themselves by trying to settle independently of the courts. Indeed, judges are increasingly looking for evidence of attempts to settle disputes when giving judgements and making awards to parties bringing disputes before them.

Toolkit for individuals – key process and skills for dealing with boardroom conflict

Individuals can also take straightforward steps to handle boardroom conflict: this can not only help remedy a damaging conflict situation, it can do much to ensure that the individual remains in a healthy mental and emotional state. When considering the tools available for board members or others within the organisation to use to resolve disputes, it is helpful to think of the toolkit as having five compartments, which are the structure or process for resolving conflict, and within each compartment there are specific skills which you use as the tools to unlock disputes.

So let's first start with an overview of the compartments of the toolkit – the dispute resolution stages. The diagram below shows CEDR's mediation phase model diagram with five phases: preparation, opening, exploration, problem solving and concluding.[3]

CEDR Mediation Phase Model

PREPARATION → OPENING → EXPLORATION → PROBLEM SOLVING → CONCLUDING

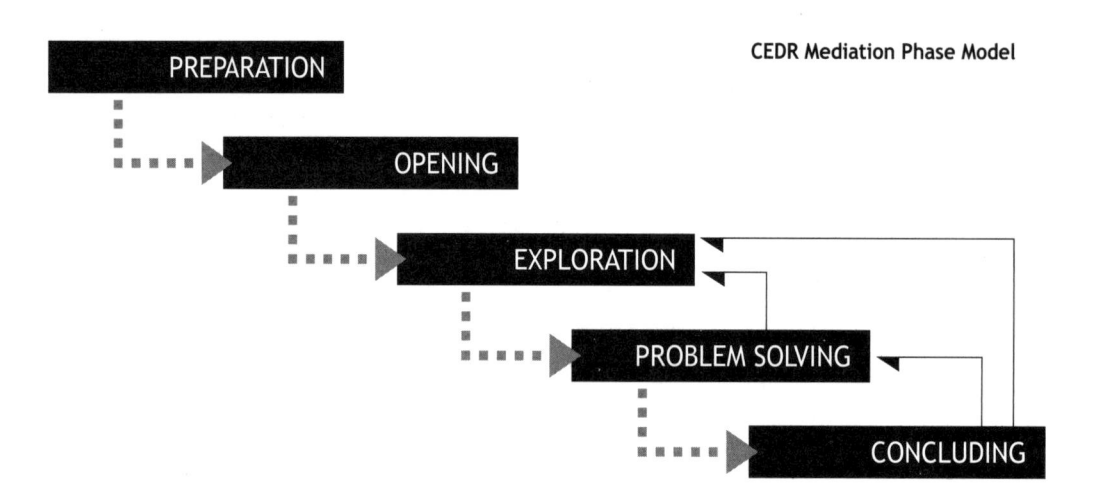

Figure 3.2: CEDR Mediation Phase Model

Years of dispute resolution experience show that it is important for those attempting to resolve conflict to keep the process above clearly in their minds when attempting to sort out disputes. This is particularly important for those internal to a board or organisations that are engaging in dispute resolution with others. When you are involved in conflict either as a party or an intermediary, where you have detailed knowledge of the content matter, background issues and personalities involved, it can be very tempting to assume you know what the answer is and jump straight into 'problem-solving' mode. After all, that is where most professionals feel comfortable, as most professional jobs require individuals to solve problems as part of their duties.

However, when looking to resolve conflict, this is almost always a mistake. Often the stated problem or position is not the actual problem, and time must be taken to understand these underlying 'interests' before beginning to look for solutions. In addition, conflict by its very nature causes personal stress and engages people's feelings. Attention needs to be given to these if people are truly to move on and engage in effective problem solving.

So what are the skills that you should deploy throughout these stages to effectively resolve the dispute? The following section outlines some of the key skills used within each stage of the dispute resolution process, with particular focus on the exploration and problem-solving phases.

Preparation

Understand the content of the dispute

The easy part of preparing is to focus on the content of the dispute, particularly because you will have background knowledge of the issues and will know quite a lot about the background to the conflict. However, equally important when preparing is to explore the assumptions you are making in this respect and ask yourself – 'what don't I know and what do I need to understand more about?' This will broaden your preparation and allow you to explore these issues during later discussions further along the process.

Consider how to handle personality issues
While understanding the content of a dispute is crucial, it is also important to consider the personalities involved in the dispute. How have they reacted in the past and currently in this respect? What is their likely approach going to be to negotiating an agreement? And finally, how are different individuals likely to react to one another? By paying attention to these issues during preparation, you can at least have some outline ideas about how you might manage them should they arise.

Think about the process
Having prepared the content and the personalities, your final task is to consider the process you are going to use to navigate your way from disagreement to agreement. Having the five-stage model set out above in mind is a start. However, consideration needs to be given to specific issues within each stage. How you will open discussion; set the agenda; record agreement; what ground rules should be adopted; and which combinations and methods of meetings will be most effective are but a few of the thoughts around process that should be considered while preparing.

Opening

Be clear of the purpose of the meeting/discussions
In any business meeting, the first thing that should be done to focus proceedings is to be clear about the purpose of that meeting. It is amazing therefore that when parties come together to meet about resolving a dispute, they too frequently skip discussion about the meeting's purpose and get right down to arguing. By starting out with a statement that the purpose of the meeting, for example, 'is to resolve the dispute by understanding each side's issues and then looking to consider options to resolve those issues', you have clearly set out what you are going to do, but also how you are going to do it – both in terms of process and style – collaboratively.

Set an agenda
This simple technique can be enormously beneficial throughout the rest of the resolution process: by establishing the issues that need to be discussed (as opposed to their solutions), it serves as a guide to all future discussions. Agreement can be sought on how to tackle the agenda items once formulated, with some perhaps benefiting from being tackled sequentially, and others grouped by common issues. Whatever the approach, the formulation of an agenda forms the backbone of future discussions and can help get them back on track when things digress. Finally, it can also be used as a way of charting progress, as you begin to resolve issues to everyone's satisfaction.

Adopt a collaborative tone
When beginning to discuss intense disputes, emotions are normally running high and the tendency is to want to blame someone else for the problem. If through the use of your language and your tone, you can indicate that the problem is a combined one, as is the resolution, it begins

to change the nature of discussion from positional to collaborative problem solving. One simple technique is to reframe language where possible from using 'you' and 'I' to the use of the collective 'we'.

> e.g. 'I want you to/you need to' to 'We need to consider.'

Exploration

Understand interests rather than focusing on positions

One of the major mistakes parties involved in a dispute make is that they focus exclusively on what they want and what the other side say they want. The parties' positions are often framed in a legal way if the dispute has escalated to involve lawyers. The problem with focusing on positions as a basis for resolution of a dispute is that almost by definition, they are going to be polar opposites and not provide much space for collaborative problem solving.

> e.g.: Party A: There has been breach of contract by you, therefore you owe me £100,000 in damages.
> Party B: There has been no breach of contract by me, therefore I owe you nothing.

The other point to make about positions is that they are really only the visible tip of the iceberg, and that underneath what is really important to parties is what is motivating these positions – their needs and feelings. These are termed the 'parties' interests' and by definition are normally much broader, encompassing both commercial and personal interests as well as legal aspects. Accordingly, those involved in the dispute or a third party intermediary need to understand everyone's interests and reveal them to each other to provide a broader basis to begin the task of meaningful problem solving.

Active listening

The capacity to be a good and understanding listener is the basis of effective communication. Parties come to a dispute with varying degrees of distress, anger, fear and optimism. The knowledge that they are listened to and understood will help to build trust and enable parties to consider more openly the options for change, and to take their share of the responsibility for resolving the situation.

Listening is an active process that entails not just hearing the words, but also being sensitive to vocal clues, tone, pitch and inflection, observing movement, taking into account the context, and communicating understanding. In this way, parties not only know they have been heard but can also hear their own messages more clearly. There are a range of active listening skills that can be used to demonstrate you are listening and these are summarised on the continuum below.

As can be seen from the continuum, active listening skills are both verbal and non-verbal in nature and if used well, can demonstrate understanding and pave the way for more effective problem solving.

The spectrum of skills needed for effective active listening

The process of active listening requires a range of skills, which can be described in a continuum:

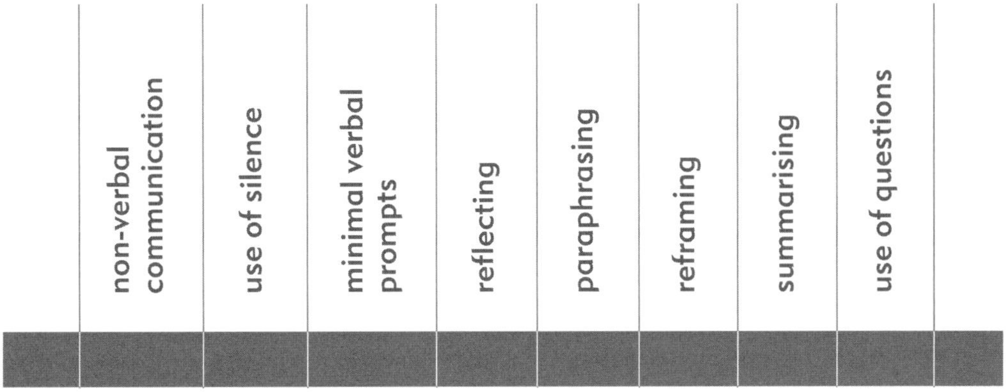

| non-verbal communication | use of silence | minimal verbal prompts | reflecting | paraphrasing | reframing | summarising | use of questions |

Figure 3.3: The active listening skills continuum

Be curious – ask open questions

There is one active listening skill that is worth specific mention in order to engage in exploration of the interests of disputants. Open questions are best thought of as broad invitations to talk: they can be very illuminating as people volunteer information from a position of feeling comfortable, which they might not reveal in response to direct questioning. The temptation for us as problem solvers is to ask closed leading questions in order to funnel discussion to an outcome we have in mind or that is pre-determined. This therefore misses the opportunity to uncover interests as it focuses largely on stated positions. Good open questions allow the party being questioned to control the direction of the discussion, to present views and ideas from their own perspective, to highlight concerns and, importantly, to tell their story. Such questions encourage wider discussion of the current situation and facilitate ideas for change and options for action.

Examples of good open questions include: How do you react to what they say? What do you think are the likely consequences? What suggestions do you have? Why is that important?

Allow the 'feelings' conversation to take place

The final skill that needs developing for effective exploration is the ability to actually have the conversation about how people felt in the past and present and, importantly, why. Often our instincts, particularly in business-related disputes, are to want to remove all discussion and expression of emotion from the resolution of disputes. The 'ignore it and it will go away' approach does not work. It is much more effective to name the emotions you are seeing being expressed by disputants and then engage in a respectful conversation about why they are feeling the way they do. This will result not only in catharsis for the one feeling the emotion, but will also demonstrate a willingness to listen as well as possibly uncover additional interests necessary to address in any problem solving.

Problem solving

First generate options before evaluating

Once there has been a full discussion about the underlying interests of each side that need to be addressed in any agreed solution to the dispute, then the parties can begin to discuss options for addressing those issues. However, parties often go wrong as options are raised by one party. These options are immediately evaluated and debated, normally favourably by the side proposing the solution and unfavourably by the other side.[4] As someone involved in a dispute, either as party or intermediary, it is better to hold off on the evaluation of options until all the possible options are on the table. Once parties can see the full picture and have the range of options in front of them, they will be able to see where trade-offs are possible and where there are convergent options which may be easy wins.

Manage negotiations actively

Whether acting as an intermediary or a party to a dispute, it is easy to get lulled into a simple horse-trade at the stage where offers and options are being discussed. It is important to manage this negotiation for the active resolution of a dispute. You can do this in a variety of ways including:

- focusing on where parties want to be, not where they are
- managing parties' expectations and helping them through disappointments
- using creative problem-solving techniques to work up deals in principle
- understanding negotiation tactics being used by parties, and using suitable strategies for creating movement
- protecting the parties from loss of face, and assisting in overcoming other common problems that impede negotiations; see below for further detail
- recognising value differentials as a potential for settlement; what is of value to one party may be easy for another to provide
- communicating offers and exchanging information tactfully
- helping the parties past the hurdle of making the first offer
- avoiding parties committing too early to a bottom line
- recognising 'magic numbers' and the psychology of numbers
- working with global sums or numerical boundaries
- assisting parties to work through apparent deadlock.[5]

Pull back when stuck – consider risks of not reaching an agreement

Often, despite considerable progress having been made toward resolving the dispute, there comes a time, where parties can appear deadlocked. The first thing to say here is, don't give up! It may be getting difficult, but if parties are nearly there they will often want to go the extra mile to get an agreement. One specific technique to be used at this stage to get parties to move is a re-evaluation of the risks of not reaching an agreement. Parties often wildly underestimate the risk to them and their companies if the dispute continues. If they are 90% of the way to an agreement, then those risks will loom even larger. Accordingly, at this stage if you pull back from discussion about the emerging agreement, and instead focus on a re-evaluation of the risk of not settling, and then put these in the context of the remaining gap (in this example, only 10%), this will often suffice to assist parties in bridging the final gap. Remember that when engaging in this risk re-assessment, it is better to ask open questions to get them to re-evaluate their risks themselves rather than you telling them your evaluation. Telling rather than uncovering risk can result in parties hardening their positions, which is the exact opposite of what you as a neutral facilitator want to achieve!

Tactful uncovering might be prompted by asking questions such as:

'Tell me how likely you would be to succeed if this matter were to go to court?'

'What are the costs involved?'

'What impact would the continuation of this dispute have on the business?'

'How would you feel if this dispute wasn't resolved today?'

Concluding

Record it and agree follow-up
If an agreement is reached, the main priority is to ensure that it is properly documented and that proper consideration is given to how and by whom it is to be implemented. It is important to ensure that there is a follow-up mechanism to confirm compliance – perhaps agreeing to have implemented steps within a defined time period, or having both sides check back in with the neutral facilitator at regular intervals to preserve a neutral communication channel until specified steps have been taken and achieved.

Remedying board disputes: summary checklist

- **People and processes** can cause boardroom warfare – the particular dynamics of any given dispute can and often are particular and nuanced. In practice, triggers can include mergers, attitudes to crisis management and succession planning, adverse regulatory findings or the installation of a new CEO. Typically, these triggers expose underlying board tensions and frustrations.
- The **five organisational tools** for handling boardroom conflict:
    1. embracing the dispute resolution idea
    2. being aware of peacemakers
    3. making a policy
    4. monitoring the effects
    5. having faith in the policy's success

- **Individual tools** for handling boardroom conflict follow the CEDR Mediation phase model:

Preparation –	a) understanding context
	b) awareness of personalities
	c) thinking about processes
Opening –	a) be clear
	b) set the agenda
	c) adopt the right tone
Exploration –	a) interests rather than positions
	b) active listening
	c) have the 'feelings' conversation
Problem solving –	a) opinions before evaluations
	b) actively manage negotiations
	c) consider the risks of not agreeing
Concluding –	a) record everything
	b) agree follow-up actions

Case study: the family boardroom fallout

A board mired in dispute cannot provide management with the direction it needs for long-term, sustainable growth. Indeed, board infighting can be very damaging: the paralysis, lack of attention and increased stress levels accompanying a dispute hurt parties far beyond those directly involved with the conflict. As this case study illustrates, boardroom conflict can damage companies and families alike over time frames spanning many years. Mediation in this case provided an excellent framework to address the commercial, personal and emotional issues at play in the dispute, reaching a solution that provided closure for all of the parties involved. The case study highlights many of the personal toolkit pointers mentioned previously, illustrating how they might work when applied practically.

The dispute[6]

Two cousins began a software development business. Anthony was the technical brains behind the development of the software, while David had the business, marketing and sales experience. David was both chief executive and chairman of the board, leaving Anthony free to focus on his software development role.

In its first few years, the business was a success. However, to match the ambitious plans the founders had for long-term growth, the business required more capital to expand. After some time, two different institutional investors agreed to supply the necessary funds – in recognition of their important contribution, the investors each took seats on the board of the company.

The company then experienced eighteen months of difficult trading, affecting the company's revenues and future growth prospects. To solve the problem, the cousins decided to ask the institutional board members to supply the business with additional funds. The two board members agreed, but imposed conditions in return for their cooperation. They requested that the chairman and chief executive roles be split, and a non-executive chairman be appointed. David was immediately unhappy with these conditions and did not want to agree: he ultimately gave his consent because he realised there was no other source of funding, without which the business would be in danger of failing.

An existing board member was appointed as chairman, and from the beginning the relationship between him and David, now just the chief executive, was very difficult. The two men had very different approaches to the business, and David also found it difficult to accept the loss of the chairman title.

The company's fortunes began to improve, but not quickly enough for the board, who decided one year later at a very tense board meeting that David should be dismissed as chief executive. A difficult, demanding period in the organisation followed. David eventually began legal proceedings over a number of issues, including unfair dismissal, breach of fiduciary duty by the board, and for the repayment of loans David said he had made to the company. The total amount claimed was £3,000,000.

What impact was the dispute having on the company?

Before considering the elements of this dispute in more detail, it is important to set out the considerable effect the dispute was having on the company. While turnover was strong, with only 100 staff, this was a fairly small company, and the dispute had been going on for over three years. During the course of the mediation, all parties identified the following detrimental impacts of the dispute.

Paralysed decision-making

Given the uncertainty around the outcome of the litigation, the accompanied potential risk, and the time the board was spending on pursing the conflict, important business decisions had been delayed. This was having a clearly damaging effect on the company's ability to develop and grow.

Poor staff morale

As this was a small company started by the two cousins, the departure of one of them in such difficult circumstances had very badly affected staff morale. Many staff felt a strong sense of loyalty to David and the ongoing litigation created a tense atmosphere in the workplace. The heavy, pervasive feeling of discomfort led to staff feeling demotivated and resulted in a sharp fall in productivity.

Distraction to the board's focus on improving the business

The dispute and accompanying litigation process was a distraction to the board's attempts to secure the financial position of the company and focus its growth and development. In addition, there was a significant personal impact on each of the board members, as many of them were personally involved in the dispute. Anthony, who was still at the company, felt particularly strained. Stress levels across the board were very high.

Reputation

The dispute had become public knowledge in the industry and many damaging rumours were circulating about what had happened and the ongoing financial viability of the company. The company was in a sound financial position but the ongoing dispute was starting to affect how customers and other businesses viewed the company. As a consequence, selling the product was becoming much more difficult as public goodwill and confidence in the company faltered.

What elements of this dispute needed addressing?

Often, in corporate governance disputes, claims made in the litigation are only the tip of the iceberg. In this case, financial compensation was important to David, but there were many more issues driving this dispute. We will consider a few of them:

Divergent interests

One of the key issues in this dispute was the divergent interests between the institutional investors and David. The institutions thought that given the stage of development of the company, a new vision was needed to drive through the necessary changes. As such, they saw it in purely commercial terms. However, David saw this dispute as having both commercial and personal dimensions. He saw his dismissal not only as unjustified from a commercial perspective but also as an attack on him personally. He viewed the company very much as being his and any attempts made by others at getting involved as a personal reflection of his leadership abilities.

Sense of professional identity

David was a self-made man who prided himself on his business acumen. Along with a sense of personal responsibility for how the company was performing, he also saw himself as a good chief executive who could bring the company through what he described as 'growing pains'. Being dismissed by the board was an especially painful blow because it challenged his sense of professional identity.

Loss of status and control

As well as challenging his professional identity, David's feeling that he had lost control of what he saw as 'his' company was a major motivating factor in the dispute. His view was that these institutional board members used their financial power to essentially oust him from his own company and parachute in one of their own supporters instead.

The board saw things differently and insisted that dismissing David was purely a business decision. They saw the decision as the best way to ensure the survival of the company and to maximise its profits, reflecting the fact that the relationship between the board and the company had less personal overtones than David's relationship with the company. In the board members' words, 'this was not personal'.

Breakdown of family relationship

The fact that this company started off as a family business added another layer of complexity to the dispute. Anthony, the technical expert, was still with the company and the dispute had deeply affected the relationship between the two cousins. David no longer spoke to Anthony, who he felt had betrayed him, leaving Anthony feeling confused, hurt and torn between his family and the business he had also helped to build.

The effects of the dispute were not limited to just the two cousins. The hostility between the two men had infected members of the extended family and they were now divided into two camps, both sides blaming the other for what had happened. The close links between business and family served to amplify aspects of the conflict, while escalating it into areas far beyond the initial scope of the dispute. While the decision was 'not personal' to the board, there were clear personal implications for David and Anthony's wider family.

Wanting justice/retribution

Given the above factors, there was a very strong sense from David that he wanted justice and for the board to be shown that they were in the wrong. Resolving the dispute had become as much about publicly restoring David's reputation as winning financial compensation or enforcing his legal rights, as he sought to remedy the emotional and psychological effects the dispute had caused. He felt that litigation would give him this even though his own legal team had advised him that on some aspects of his claim he only stood a 50% chance of success. David was therefore determined to negotiate very hard in the mediation.

Interestingly, the board had also begun to take this dispute personally, even without David's close family ties to the company. They felt that a lot of the problems with the company were down to David and there was a real sense of wanting to make him pay for 'the state he left the company in'. They were angry with the growing rumours about the company's future and blamed David for the mounting problems the ongoing dispute was creating at all levels of the business.

What happened in the mediation to move the parties to agreement?

We have considered some of the issues that needed to be addressed for this dispute to settle. It is clear that litigation would not provide adequate means for redressing many of the issues. A court is not concerned with the breakdown of the family relationship or the sense of professional identity and the loss of power and control. Rather, they look at the legal rights in respect of the claims David made against the company. The impersonal court system was not fully equipped to deal with the detailed personal issues at play in David's case.

The huge benefit of mediation is that while it can discuss the legal aspects of a dispute, it can also address some of the wider elements influencing people's motivation and behaviour. A purely legal assessment of a dispute might not result in a satisfactory resolution, but approaching a dispute with *mediation*, and taking other factors into consideration, may *unlock* a settlement. Such factors might include:

Letting people tell their story

Often in difficult dispute negotiations, parties make a fatal mistake by jumping straight into substantive negotiations on a settlement figure. Doing this misses an opportunity for parties to talk through 'what happened', from their perspective as well as expressing their feelings about the situation. Allowing people to have an opportunity to tell their story, and to express their feelings about it, is a crucial part of having a difficult conversation and allowing people to feel understood.[7]

Therefore, in this dispute, it was important that the mediation allowed time for these conversations to happen. This was achieved by having an initial joint session when each party got to tell their story. It was also important that Anthony was given his chance to tell his story privately to the mediator: this process uncovered a lot of anger, frustration and upset which was expressed in quite a forceful way.

At this stage, creating space for Anthony to explain the situation from his point of view and discuss how it had affected him was significant. Before the mediation process began, Anthony did not have a constructive outlet for his feelings, and his unique position in the dispute was not being accounted for. The mediator's presence offers a solution to this problem. Mediators are trained to act as a 'sponge' for these sometimes tumultuous feelings, allowing the parties to achieve catharsis by expressing feelings that may have been bottled up and hidden for a long time. Additionally, the mediator can help the parties in dispute manage their emotions productively. This breaks the retributive cycle and instead channels each party's energies towards a forward-looking plan of action.

What became clear from the private conversations with both cousins was that their respective version of what happened during the time of the removal of David as chief executive was very different. Understanding this pointed to a clear action plan: convening a meeting between the two cousins to address the different perspectives on the story, and work on beginning to restore the family relationship.

Beginning restoration of family relationship and dealing with betrayal

When discussing the restoration of the family relationship, it is important to say from the outset that mediation is not a miracle process that will magically fix acrimonious relationships between parties, especially these family members. What mediation can do, however, is ground a dispute in reality. It is a practical approach that finds common ground between parties, as a precursor to discussing areas of difference and finding realistic ways of navigating them.

In this particular case, what was possible was for the mediator to set up a process where both cousins could tell their version of the story in a respectful way. After this, the cousins could then begin to re-establish communication and discuss the very real issues that had led to the breakdown of their relationship.

Once it was clear that both cousins had different versions of what had happened at the relevant board meetings and offshoot meetings after these, the mediator was able to tell each cousin these new details. The mediator also suggested, and gained agreement to, a private cousin meeting chaired by the mediator to explore how the new details affected the dispute. They agreed to this and, at the start of the meeting, set some strict guidelines for the conduct of the meeting which meant that they could initially talk uninterrupted. This enabled both sides to tell their story from start to finish without getting side-tracked into debates with each other. As mediation is a voluntary process, the agreement of each cousin to all suggestions was crucial.

Once the stories had been told, the mediator identified five key issues from their stories which needed to be discussed further, and invited the cousins to comment. This began a constructive discussion between the two cousins, and, importantly, allowed them to begin communicating again. Halfway through the discussion, Anthony was able to say how much he regretted the situation and the impact that it had on their family. David agreed with this but made it clear he still felt betrayed by Anthony's actions. This enabled Anthony to explain that that was not his intention and reiterate that he had actually voted against the resolution to replace David as chief executive.

The meeting ended positively, with both cousins finding common ground over a desire to spare their family further heartache. David and Anthony agreed that for the sake of their family, reaching a settlement at the mediation would be the best way forward rather than pursuing a drawn-out court battle. Anthony said he would do all he could to ensure that the company would commit to the mediation process.

Managing a tough negotiation on both sides

Mediation is often derided by its critics as a 'soft' process: nothing could be further from the truth, especially in the case of mediations involving corporate governance issues. Representatives of parties in corporate governance disputes are normally very senior within the organisation and have many years of business experience. They are also normally very accomplished in their field of expertise. Accordingly, negotiations to settle these disputes are seldom soft and are often very tough.

In such situations, the mediator plays a key role in assisting the parties to negotiate in a way that is most likely to achieve settlement. There are many aspects to this, much of which centres on the 'hard', business-like way party representatives make, frame and respond to offers. Parties in these types of disputes, for example, often want to begin negotiating from the extreme of their negotiation range without much thought given to how the other party may receive this and how they might reciprocate. Offers are often expressed in global amounts with parties not wanting to provide a breakdown, framed poorly and therefore not likely to be received well by the other side, and often parties are unsure what their next move should be.

In all these situations, the mediator can be an asset in articulating messages to each party without putting words into either party's mouth. The mediator can, for example, coach the parties through the negotiation process by assisting them to frame offers appropriately, getting them to explain the rationale for offers and testing how such offers are likely to be received by the other party. This all takes place without the mediator compromising their neutrality by telling the parties what their offer should be.

The negotiation in this case was very tough, with both sides taking strong negotiation positions from the outset and only making concessions slowly. This form of positional negotiation[8] was particularly evident with the representative from the company, who clearly had decided to adopt a firm negotiation strategy at the outset. His intended opening offer to David was very nominal in the context of the claim, which was likely to be received quite badly by him and risked prompting him to walk out. In this case, particularly, the hidden messages conveyed by each communication had the potential to speak very loudly indeed, overpowering the goodwill each party had brought to the mediation process.

Accordingly, a lot of time was spent talking though the rationales for this first offer and how David might respond to it. In doing this, the mediator sought Anthony's view, and asked him in the light of the cousins' discussion earlier in the day how he thought David would react to this opening offer. He helpfully indicated that it would not be received very well and that he would prefer them to consider making a higher opening offer. This comment was enough for the mediator to suggest they discuss this privately amongst themselves, while the mediator spent some time reflecting with David. After the 30 minutes had passed, they had a new opening offer which was considerably higher and when conveyed to David got the response, 'at least they are treating this seriously.'

This was just the beginning of what turned out to be quite a difficult negotiation which lasted over five hours. However, if the parties had not had the assistance of a mediator in managing this process, the chances of reaching agreement would have been greatly reduced. As an impartial third party, the mediator enjoyed more flexibility to consider the wider implications of each party's actions and communication, such as thinking about the range of possible ways David might respond to the company's token opening offer. Asking for Anthony's input at this stage was a creative way of engaging him as a stakeholder, and using his insight to head off a potential problem before it had the chance to take hold. In this case, mediation's ability to respond to particular circumstances was a tremendous asset in handling each party's likely reactions.

Balancing retribution versus risk

Despite having a mediator assisting in the negotiations, and despite both sides having made substantial movement, there was still a gap, which looked like it could not be closed. At this stage, when parties think they can move no further, it is usual for them to return to focus on their legal rights and the fact that they can simply go to court and get their retribution by being proven right in a court of law.

So it was in this case. The parties had managed to negotiate so that they were only £25,000 apart, but neither side said they were prepared to go any further. Because of David's desire to be proven right, his fall-back position when this gap presented itself was, 'well let's go to court then and I will be proven right'.

In this situation, the mediator's job is to assist the parties in examining the risks of pursuing this course of action. The initial risk in this case, as with others, was that the law was far from clear and that David's lawyer, who was present at the mediation, had already made it known that some points would be more difficult to succeed on than others. Accordingly, some time was taken to talk through these points, examining the likelihood of succeeding or failing and the full implications of this.

The second risk to be discussed at some length was the costs involved in taking this dispute to trial. When discussing costs, the parties looked at not only financial costs, such as legal fees, but also transactional costs on both sides. The legal costs in this case were likely to be quite high and whichever side lost would not only have to pay their own costs but the majority of those of the other side.[9] The uncertain outcome of several of the legal points in this case therefore represented a significant financial risk to both parties. Ironically, creating financial security was one of the reasons the board members took the decision to dismiss David. The long-term repercussions of saddling one party with significant financial liabilities were likely to entrench hostility and instability rather than alleviate it.

For David, there were other costs associated with trial as well. These included:

- a delay in getting a financial settlement,
- the stress of the ongoing litigation, and
- the impact on the family relationship.

For the company, the other non-monetary costs of this dispute going to litigation included:

- the ongoing impact that the dispute was having on staff morale,
- the time spent by senior members of the company pursuing the litigation process, and
- the risk to company and personal reputations if the dispute went to court.

After discussing these risks with both sides and reiterating that the gap between the parties was only £25,000, the mediator allowed them some time in private to discuss whether they would like to make another offer. Giving them time was crucial at this point. The parties had been working for some eight hours in stressful circumstances and they needed space for reflection. Furthermore, because issues of identity and personal dignity were so acute, building in an opportunity for each party to step back and reconsider without losing face was especially important.

In this case, allowing time for each party to re-evaluate the situation and their respective positions generated a positive outcome. Following one more round of trading offers, David and the board reached a respectful, reasonable and practical agreement.

Notes

1. *Toolkit 4: Resolving Corporate Governance Disputes*, 'Volume 1: Rationale', International Finance Corporation (ed. James Spellman), Maryland 2011 pp. 11–18.
2. Summarised from 'What Skills are needed for CG Dispute Resolution' module 1 of volume 3 of the 'Resolving Corporate Governance Disputes Toolkit'; Global Corporate Governance Forum/IFC.
3. CEDR mediation phase model diagram, *The CEDR Mediator Handbook* (5th Edition), 2010.

4. This dismissal of an offer made by another party is called reactive devaluation and is hardwired into human psychology.
5. Taken from the *CEDR Mediator Handbook* (2010 edition).
6. To protect the confidentiality of parties, names, dates and specific details have been altered and anonymised.
7. For more information on the 'what happened' and 'feelings' conversations implicit in any difficult conversation, see Douglas Stone, Bruce Patton and Sheila Heen's book *Difficult Conversations*, 2000, Penguin Books.
8. For more discussion on the hallmarks of positional negotiation, as well as the other main approach to negotiation, principled or collaborative negotiation, see R. Fisher and W. Ury *Getting to Yes*, Random House, 2007.
9. This is the legal rule in England and Wales, where the loser must pay the other side's costs, see Civil Procedure Rules of England and Wales, Rule 44.

4
Managing emotional turbulence – the psychology of organisational conflict

Dr Karl Mackie CBE and Tracey Fox

'Who is the company secretary?'

This question, or one like it, is one that many readers have probably heard when explaining their role to others. Few people outside of the boardroom know what a company secretary is or what their role entails; those who have heard perhaps think of a person who takes minutes, writes reports and performs administrative tasks. This observation is both true and falls short. This person does note, write and dispense: they are also a stable, cool and centred influence on those around them, and without their composed presence much of the essential and visionary work of each organisation's directorial team could not be accomplished.

When we ask 'who' this person is, however, we are interested in the typical characteristics and traits of the company secretary, and how these help or hinder their ability to effectively discharge their duties. Our traditional image of the company secretary is of a person who is, among other things:

- Stable
- Detail-oriented
- Calm
- Organised
- Pragmatic

This depiction of a somewhat self-contained person might admittedly be a little outdated – diversification of the role (to combine it with that of a company's legal director, for example) means that people with different traits, backgrounds and expertise can also serve boards in this capacity. Neither would we wish to caricature all company secretaries as solitary people with a propensity for pedantry: the richness of each individual comes from their nuances and foibles. However, we notice that generally speaking, company secretaries tend to be adept at adopting a less emotionally driven position in business. When dealing with larger than life, sometimes antagonistic directors, or managing a volatile change situation such as a hostile takeover bid, this cool face is invaluable.

However, the situation under the surface may be quite different. Even the calmest person will eventually feel the effect of playing 'piggy in the middle' to sniping directors, and even the most professional person is likely to feel emotions in a difficult or stressful situation. This chapter is devoted to looking at the professional and private faces of the company secretary: how they can be aware of their emotions, how they can learn to manage their emotions, and how they can effectively manage the emotions of others.

The company secretary's role in managing emotions

The role of the company secretary is well defined with respect to its legal, technical and administrative responsibilities, and there are role requirements in place to ensure that the company secretary is appropriately qualified by profession or experience to discharge these duties effectively. However, there are also more subtle qualifications and attributes that a company secretary should be able to summon in order to work effectively. Section 4.25 of the 1992 Cadbury Report into corporate governance states (with our emphasis) that:

> 'The company secretary has a key role to play in ensuring that board procedures are both followed and regularly reviewed. The chairman and the board will look to the company secretary for guidance on what their responsibilities are under the rules and regulations to which they are subject and on how those responsibilities should be discharged. *All directors should have access to the advice and services of the company secretary and should recognise that the chairman is entitled to the strong and positive support of the company secretary in ensuring the effective functioning of the board.*'[1]

This statement indicates that as well as technical duties, the company secretary also delivers more interpersonal levels of support to the board. It is likely that board members, including the CEO, will approach the company secretary with questions, uncertainties, frustrations, upsets, etc. before airing these issues to other directors in either a formal or informal environment. It is also likely that at least some of these approaches will involve high emotions, which can be intensified or apparently justified by responses that do not adequately address the emotion and its cause. Considering these issues, it is important that the company secretary understands something of the psychology of conflict, the science behind high emotion and the strategies for dealing with these things.

The science of conflict

The study of conflict is something of a growth area for psychologists and neurobiologists, and ongoing research presents intriguing possibilities for this field of scholarship.

What is an emotion?

This question has long vexed the brave and the brilliant of the thinking world. In the 1880s, affective neuroscientist William James proposed in his paper 'What is Emotion?' that:

> 'emotions are no more than the experience of sets of bodily changes that occur in response to emotive stimuli. So, if we meet a bear in the woods, it is not the case that we feel frightened and run; rather, running away follows directly from our perception of the bear, and our experience of the bodily changes involved in running is the emotion of fear. In other words Bear ➔ Run ➔ Fear vs Bear ➔ Fear ➔ Run. We interpret our physical reactions and conclude that we are frightened. Different patterns of bodily changes thereby code different emotions.'[2]

In the following century, different neuroscientists and psychologists posed alternative theories to what eventually became known as the James-Lange theory (acknowledging the work of Carl Lange, who developed similar ideas to James' at a similar time), but modern neuroscience has turned back to James-Lange, with some modifications. Research scientist Tim Dalgleish of the University of Cambridge suggests this summary as part of his paper on 'the emotional brain':

> 'The James-Lange theory has remained influential. Its main contribution is the emphasis it places on the embodiment of emotions, especially the argument that changes in the bodily concomitants of emotions can alter their experienced intensity. *Most contemporary affective neuroscientists would endorse a modified James-Lange view in which bodily feedback modulates the experience of emotion.*'[3] (our emphasis)

The Concise Oxford English Dictionary defines emotion as:

> '*n.* a strong feeling, such as joy, anger, or sadness. › instinctive or intuitive feeling as distinguished from reasoning or knowledge'[4]

For the purposes of this chapter, it will be helpful to bear both definitions in mind. We hope to convey in this chapter that one of the keys to managing emotions successfully is to recognise their deep and broad impact. Emotion itself may be intangible, but it is linked with measurable physical effects, and carries implications for our personal, social and business relationships. These factors, and the ease with which they interlink and amplify one another, make learning how to manage emotions successfully a key skill that few people can afford to ignore.

The brain in conflict situations

Firstly, let us look briefly at how the brain works when confronted with a conflict situation, and what that might mean for the way in which we respond emotionally to conflict. Most neuroscientists agree that the brain can be thought of as having three 'parts' – the rational, the emotional and the primitive. Broadly speaking, each part of the brain controls different functions and abilities; the 'primitive' parts of the brain such as the brain stem, for example, regulate essential functions such as breathing or heartbeat.

Our emotional experiences are governed by the limbic system, a primitive part of the brain which regulates short and long-term memory, among other things.[5] In particular, it is thought that one part of the limbic system – the amygdala – acts as the volume button or guardian of the data flowing between the rational, emotional and primitive parts of the brain. How efficiently the amygdala functions affects and is affected by our experience of stress and conflict, which has implications for the emotions we feel and express. In relatively unstressful situations, the amygdala functions effectively and decisions are made with input from different brain centres; in stressful situations like a conflict, the amygdala becomes overwhelmed, and communication between brain centres is interrupted. Information enters the brain and is processed by the emotional part, but this is not counterbalanced by rational brain processing, leading to an emotion-heavy reaction and response.[6]

Another significant piece of neuroscientific thinking to be aware of is emotional contagion – individuals can 'catch' emotions subconsciously through the working of mirroring neurons in the brain that mimic what others seem to be feeling. This is highly significant when thinking about the role of emotions in difficult dispute or conflict situations. Firstly, contagion carries potential for escalation – if one person is visibly agitated, angry or upset, it follows that others in the room will experience similar emotions also. It is very easy to become quickly caught in a round robin emotional spiral in this situation, creating an environment that hinders rather than helps calm communication. Secondly – and conversely – it follows that if emotions are contagious, the example set by a calm, measured person can also bring about environmental and situational change. Essentially, it is possible to actively influence how people respond emotionally to conflict.

The effect of exposure

The second fascinating phenomenon to note is the effect of exposure, also known as the 'mere-exposure' effect or the 'familiarity principle'. Research and thought has been conducted in this area since the 19th century, but the work of figures such as Robert Bornstein has done much in the last 30 years to develop understanding of subliminal perception and its effects.

In their 1987 study, for example, Bornstein and his colleagues found that prior exposure to pictures of faces not only affected preferences for those pictures, but also the interpersonal behaviour of subjects toward the pictured individual.[7] Specifically, subjects subliminally exposed to a picture of an accomplice subsequently displayed a more positive attitude toward that person.[8] Even more remarkably, those subjects were much more likely to agree with that accomplice later when they engaged in a judgement task, even though they did not consciously recognise them.

For anyone interested in the study of conflict or negotiation, these findings have significant impact on the way we approach difficult or emotional situations. Bornstein's research suggests that what we consider to be independent judgement is affected by earlier exposure – prior negative associations with a person are likely to produce a negative bias towards that individual's position, and prior positive associations are likely to positively influence the way we see that individual and their position. Associations in this case might be formed in business or social environments; they will almost certainly be situations that evoke an emotional response (e.g. walking away from a business negotiation feeling that we have, or haven't, been treated with fairness).

Notably, Bornstein's study does not look at prior encounters that elicit emotional neutrality – situations such as seeing a columnist's photograph in a newspaper above a strongly biased article, for example. Furthermore, we have relatively little scientific understanding of how context affects prior exposure and subliminal perception. While Bornstein's study produced results in a neutral, scientific test environment, conflict and negotiation situations are by definition more adversarial and partisan in nature, and further testing would be helpful in ascertaining more precisely how context affects these subliminal reactions.

For our purposes, however, we can usefully take the exposure effect and deploy it in managing ours and others' emotions. For us as individuals, awareness of the exposure effect can help us to operate more mindfully – knowing that the exposure effect is at work can help us decide whether we are really looking at a situation or person neutrally. For us as third parties, or neutrals, in the conflicts of others, awareness of the exposure effect can give us insight into the situation's dynamics. What might seem like irrational, exaggerated dislike between individuals might have roots in an interaction from years ago, or a seemingly trivial social meeting that hit home for one, some or all of the individuals involved. Understanding this adds to the dispute landscape the neutral third party is painting, providing shade, tone and depth to the 'big picture'.

Mind into matter – the impacts of emotion

The neurobiological effects of emotion affect your body, thoughts and behaviour – and in the confines of the boardroom, despite how measured the company secretary might be, these things cannot be ignored. As Roger Fisher and Daniel Shapiro note in their excellent book *Beyond Reason: Using Emotions As You Negotiate*, the total impact has various aspects:

Physical impacts include causing you to perspire, blush, feel butterflies in your stomach, laugh, tremble, etc. Even if you try and suppress the emotion, your body still experiences physiological change, and in fact, the stress of trying not to show an emotion can be an extra distraction. In a serious, detailed or high-stakes situation, this extra distraction can significantly impair your ability to focus on the task in hand.

Thinking impacts come in two parts, depending on whether the emotion is positive or negative. ***Positive emotions*** have an expansive, affirmative effect on the way you think: you are more likely to focus on the 'right' and good in you, others, ideas and situations. Your thinking is likely to be creative and flexible, and you are more likely to approach situations with a 'can-do' attitude. In terms of how you perceive others, positive emotion is sometimes described as 'the halo effect': if you remember a person having done something good, noteworthy or helpful for you, you tend to see their subsequent actions in a positive light. This might lead you, in practice, to make allowances for a person or give them the benefit of the doubt in situations where you are called on to make a judgement or evaluation.

Negative emotions, by contrast, shrink your horizons. You are more likely to see the bad in things, and become blame-happy as you, others or situations don't match your expectations. The negative thoughts mushroom, taking up space, time and energy that could otherwise be devoted to remembering, thinking and learning. In contrast, when applied to your perception of others, this is sometimes called 'the horns effect': you might have got off on the wrong foot with someone, and now you can't help but look for the murky 'something else' lying behind their subsequent actions. If you can't quite put your finger on why you keep seeing the ulterior motive behind someone's actions, even when they are pleasant and professional with you, it may be that a brief, early misstep has earned them a 'horn headband' in your mind.

It is very possible that you have encountered this sort of paradigm before: positive psychology is a growing frontier of study and an increasingly attractive subject for psychology and business writers. Martin Seligman's book *Authentic Happiness* is a modern classic of the genre, in which Dr Seligman explores the effect of positive psychology – essentially looking at how people can 'live in the upper reaches of your set range of happiness'[9] – on the way that people respond to their environment. Malcolm Gladwell's *Blink*[10] is another book worth dipping into on the subject of split-second impressions, and how it is possible to make accurate judgements on a limited period of exposure.

Behaviour impacts are the most expressive display of the emotional experience – when you feel a strong emotion, say anger, you are motivated to take action, say banging the table in front of the person who has angered you. In most cases, we can control these impulses before they find expression, but while caught in this mindset, careful thinking is all but jettisoned. While we might not physically lash out, we could easily say or do things which we later regret, and which we would not do under the guide of careful thinking.[11]

We could also look at the effects of negative emotion in terms of:

- physiology – when angry or frustrated, our heart rate increases, for example
- cognition – we tend to think of negative thoughts when we are angry
- action – we tend to act in certain ways when we are angry or frustrated
- feelings – we feel anxious, for example, when we are angry or upset.

Acting under the influence of negative emotion is like being trapped in a rat run of ever decreasing circles: the atmosphere is dark, constrictive, jittery, tense, rigid, uncomfortable, breathless, and airless; our perspective is narrow and dim, our focus shattered. We do in fact develop 'tunnel vision' because negative emotion affects neurotransmission so significantly; wider issues and the big picture fall out of focus and rapidly out of the scope of our vision because the only information being transmitted falls within the ever-decreasing bounds set by negative emotion. Everything becomes 'smaller', and for people working at board level, who need to be able to take a long and broad view, this restrictive landscape is personally and professionally damaging.

Evolution vs employment – when emotional reactions become difficult

There is no doubt that emotions are powerful: they have served us well historically by sending survival signals, and continue to act as a personal bellwether for how we can or should react in varying situations.

Unfortunately, the correlate symptoms generated by emotional reactions are often misplaced when it comes to working in groups for effective problem-solving or collaborative working. The modern workplace prizes the ability to be flexible in how we work: we might be called upon to work on a project independently, collaborate closely with others for a fixed period of time, or work more fluidly on an ad hoc basis, alongside people with whom we share a looser professional bond. At board level, particularly, board meetings may be infrequent assemblies of diverse personalities – because the typical director has expectations about being listened to, there can be strong clashes when others' agendas dominate proceedings.

These changing conditions offer increased opportunities for productive synergy, but also for miscommunication and frustration. Inevitably, emotions will rise to the surface and it is more important than ever that we:

- anticipate emotional responses
- recognise our emotions' physical manifestations
- have an action system in place for handling the emotion(s) appropriately.

Reconciling science and society

There are, however, ways of accommodating both evolutionary and intellectual approaches, and they rely heavily on:

Recognition of the emotional experience – this means paying attention to both your own and the other person's physical symptoms and, crucially, acknowledging them. This may not be an obvious display but a more subtle clenching of the fist, tightness of breath or subtleties in eye movement, for example. As we have already seen, trying to ignore or hide emotional feelings is likely to do more harm than good.

Reflection on what those symptoms might mean. If you are acknowledging stress and frustration signals, for example, towards a colleague who is always late for meetings or handing on important documents, you might try probing that feeling a little more – *respect* the signals as real and meaningful to your situation. Let's say your colleague's actions cause you to be ten minutes late out of a meeting, or you to circulate a proposal in the afternoon rather than before lunch. You might be frustrated because you end up missing your train home or because others ask you 'why didn't we get the proposal earlier?' – but you might also feel this way because the lateness disrespects your time, your contribution, and you more generally. The issue of timekeeping, in reality, creates both effect and impact which should be considered.

Response in a measured way – a good response is proportionate to the instigating action, is focused on the problem and not the person, and looks for workable ways to meet the needs raised by you and/or those people in conflict. In complicated situations, it is worth trying to identify what Fisher and Shapiro describe as 'core concerns': Appreciation, Affiliation, Autonomy, Status and Role. These factors are discussed elsewhere in the book in more detail, but for our purposes it is important to say that most emotional conflicts pivot on one or more of these five factors. Acknowledging these elementary conflict causes, even if you cannot address the specific concerns at play, is likely to have an ameliorating effect on the situation.

We suggest that the response process is itself a series of decisions – to fight, flee, freeze, or think.

Fight, flight, freeze – or think?

Most people are familiar with the fight/flight paradigm, where an individual assesses and responds almost instantly to a threatening situation with a decision to stand and fight, or run and escape – both options are born of an optimistic view of our ability to do either in a given situation.

Recent thinking also adds 'freeze' to this list – essentially, when an individual feels that there is no hope of successfully escaping a situation, they respond by freezing their physical and mental responses to stimuli. In some cases, this may result in a person physically 'playing dead' – for example, if they were to be attacked by a large wild animal, freezing would likely result in significantly lowered blood pressure to minimise blood loss from wounds, large volumes of hormones being dumped into the bloodstream to deaden pain, and slackening muscles to achieve a lifeless appearance. For our purposes, however, 'freeze' is slightly less extreme – confronted with a stressful or traumatic situation, an individual is likely to act like the proverbial deer in the headlights, experiencing memory blots and losing the ability to think clearly about complex issues.

From these patterns, we can see clear potential for difference between innate emotional, neurobiological responses and socially optimum, contemporary ways of handling difficult situations. Our evolutionary fight, flight or freeze reactions equip the body for a rapid response to danger and difficulty, but these same responses seriously inhibit our ability to solve problems intelligently. There is a direct conflict between what your consciousness thinks you should do in the abstract, and what response your brain is likely to actually direct you towards.

William Ury elegantly describes the recognition, reflection and response process in his book *Getting Past No* as 'going to the balcony'[12]: not necessarily a physical outside space, but a state of enforced mental detachment from an emotionally difficult situation. Going to the balcony differs from the freeze because it is a conscious technique – the act of mentally announcing (or indeed, vocalising) an intention to go to this place recognises that one's emotions surrounding a situation have gone beyond a 'safe' point, creates a break for reflection, and not only promises a considered response, but is itself a response.

Global opportunities, high stakes

How business structures amplify emotional turbulence

We have looked at the science of managing emotions and how a rational response can collide with evolutionary impulse; it is clear that the potential consequences of this collision make formulating a handling strategy a worthwhile investment.

This need becomes even more apparent at board level: in this kind of environment, there is ample opportunity for emotional responses and consequences to be generated and make an impact. The board must not only navigate its own difficult landscape, but also those of the wider business environment and the sum total of factors which affect it. It is imperative that the board is at its best so it can deal with those external influences – and that means dealing with turbulent emotions successfully.

Shared needs

Although boards are in some ways distanced from the rest of the organisation they serve by increased levels of responsibility, there are common threads that unite every member of a business from the most junior staff member to the most senior. One of these threads is the experience of needs: the different things an individual must have realised at a given time, and the consequences of these needs going unsatiated.

Psychologist Abraham Maslow (1908–1970) suggested that everyone essentially shares the same motivation to have their needs met. He initially identified five – later eight – levels of need, and outlined that humans are on a quest to have these needs met in sequence. Once a level of need has been satiated, attention turns to the next need level; this continues until the individual reaches and satisfies 'transcendence' – a need to help others in their quest for self-actualisation. If needs are not met, or are otherwise frustrated, we are apt to become angry, upset, aggressive and favourable to risk.

People at board level are likely to fall in the top half of the needs triangle, with their basic biological, physiological and safety needs met. The question of meeting esteem needs, however, and needs above this, resonates clearly in a boardroom environment. In particular, status and reputation are areas that can be challenged and tested spectacularly in this arena, and especially so in the modern global workplace. The 'war for talent' is worldwide, and increasingly C-suite positions are filled by 'inspired' and 'creative' cross-industry placements, where your new chief information officer is someone else's old chief marketing officer. Workplace pressures have never been greater, with more and more diversely gifted people competing for recognition and reward. In such an environment, it is little wonder that conflict can sometimes take on deeply personal, emotional aspects.

Given these pressures, it is not surprising that the boardroom is an incubator of political stress, manipulation and manoeuvring. In all of this, the company secretary must keep a cool head. The board team, after all, are assembled for the purpose of steering the company they serve towards success – they are talented and experienced people with beneficial contributions

MANAGING EMOTIONAL TURBULENCE – THE PSYCHOLOGY OF ORGANISATIONAL CONFLICT   67

Hierarchy of needs
adapted to eight levels,
based on Maslow's theory

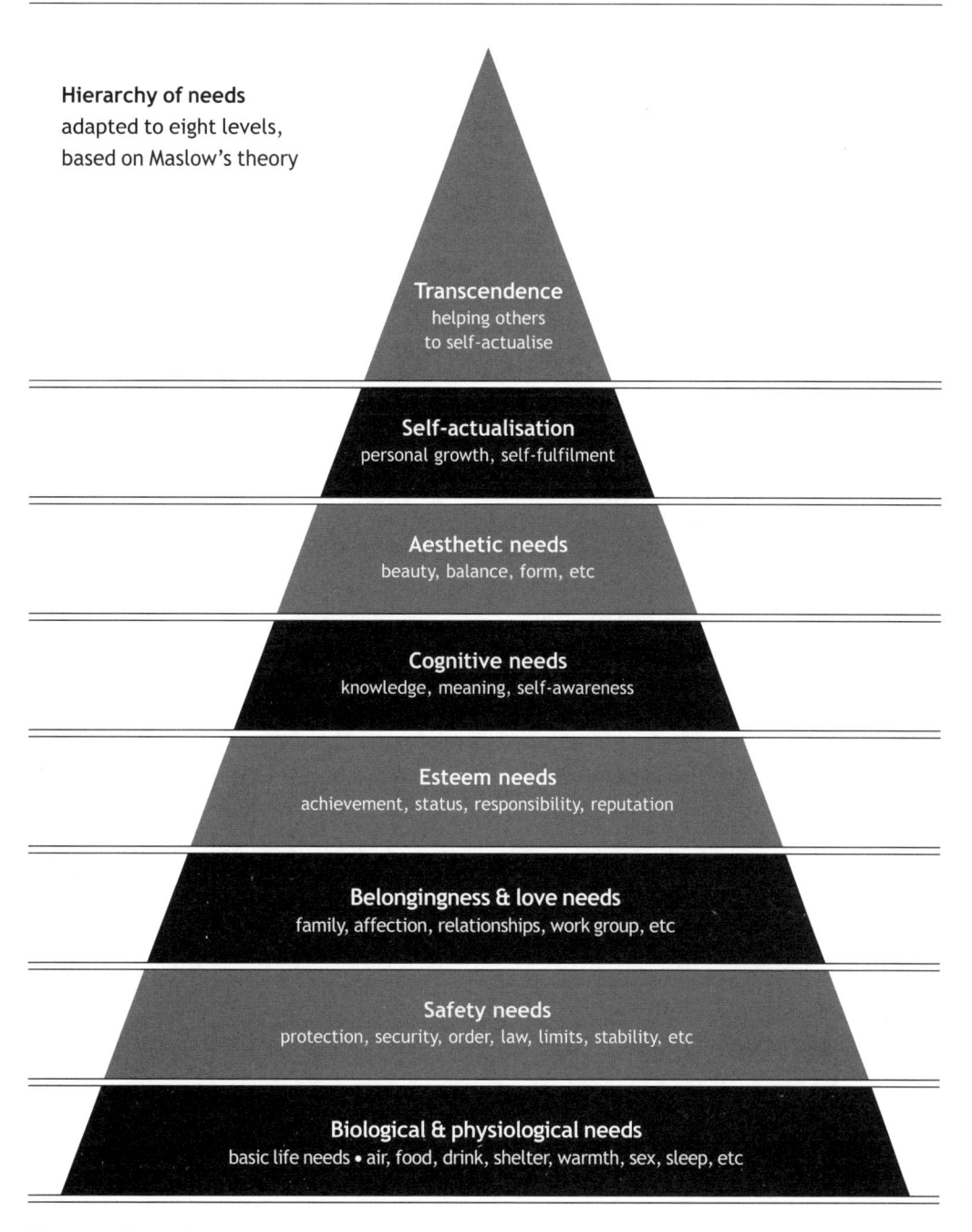

Transcendence
helping others
to self-actualise

Self-actualisation
personal growth, self-fulfilment

Aesthetic needs
beauty, balance, form, etc

Cognitive needs
knowledge, meaning, self-awareness

Esteem needs
achievement, status, responsibility, reputation

Belongingness & love needs
family, affection, relationships, work group, etc

Safety needs
protection, security, order, law, limits, stability, etc

Biological & physiological needs
basic life needs • air, food, drink, shelter, warmth, sex, sleep, etc

Figure 4.1: Hierarchy of needs adapted to eight levels, based on Maslow's theory.

to make. They are professionals, and should know how to conduct themselves appropriately in the board environment. They are also human beings, with individual challenges, strengths, motivations and weaknesses that affect their attitudes and behaviour. They are all motivated to have their needs met, and at times this can cause conflict rather than collaboration. The company secretary's task is to understand the common human needs for status and acknowledgement, recognise when these needs might cause conflict, and take the right action to deal with the situation.

What can a company secretary do to manage turbulent emotions?

The theory – recognising conflict styles, emotional intelligence, and 'the dark side'

The key for a company secretary in managing their own and others' turbulent emotions lies in self-awareness: without accurate personal application, theories will only be partially useful to you. Cultivating self-awareness will help you to become more understanding of your own strengths and areas of development; in turn, you will be in a better position to pick up on aspects of others' behaviours and respond effectively.

Everyone has a conflict style, even if they are not aware of it or do not recognise it. Not only does everyone have a conflict style, they are able to alter it to suit any given conflict scenario. This is important to note because it means that, unlike the previously immovable fight-flight-freeze response, we can, with consideration, adapt the way we respond to others' emotions to achieve a productive and satisfying resolution.

Conflict styles

Conflict management theorists Thomas and Kilmann developed the idea that there are five different modes of handling conflict which can be plotted on an XY axis. The Y axis represents a range in level of 'assertiveness' and the X axis a range in level of 'cooperativeness'.

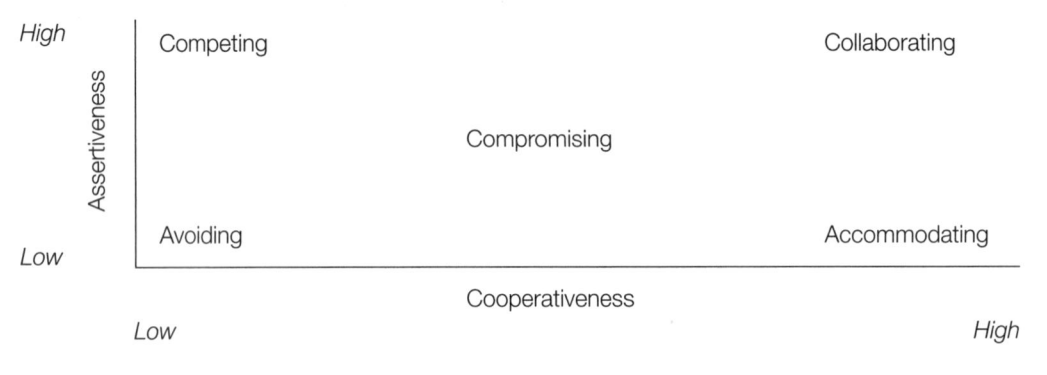

Figure 4.2: Conflict styles

In the following descriptions, the word **assertive** means 'the extent to which the individual attempts to satisfy her/his own concerns' and **cooperative** means 'the extent to which the individual attempts to satisfy the other person's concerns'.

Accommodating (Ac:)

This approach is unassertive and cooperative; it is the opposite of Competing. It involves accepting the other person's position, either by backing off or tolerating the behaviour and neglecting your own concerns.

Avoiding (Av:)

This approach is unassertive and uncooperative; the individual does not immediately pursue their needs or those of the other person. They do not tackle the conflict.

Avoiding might take the form of diplomatically sidestepping an issue, postponing an issue until a later time or simply withdrawing from a threatening situation.

Competing (Cp:)

This approach is assertive and uncooperative; an individual pursues their own concerns at the other person's expense. This involves trying to win. It is a power-orientated mode; using whatever power you have – economic, intellectual, physical, status – in order to win one's own position.

Competing might mean standing up for your rights or beliefs, or it might simply mean trying to win.

Compromising (Cs:)

This approach is between assertive and cooperative, on a middle ground between Competing and Accommodating. This approach finds some solution that partially satisfies both parties. Compromising might mean splitting the difference, exchanging concessions or just seeking a quick, bland solution.

Collaborating (Cl:)

This approach is both assertive and cooperative; it is the opposite of Avoiding. Collaborating might involve exploring a situation in which the parties would otherwise be competing for resources, or it might involve trying to find a creative solution to an interpersonal problem.

This approach involves exploring mutual positions to try to find a solution that fully meets the interests of both parties. It usually requires some trust and an explanation of each other's needs and demands, time, creativity and energy.

For more information on conflict styles, see Appendix 1.

Adapting your conflict style

In high-emotion situations, if you are aware of what style an individual is adopting, you have the ability to position yourself in such a way that responds most fully to that person's state. Determining a person's conflict style, and which style would be appropriate for you to adopt, are observations that you could make while on William Ury's balcony. Adapting in this way should not be seen as capitulation or weakness – in fact, if done properly it can be a great strength. Your specific goal when adapting may change according to circumstance, but broadly speaking, the reason for adapting is to achieve a positive outcome where each emotional party feels recognised and respected, and each party is able to turn their emotions into a constructive platform for discussion.

A person's 'raw' conflict style – their first response – can in turn be influenced by a) their level of emotional intelligence and b) their score on the Hogan Development Scale. Emotional intelligence (EI), or the ability to identify, assess and control our emotions, is probably a familiar concept.

What is emotional intelligence and why is it important?

How well do we understand ourselves and other people? Much of our work success is based on our skills, knowledge and experience; but another part depends on how we get on with colleagues, managers, staff who report to us, suppliers and customers. We need to understand ourselves and how we appear to other people, as well as understand what makes other people tick. We can then use this knowledge to achieve our goals. Emotional intelligence is not about being nice or soft. It involves interacting effectively with other people to get a job done or to achieve the kind of life we want.

It is important here as a signifying trait and tool – EI as a trait indicates how well we can deal with emotions, while as a tool we might think of it in terms of successfully articulating and applying feelings and ideas about emotional situations.

Tools such as the Thomas-Kilmann Emotional Intelligence Questionnaire (TEIQ) measure our understanding of ourselves and of other people, and our ability to use this knowledge to achieve our goals. TEIQ measures facets of behaviour which include *adaptability* – being flexible and willing to adapt to new conditions, *emotion regulation* – being capable of controlling emotions and *trait optimism* – being confident and likely to 'look on the bright side' of life.

It is definitely possible to improve our EI ability through practice, for example creating a habitual space in conflicts to say how we feel about a situation or a given person, and how different outcomes might change this.

The Hogan Development Scale (HDS) is perhaps newer ground, and is particularly pertinent for board-level emotional situations. Based on literature around leadership failure,

> 'the HDS focuses on eleven dispositions that would generally be considered desirable attributes but which flip into destructive mode if not managed well. These dark side qualities typically become apparent during novel or stressful periods, or when the individual feels

Facets	High scorers perceive themselves as...
Adaptability	...flexible and willing to adapt to new conditions.
Assertiveness	...forthright, frank, and willing to stand up for their rights.
Emotion perception (self and others)	...clear about their own and other people's feelings.
Emotion expression	...capable of communicating their feelings to others.
Emotion management (others)	...capable of influencing other people's feelings.
Emotion regulation	...capable of controlling their emotions.
Impulsiveness (low)	...reflective and less likely to give in to their urges.
Relationships	...capable of having fulfilling personal relationships.
Self-esteem	...successful and self-confident.
Self-motivation	...driven and unlikely to give up in the face of adversity.
Social awareness	...accomplished networkers with excellent social skills.
Stress management	...capable of withstanding pressure and regulating stress.
Trait: empathy	...capable of taking someone else's perspective.
Trait: happiness	...cheerful and satisfied with their lives.
Trait: optimism	...confident and likely to 'look on the bright side' of life.

Table 4.1: Behaviour facets and typical characteristics, Hogan Development Scale

relaxed or invulnerable...We all learn to vary our behaviour according to the pressures we are under and the situations we face and we all exercise restraint over socially undesirable impulses. Cloaked by their positive and attractive aspects, dark side characteristics promote the high flyer's success, and support his or her journey to the top table.'[13]

The HDS is important because it acknowledges how circumstances can alter a person's behaviour, changing the strengths that catapulted them to the boardroom into deadly 'dark side' tendencies that cause problems. For example, your chief operating officer's (COO's) diligence is likely to be an asset in normal circumstances, but under strain this may turn into perfectionism that is difficult for others to work with. Unable to delegate and coming across as hypercritical, the diligent COO could inadvertently infect those around them with stress, in turn bringing out the dark sides of others. The 11 dispositions also fall into clusters – under stress, people move away (such as from independence to detachment), move against (such as from confidence to arrogance) and move towards (from dutiful to dependent) others.[14] Trickey and Hyde describe this dynamic at board level as akin to 'the bubbles in a champagne flute',[15] where the tiny specks of behavioural traits at the bottom of the flute (or organisation) increase in size as they rise, until bursting as they hit the top. The uncomfortable paradox is that these double-sided traits are valuable and useful, and to function well at board level they are likely to be particularly vivid: prizing the good means accepting and managing the downsides.

The practice – how can a good company secretary respond?

Relationships, process, context

The theories and ideas we explored in the previous section should provide you with some starting points for thinking more deeply about what attitude you bring to conflict, and how you might look differently at conflicts that raise emotions. This final section aims to provide you with practical tips and tactics that you can begin to deploy immediately when faced with conflict situations likely to result in high emotion.

We see the practice of managing emotions as having three main elements: relationships, process and context.

Relationships – relationships are key to handling disputes and managing the emotions that they provoke. How would you describe your relationship with the directors, the chairman, the CEO you work with? Do you keep up to date with their news and views? Do you feel able to approach them about a difficult issue – and can you predict how they might respond?

If you feel that your relationships with various board members could be better, there are immediate steps you can take to change that. Pick up the phone and arrange a one-on-one meeting: this does not have to be formal, and you might even see a different aspect to their personality in a more relaxed environment. Once you've taken this first step, nurture the relationship – perhaps aim to have lunch or a long, relaxed phone call once every six weeks with each director. Scheduling this with several busy people may well prove challenging at first, but the value and benefits each cultivated relationship can bring are worth the effort.

Process – the company secretary is ideally placed to introduce new ways of working to the board, and this can be used advantageously to manage emotional conflicts, conversations and situations more effectively. You could consider using:

- sidebar conversations – adapted from the legal world, sidebar conversations can be effective tools when used appropriately. If a person is becoming visibly upset or angry, for example, inviting them to take a couple of minutes outside with you can be a good way of taking the heat out of the room, allowing everyone time to refocus, and allowing you to find out why the person is so emotionally reactive. This information will help you assess what your next steps should be, e.g. whether to reconvene or postpone the meeting.
- executive coaches – outside help of this type might be appropriate if a particular director seems to experience long-term difficulty in handling their emotions. This should not be limited to thinking about 'anger management' – directors who frequently experience shyness, nervousness, sadness, anxiety, etc count as having difficulty managing their emotions, and could benefit greatly from external support and coaching. As well as bringing personal benefits, there is strong business justification for helping talented executives work at their fullest potential.
- external neutrals – this covers neutral chairs and independent investigators as well as mediators. Some cases do benefit from the independence and focus an external peacemaker can bring to the situation; an external neutral will also be experienced in acting as a sponge for

people's emotions and can offer everyone, company secretary included, an outlet for their feelings. A good company secretary should have the knowledge and judgement skills to identify situations that might need external help.

Context – springing new or vast quantities of information on a person at a time when they may not be in a position to process it can be overwhelming, increasing the chances of that individual responding in a difficult, emotion-led way. Making sure that everyone has access to the information they need is a good way of anticipating high emotions and building in a way to handle them. Some examples of this might include:

- thorough ideas testing – new ideas or ways of working are looked at closely, perhaps using a Strengths, Weaknesses, Opportunities and Threats (SWOT) framework. The company secretary's role here, as well as giving advice, might be to act as the 'keeper of the flame', ensuring that everyone can have their say, understand the issues and ultimately stay on task.
- managed 'futures' conversations – part of your administration as a company secretary may involve knowing when directors are due or likely to stand down from their positions. This can be distressing and stressful for the individual in question (as discussed in later chapters), but can also be managed by spending time with the individual to talk about 'life after the directorship'. Creating space for this delicate conversation to happen will help to channel the emotion surrounding an exit to a more effective, forward-looking conclusion.
- storytelling – using tools such as metaphors, personal experiences and labels can help to reframe an idea or issue, and create new understanding and perspectives. This is also a way of engaging with people on a more personal level – sharing experiences, for example, will give you more insight into their motivation and reasoning, and help to develop a more trusting relationship.

The overall practical aim of using these tools, together with the theoretical and scientific ideas we have presented, is to create an environment conducive to good emotional management.

Handling high emotion: summary checklist

- the company secretary has a necessary and important role in managing their and others' emotions.
- our brains 'short circuit' the reasoning part of thinking in highly stressful and pressured situations, leading to emotional decision-making.
- emotions are contagious – and this means you can influence positively as well as be influenced by others.

Do

- **recognise, reflect, respond.** Self-awareness is your invaluable key to monitoring and managing your emotions and those of others.

- consider the conflict styles of everyone – including you – involved in an emotional situation. Do they have an adequate conflict vocabulary to express how they feel? Has the 'dark side' taken over momentarily? Can you shift people towards complementary conflict styles?
- foster good practice – think about the relationships, processes and context, or who else might be involved, in an emotion-led conflict.

Don't

- react on impulse – recognise when you are making emotion-led decisions and take time to consciously balance this by calming down and regaining a rational perspective.
- get stuck on one conflict-handling style – vary your approach depending on how a conflict develops. Emotional situations are not governed by reason, and matters may develop in a way you hadn't foreseen. Mitigate this risk by being an active, curious listener.
- get caught out! Start to develop good relationships, information and handling systems now – this will help you to better anticipate conflict and deal with it more effectively when it does arise.

Case study: handling high emotions

This case study illustrates a conflict situation in which managing emotions effectively was a key priority for reaching a resolution. We hope that this will show how the concepts from the chapter can be deployed in practice, and that readers will be able to take this as a model for how they can handle high-emotion conflicts.

The dispute

An industrial company, after years of intensive research, developed a promising high-specification machine with strong take-up potential in wider industry and areas of the commercial sector. Excitement was high, but disappointments ensued when the machine's early potential began to unravel. Technical problems arose and although these were corrected by the industrial company, damage had already been done. The technical problems caused delays in marketing the product: promotional material had to be amended, and the machine's launch had to be put back by eight months. Even after the machine had been introduced to the market, the problems that had dogged the launch did not abate. More technical faults were found, damaging an already weaker than expected customer take-up. Word spread that the machine was an expensive failure, and its parent inventors a soon-to-be busted flush. The swirling rumours about the industrial company fulfilled their own forecast, and soon the company faced liquidation.

The company was saved by one of its suppliers, who agreed to purchase the company under a share sales agreement. The supplier acted as much from conviction as business sense. They had not just invested significant sums of money in the company and its machine; they had wholeheartedly subscribed to the transformative, cutting-edge potential of the machine and its associated research. The supplier strongly believed that with stable funding, guidance and a little luck, the machine could take its rightful place as a market-changing, industry-leading product.

After the purchase, serious problems began to emerge. The supplier alleged that after investigating the industrial firm's accounts and history, it found that the company's stock was worth around £6 million less than was paid, which was not disclosed prior to the purchase. The supplier also claimed that the beleaguered company had additional creditors that were not listed in the management accounts, and that additional liabilities existed in relation to the sale contract for the machine. From the supplier's perspective, what they had thought was a cluster of gold nuggets were in fact, on closer inspection, shrivelled lemons. The amount in dispute was given as £26 million, the total sum the supplier had invested since the purchase to keep the industrial company solvent.

To complicate matters, the original board of directors of the industrial firm still had strong links to the firm following its purchase: the vendors had continued as employees – but not directors – of the industrial company. This kept them in close proximity to the ever-worsening fortunes of the company, and gave them a continued personal investment in the eventual success or failure of the firm. The suppliers were furious. They claimed that not only had the ex-directors misrepresented the state of the company, but that they had also failed to disclose concerns that they could reasonably have had once the sale had been finalised, and the ex-directors given new roles as employees. After a year, the ex-directors were dismissed for gross misconduct on the basis of the alleged misrepresentations. The ex-directors responded by starting proceedings for unfair dismissal at an employment tribunal.

Analysis

This case study is a strong illustration of a conflict situation in which emotional responses play a significant role in prolonging, escalating and to some extent distorting the original dispute.

The suppliers

The suppliers intervened to save the industrial company on both a financial and emotional impulse. Their financial investment was considerable and provided a 'point of no return' moment, in which their outlay tied them to staying the course with the industrial firm irrespective of the outcome. This in itself is also a type of emotional attachment, where adhering to a particular course of action signifies 'staying power' and resilience; many individuals and organisations display behaviour like this.

The emotional dimension of the supplier's involvement, however, went deeper. The directors of the supplier firm had invested themselves personally in the success of the industrial company and its machine, distorting their view of the company's prospects. The company's future had become a vehicle for achieving status and recognition, meaning that failure would not only deny the directors their need fulfilment but actually detract from their sense of status, achievement and recognition. When the industrial company was ultimately unsuccessful, the effect on the suppliers was deeper and more personally hurtful than it might otherwise have been. The industrial company's failure seemed to challenge the supplier firm's ability to make sound judgements, with outsiders saying that they 'should have seen it coming' and ought to have made more thorough inquiries into the industrial company before committing to the purchase. Therefore, what should have remained a purely business matter became an issue that called the directors' personal judgement and values into question.

To look even more deeply, we can see that much of the anger shown by the supplier firm's directors stems from worry that needs that had been met might now be compromised. In ascribing more value to the industrial company and its product than it might have deserved, and then stepping in to rescue the company when it encountered financial trouble, the supplier firm cast itself in the role of saviour. Thinking back to Maslow's Hierarchy of Needs, this action fulfilled many of the fourth-level needs – achievement, self-esteem, gaining the respect of others, etc. The industrial company's continuing troubles threatened the secure meeting of these needs – should the buyout fail, there would be no achievement, people might not respect the decision-makers involved, and subsequently self-esteem would be threatened.

The spiralling fury felt by the suppliers would have been exacerbated by the decision-making short circuit caused by informational and emotional overloading. At the point where the industrial company's accounts were revealed, the suppliers would have felt a full range of emotions, including:

- Shock at the perceived scale of the accounting discrepancies
- Worry on realising that the situation was really 'happening to them'
- Anger and hurt at being 'duped' by the directors of the industrial firm
- Embarrassment that they had been 'taken for a ride'
- Sadness at the thought of losing what had previously been a good, trusting relationship with the industrial firm's directors

One director at the supplier firm later recalled feeling dizzy and unwell when he heard the news about the industrial firm's accounts, while another said they felt short of breath as the situation unravelled – this highlights how being emotionally overwhelmed frequently manifests itself as a range of physical complaints. Assailed by conflicting emotions, and coping with their physical expression, it is perhaps not surprising that the decision-makers at the supplier firm responded angrily and sought opportunities to 'get back' at the industrial firm's directors.

The ex-directors

From the ex-directors' perspective, Maslow's Hierarchy of Needs illustrates that their dismissal threatened need levels two, three and four. Withdrawing employment introduced insecurity, threatening the ex-directors' ability to be physically safe in terms of paying bills, buying food, securing shelter, etc. The third level – 'love and belonging' – relates in terms of the dismissal to the withdrawal of colleagueship and corporate belonging. Consider how strongly people can identify their personhood with their occupation; taking this away poses a crisis of self-image, while at the same time diminishing the number of peers with whom to compare and reassure oneself. Finally, ex-directors' fourth level needs of achievement and self-esteem were severely compromised by the dismissal. From being board members of a promising company, the ex-directors had been stripped of their directorship, seniority and ultimately their employment entirely. From a position of authority and respect, the ex-directors found themselves in a position of powerlessness, unable to command the respect that they had done before. Seeking redress at an employment tribunal offered a way of publicly and formally meeting these needs, restoring the ex-directors' comfort and self-image.

The question of how much the ex-directors knew about the problems the industrial firm faced, and why they did not disclose these problems to the new buyers, is problematic. As directors, it is unlikely that they had no knowledge of issues like undisclosed creditors and additional liabilities, but it would be very difficult to prove the extent of their knowledge and understanding. A possible explanation might be that, under pressure, the ex-directors 'froze' in the same way a cornered animal might. Consider the situation before the buyout – it had become clear that the international marketplace would not adopt their product, that other firms could produce similar research and products at a more financially competitive rate, and that their reputation as a firm was significantly damaged. Faced with these threats, and paralysed by what in business terms were life-or-death decisions, the ex-directors may have simply elected to do nothing as an attempt at psychological self-preservation.

An alternative view suggests that the ex-directors' needs for security, belonging and self-esteem were being met by the status quo at the industrial company. Logically, in seeking to preserve this status, the ex-directors would not raise difficult issues for fear of jeopardising the meeting of their needs. They may have been unable, or unwilling, to see that in the long term, not addressing the issues the industrial company faced would not be in their interests. The concept of 'wilful blindness', covered extensively by Margaret Heffernan's book of the same name, applies here: 'we mostly admit the information that makes us feel great about ourselves, while conveniently filtering whatever unsettles our fragile egos and most vital beliefs'.[16]

On the basis that people tend to do things that they see others doing, it is probable that anyone who did privately harbour reservations about the company's finances or liabilities would have kept quiet in order to conform with their peers. Additionally, even if a director felt uncomfortable with the company's health, they might have felt that if those they perceived to be authoritative – perhaps with longer tenure, more formal qualifications, or even with more assured mannerisms – had not raised the issues, then there was no scope to do that at all.

Things come to a head

It was clear that the complex and deeply felt emotions experienced by everyone involved in this dispute would make finding a resolution very difficult. Early suggestions by each party to talk things through were met with stony silences, delays and rising resentment, which only served to damage the already fragile relationship further. Once the possibility of an employment tribunal had been raised, the relationship collapsed. With emotional decision-making dominant, each person's perspective narrowed and hardened. Furthermore, the consequences of emotion-led decision-making became self-perpetuating: high emotions generated emotional decisions and actions, which in turn provoked further feelings of hurt, anger, worry and upset. External intervention was necessary to unpick the knots in the situation.

The parties eventually agreed to try working with an external mediator before pursuing an employment tribunal or litigation, on the grounds of cost. The mediator was faced with several problems:

- How to establish trust – between themselves and each party, and between the parties. Trust between the parties had been shattered by the dispute and its impacts, and for a mediated discussion to be successful, the mediator knew that the parties would need to feel confident that any agreements or settlement would be followed through by the other party.
- How to break the emotional spiral – the dispute was self-perpetuating and indeed growing because of factors such as neurobiological short-circuiting, emotional contagion, and strong personal alignment with the issues causing the conflict. To stand any chance of reaching an agreement, the mediator saw that one of their primary roles would be to reintroduce reason and objectivity to each party's thinking process.

- How to build a working relationship – even though the relationship between the parties had deteriorated greatly, it was important to build some kind of bridge between the parties that would allow them to implement what they could agree at the mediation. Trust and putting a break on emotion-led decisions were a large part of bridge-building, but working out ways of developing these things in practice was a challenge.

Recognising that trust would be an especially important quality to foster in the mediation, the mediator spent a lot of time speaking with the parties via telephone in the weeks before the mediation date. This allowed each party to feel comfortable working with the mediator, and gave everyone a chance to digest possible risks associated with particular issues. This extensive pre-mediation contact was given to ensure that on the day of the mediation, each party got the most out of the process.

Generally speaking, problematic relationships require a three-stage approach:[17]

- Mitigating poor relations by de-escalating conflict and gradually building trust – for example, this could be done by exchanging letters stating the parties' intentions to collaborate by exchanging information.
- Bridging relationships by identifying the need for collaboration.
- Highlighting the incentives/benefits for participation – even parties with a history of confrontation can move on to collaboration when cooperation is required to achieve a valuable benefit.[18]

The mediator's tactics

The ambiguity of some aspects of the dispute, coupled with each side's strong emotions, meant that the mediator had to be imaginative in structuring the session, allowing each side to have their say while also keeping matters grounded in reality. This was achieved by beginning the mediation in a joint session, involving both parties and the mediator in the same room. The joint session made clear that two main factors would be key to reaching agreements: as well as a financial settlement, both sides expressed a need to save face and address the feeling of being 'cheated' by the other party. More generally, a joint session inherently sent a message of 'no secrets' – everyone is party to communications, and can contribute to the discussion. For a dispute fuelled by non-disclosure and withheld information, the open joint session set a tone of fairness, honesty and communication.

The mediator leading the session helped the parties to identify these issues as a first, significant task. Having agreed these points, the mediator then grouped together the principal figures in one room and the legal representatives in another to work through these issues from all angles in parallel sessions, run by an assistant mediator. The presence of an assistant mediator in this case served a useful double function: as well as the practical advantage of having another person to run a counterpart session, the assistant mediator was able to act as a second pair of eyes and ears to pick up on details that might otherwise have been missed by the lead mediator.

An interesting feature of this dispute was the existence of personal guarantees by the ex-directors for the debts of the company, which could be called in at any time by the purchasers. This led to an unusual situation where the parties' legal positions were secondary to the commercial and personal interests of the parties. The mediation, therefore, focused almost exclusively on exploring issues such as why the ex-directors' positions at the industrial company were felt to be untenable, and the commercial future of the company. The mediator approached the discussion with the intent to be robust, creating space for emotional expression but keeping an overall focus on achieving a productive discussion.

In keeping with the personal tone of the mediation, it became clear that storytelling was a key way of gathering information and piecing together each side's version of 'what happened'. Storytelling was especially effective and appropriate to this dispute:

- Each side had a chance, working with the mediator and their assistant, to tell their version of events and come to terms with how they were feeling – saying out loud thoughts like 'I feel betrayed because I thought we had a good relationship – was I wrong?' was cathartic and mentally clarifying. This was very important, as it acknowledged people's feelings in a non-partisan way.
- Each side had a chance to tell the other how they saw the dispute and what they were feeling – this allowed each side to learn about the other's point of view, interests, and needs.
- After the exchange of stories, the parties broke away into separate groups to reflect on what they had shared. Although many individuals in each party still felt that they had been treated badly, the mood of each room changed as each individual started to say things like, 'I understand why they didn't tell us that' and, 'It must have been difficult for them – I know I'd find dealing with that hard'.

As a general point, the neutrality and information exchange offered by storytelling make this a good tool in approaching disputes which are emotionally driven. Adopting a curious, non-judgemental position cools any perception of taking sides, while giving people a platform to talk about how they feel encourages them to a) acknowledge their feelings and b) start to think about *why* they feel a particular way. Both of these things help change the tone of people's thinking, and use the contagion principle to create and sustain an atmosphere of curiosity rather than animosity.

Moving towards resolution

Work with the mediator happened over a two-day period, owing to the need to build trust, establish new thought patterns, and discuss the complex issues in play.

Eventually, the parties reached a settlement in relation to an agreement for lease, and a side letter containing non-binding undertakings. In particular, the parties gave feedback emphasising the mediator's skill and helpfulness in building rapport with everyone.

Learning points from this example

- Emotion acts as a multiplier – it can transform small details into looming issues, and adds layers of complexity to already detailed conflicts. While you cannot shut off emotions, it is important to recognise a dispute's emotional potential and respond accordingly.
- Some emotion-led disputes need the help of a neutral third party to unpick the issues and facilitate constructive, to-the-point discussions. This is especially true if the relationship between the parties has been damaged, or if the parties need to maintain a relationship whatever the outcome of the dispute.
- In emotional disputes and conflicts, you should try to: **build trust, break the emotional spiral and bridge the gap** between the parties so they can have a working relationship. Parties don't need to become best friends again, but they should be at a stage where they can work together well enough to discuss issues and plan a way forward.

Notes

1. *Report of the Committee on The Financial Aspects of Corporate Governance*, chaired by Adrian Cadbury, published 1/12/1992 pp. 31-32. http://www.ecgi.org/codes/documents/cadbury.pdf retrieved 12/2012.
2. Tim Dalgleish, 'The emotional brain', in *Nature Reviews Neuroscience, v5 issue 7*, July 2007 (print ed.), Nature publishing group, http://www-psych.stanford.edu/~knutson/ans/dalgleish04.pdf retrieved 13/1/2013.
3. Ibid.
4. Concise OED, 11th Edition (Revised), ed. Catherine Soanes and Angus Stevenson (OUP 2008, 2009).
5. Helen Phillips, 'Introduction: the Human Brain' taken from *New Scientist*, September 2006 http://www.newscientist.com/article/dn9969-introduction-the-human-brain.html?full=true retrieved 15/1/2013.
6. Adapted from Nadja Alexander, 'Confrontation or conciliation: does science have the answer?' taken from http://kluwermediationblog.com/2012/06/16/confrontation-or-conciliation-does-science-have-the-answer/ retrieved 15/12/12.
7. R. F. Bornstein, D. R. Leone, & D. J. Galley, *The generalizability of subliminal mere exposure effects: Influence of stimuli perceived without awareness on social behaviour*, 53 J. Personality & Social Psych. 1070 (1987).
8. *Id*.
9. Martin E P Seligman, *Authentic Happiness* (London 2003, Nicholas Brealey Publishing) p. xii.

10. Malcolm Gladwell, *Blink: The Power of Thinking Without Thinking* (London 2006, Penguin).
11. Adapted from *Beyond Reason: Using Emotions as you Negotiate*, Fisher, Roger and Shapiro, Daniel, Random House (London 2006) p. 11–12.
12. Ury, William, *Getting Past No: Negotiating with Difficult People,* London 1991 pp. 16–35.
13. Geoff Trickey and Gillian Hyde, *A Decade of the Dark Side: fighting our demons at work* (Psychological Consultancy Limited, Tunbridge Wells 2009) p. 3.
14. Karen Horney, *The Neurotic Personality of Our Time* (London 1977)
15. Ibid p. 19
16. Heffernan, Margaret, *Wilful Blindness: Why We Ignore The Obvious At Our Peril* (Simon & Schuster, London 2011) p. 4.
17. Jean Poitras et al., *"Bringing horses to water? Overcoming bad relationships in the pre-negotiating stage of consensus building"* in 19 Negotiation Journal 251 (2003).
18. Refer to studies by M Sherif et al., Inter-group co-operation and competition: the Roberts Cave experiment, University Book Exchange, Oklahoma, 1961.

5
Working with powerful people in a dispute context

Eileen Carroll QC (Hon) and Ranse Howell

This chapter looks at the distinct challenges and techniques that are likely to arise when dealing with a conflict situation involving a powerful person or people. It is clear to us that being in a position of power can change how an individual thinks, and more importantly, what their expectations might be of the conflict, how it can be resolved and how others respond to the individual. It is equally clear that one can adapt their negotiating style to manage these needs, while always keeping perspective of the dispute landscape and the end goal of reaching a settlement.

This chapter begins with a detailed case study looking at a dispute involving a powerful, executive-level person and how the intervention of a mediator successfully broke deadlock and helped the parties reach settlement. Following this, we look at some of the influencing factors in successful negotiation, such as the impact of thorough preparation and the re-establishment of trust among the parties. Naturally, while the case study is based on a real-life dispute, some details have been changed to protect the parties' anonymity.

Case study: managing a CEO's exit

The dispute

A CEO of a large multinational company was asked to leave his company following a 24-month period of poor performance. The CEO had joined the company to great anticipation, with ambitious plans to modernise infrastructure and IT systems and to break into new markets at home and internationally. His plans were welcomed enthusiastically as ushering the company in a fresh direction in a market that had undergone significant changes following rival company mergers and partnerships. Accompanying these expectations, the CEO commanded a generous compensation package from the company as the price for his talents.

In the short term, the CEO achieved cost savings which were helpful to the business. His long-term strategies, however, soon began to sour. The modernisation plans he envisaged were difficult to implement and turned out to be expensive failures when put in place. Customers and suppliers became dissatisfied with the company's ability to deliver services and began to turn to rival companies. As a consequence, the company lost market share, and from a leading business was edged out to a more modest market position.

In light of these disappointments, the CEO was asked to leave the company before the end of his contract. A new CEO – significantly younger than the exiting CEO and with a different vision for the company – was appointed, to the satisfaction of shareholders. As part of his exit package, the outgoing CEO looked forward to substantial compensation and a respectable public reference from the company.

The outgoing CEO's compensation proved to be a sticking point for shareholders, however, who reacted angrily at the company annual general meeting when the details of the compensation package were revealed. The shareholders believed that offering the specified level of compensation to the exiting CEO would be a reward for failure. Responding to shareholder anger, the company decided to change the terms of the CEO's exit package to limit the financial provisions made. The company also declined to give detailed complementary references to the exiting CEO, which drew attention to his less than stellar performance. The exiting CEO was very upset by how his exit had been managed, and after taking advice instigated legal action against his former employers.

The company suggested mediation as a way of resolving the issue quickly and privately: from their perspective, reaching a solution quickly would allow them to focus on the company's future with a new board team. The exiting CEO agreed to put his legal proceedings on hold while exploring a mediated settlement, without giving up his access to litigation.

Special considerations

Several factors made this mediation a difficult, delicate process requiring special care and attention. While these factors were particular to this dispute, they can also be taken more generally as elements that will affect the highest corporate executive level (C-level) disputes more generally.

Identity

Most exits from companies have an element of difficulty – work is a significant prism through which a person's identity is constructed, thus removing work status can prompt uncomfortable challenges to self-image and identity. In this case, the link between the exiting CEO's position and his identity was particularly pronounced. He had a very strong CV, showing years of experience and forward progression in his career. Additionally, his recent role had taken him to the top of a multinational company, with all of the prestige and respect that accompanied such a position.

Being asked to exit the company affected the outgoing CEO's sense of self as well as his career path.

Expectations of power

Being asked to leave the company immediately cut off the outgoing CEO's access to power and influence, providing a stark contrast in potency compared with his recent abilities. The outgoing CEO had difficulty adjusting to this new reality of limited power and altered sphere of influence. Additionally, the swift exit had caused his industry peers to start questioning his judgement and reputation, reasoning that he must have 'lost his touch' to be asked to leave so suddenly. The CEO had lost power within his organisation and influence among other figures in his industry.

At this point, one might consider the question of power and influence, and where it is derived from. People who, for example, gain their sense of power and influence from being able to command a high salary will respond most strikingly to situations that compromise that ability – the same is true for people who derive power and the ability to influence from their seniority within an organisation. Withdrawing access to organisational power and influence created a high-impact situation for the exiting CEO where his ability to act, and therefore the identity he had built around that ability, was swiftly and decisively undermined.

Expectations of respect

After years of being a successful, respected authority figure, both within his organisation and more broadly in the business world, the exiting CEO's expectations of how he would and should be treated were particularly defined. For many years of his career, he had been surrounded by peers at board level, all sharing similar work histories, education levels, and life experiences. He had also been used to being listened to, to having people respond to his authority, and to receiving things from information and reports to refreshments in a timely and exacting manner. Being asked to leave the company, and then to learn that his exit package would be significantly different from his expectations, made the outgoing CEO feel unvalued and disrespected. The mediation revealed that not having his expectations of respect met was a significant personal issue for the exiting CEO in the dispute.

Age

The exiting CEO was at a stage in his professional life where rebuilding a career, and achieving a role with similar prestige and responsibility, would be limited by his age. While non-executive directorships would have been appropriate and realistic options for his experience, a CEO position following his exit was a less likely outcome. This was a challenging reality for the exiting CEO to accept, making the manner of his exit from his recent employer a particularly pertinent issue.

Who to mediate

Issues of identity were a key concern for the exiting CEO and his team of advisors, even affecting the choice of mediator for the dispute. Securing the services of an experienced, prestigious mediator was an important factor for the exiting CEO, as a way of reaffirming his identity as a man of stature and importance, and as a way of helping him to feel that he was being taken seriously. Finding a mediator with gravitas was also important in terms of enabling the CEO to feel that he could relate to an equal, a person who fully understood his position and needs. Because of the legal issues surrounding the dispute, it was necessary to secure a mediator who could be relatable while also giving a robust 'reality check' on all of the positions and consequences at stake.

How to act sensitively

Every mediation is a sensitive, confidential undertaking; in this case, these qualities were particularly sought after for two main reasons. The exiting CEO's personality made sensitive handling imperative – he was a proud man used to being respected and feted for his abilities, and indeed had been taken into the company as something of a saviour figure. Participating in the mediation process was a departure from his usual way of working, and the need to 'give and take' felt like uncomfortable new ground. Achieving a productive mediation relied on the mediator handling these feelings while also remaining neutral and fair to everyone involved in the process.

To compound the issue of sensitivity, speculation about the dispute had begun to appear in news outlets. Much of the coverage was speculative, but this in itself was damaging in terms of affecting the CEO's self-image and the attitude he subsequently brought to the mediation. It also meant that awareness of the dispute reached a far wider audience than a similar dispute typically would. While the mediation was conducted with confidentiality and discretion, there was an unusual sense of being observed surrounding proceedings, as external groups were aware a) of the dispute existing and b) that attempts to find a resolution were ongoing.

Access to information

At board level, it is highly unlikely that either mediation party would enter the process without solid legal advice on topics such as legal rights, fiscal entitlements, and attaining complementary references. Mediation for these types of situations is therefore less focused on exploring a spectrum of entitlements. The process does, however, add great value in allowing the company to interface with the individual with a responsiveness and porosity that litigation does not offer.

Managing these factors

For this case, the parties agreed that co-mediation was the best choice in practical terms. Two mediators were selected who each had strong reputations in their respective fields, and who both brought experience and expertise to the proceedings. Selecting mediators with professional prestige played especially well to the identity needs of the outgoing CEO, who felt that he could find affinity with them and was being respected by their involvement. Having two mediators also enabled the complex case to be managed more effectively: separate caucuses, for example, allowed each party to have individual attention from a mediator at crucial points of the process.

It was clear that the issue of identity would be central to resolving the conflict. The outgoing CEO's identity was closely tied to his position with the company, and the unfolding mediation would be influenced by how comfortable he felt with his image and identity. Overcoming this precarious factor was critical to the mediation's success. In practice, this meant finding ways to give the former CEO a sense of control and enough confidence to proceed actively with the mediation. This strategy was necessary but not without risk: in finding ways to help the former CEO feel comfortable and in control, the mediators had to remain aware of how doing this could affect the other parties connected to the mediation.

In practical terms, the mediators developed this sense of control and confidence by deploying communication and knowledge tools. For example, the mediators took particular care to establish a strong mediator-party dialogue; to find out in detail what the former CEO's expectations were of the process; to explain how mediation negotiations might differ from other types of negotiation system. The time spent over this was not only useful in terms of helping the mediating parties understand the process ahead of them; it also gave the mediator insight into the individual personalities involved in the negotiation. In terms of deciding on effective strategies, this information was especially valuable and relatively easy to come by.

Generally speaking, the types of personality that emerge at mediations vary greatly. Some people stay very quiet and have an accompanying 'shadow negotiator' working almost as a protector-figure; these people often treat silence as a negotiation tool where they feel that engaging in dialogue will leave them vulnerable and on the back foot somehow. Others come in with bravado, determined not to be 'browbeaten' by the other side, expecting to extract concessions without having to make any themselves. The most valuable thing a mediator can do in this situation is to let the individual's personality unfold. This is actually an ideal point at which to let the exiting party take control – they gain something by setting the terms of personality revelation, and the mediator gains by observing the exiting party acting on their own terms.

One thing all varieties of personality will want to do is tell their story: it is almost guaranteed that at some point in the mediation, both the exiting party and the company representative will want to talk about 'what happened' from their perspective. The point at which this happens will be governed by each individual personality and when they want their voice to be heard. Taking a flexible approach to mediation, through letting each story unfold rather than forcing each story at a precise time, can be a subtle way of enabling each party, and in particular the exiting party, to recover a sense of dignity, authority and personal power.

As mentioned before, it is important for a mediator not to undo the value of the hands-off approach by surrendering overall control of the mediation process to one party. The mediator must strive to achieve a balance in which the parties abide by common 'rules', but also have a safe space in which to talk, think and explore. This artful balance cannot be achieved if the mediator cedes too much power to one party; it is not in anyone's interests to encourage this kind of situation to develop.

Outcome

The mediation in our case study, being particularly intricate, took place over two days. The first day was very productive, and the co-mediators helped each party to start thinking about realistic offers and possible areas of compromise. However, the issue of the outgoing CEO's sense of being paid respect was not fully addressed. The co-mediators could sense, from their experience, that fresh tactics would be needed on the second day of mediation to achieve a settlement.

Each mediator came up with an individual contribution that made a measurable difference in getting the exiting CEO to move a little more to achieve a settlement. One mediator, with a long and deep background in legal practice, used their professional reputation and experience as a way to enforce strong reality testing: his ability to approach the exiting CEO, present options and be a sounding board for possible outcomes helped the exiting CEO to see things realistically. The other mediator, conscious of the vulnerability the exiting CEO would feel when confronted with reality, arranged for a very senior director from the company to attend the second mediation day. Doing this helped the exiting CEO feel that he was important enough to warrant a 'good goodbye', from an equal at the company, casting the choice to pursue a mediated settlement as an empowered one rather than an enforced one.

The mediation was a success: by the end of the second day of discussions, a settlement had been reached and the parties were relaxed enough to celebrate the outcome together at a meal. The exiting CEO accepted a reworked compensation package, but the process had given him an opportunity to speak with his former employers, understand their reasons for ending his tenure at the company, and begin working on a personal identity that was not tied to his position at the company.

Learning points

This mediation highlights a number of learning points, which can be taken forward into other similar situations:

- Identity is absolutely paramount when mediating C-level disputes, and has a significant effect on how negotiations will play out. Factors such as finding the most appropriate mediator (e.g. one who can speak to each party as an equal) and ensuring that the 'right' people are at the negotiating table (such as the exiting-CEO's one-time board colleague) play small but significant roles in reassuring the exiting party that they are 'worth' consideration and time.
- Achieving a 'good goodbye' is a promising goal to aim for: this is an exit that respects the exiter's identity needs and offers a sense of closure as well as financial compensation. A good goodbye is not by any means painless, but offers the kind of structure that minimises painful feeling and points to a new future. Helping the exiting party envisage a future beyond the dispute offers healing, and introduces constructive, positive feelings to the negotiations.
- Developing a culture of respect should be a top priority: this includes acknowledging the achievements and status of the exiting party while also creating respect for the other parties involved in a dispute, and for the process of mediation itself. Creating respect and positive self-image is likely to yield constructive results from the mediation process, with parties more willing to engage if they can see the potential for genuine benefits.
- Treating issues of identity, respect, and achieving a graceful exit with seriousness are a worthwhile investment for a company: a happy former employee can be a formidable PR ally in years to come. Even after leaving a company, an exiting party will still have strong networks and contacts which can be used to the benefit or detriment of the company. If at all possible, promoting a graceful and dignified exit is the optimal outcome.
- Pay attention to small details: the location of mediation should be as comfortable and reassuring as possible. A C-level director may feel uncomfortable opening up to a mediator in an office but could come into their own over breakfast at a luxurious hotel, for example. Lunch at the Savoy is not a necessity, of course, but ensuring that mediating parties have access to refreshments, breakout rooms, communication equipment, secretarial services, comfortable seats, etc makes a real difference to the quality of concentration and therefore discussion that takes place.

Working with powerful people in disputes: issues of preparation, managing emotions and trust

The case study outlines a not unusual situation, where individuals have to consider past, present and future behaviours in order to achieve success. The rest of the chapter will look at the following:

- Past – focus on preparation
- Present – managing emotion
- Future – dealing with the breakdown and rebuilding of trust.

All of these have to be dealt with effectively and while these concepts will be used for illustrative purposes, there are many different concepts that could have been used in the same or similar order.

For the ease of discussion, the terms mediation and negotiation will be used interchangeably. The discussion will focus on the negotiation element of the mediation (since mediation is a type of facilitated negotiation) and not the mediation process itself.

Working with the past – preparation

Preparation is something that should be done effectively, as all who engage in any form of mediation and negotiation well know, sometimes requiring a preliminary step of 'preparing to prepare'. Individuals should take great care and effort when preparing and often there cannot be too much preparation, provided it is of the right kind. Individuals should not lose sight of the flexibility required in each and every negotiation. Some find it useful to use a preparation sheet (with simple headings or complex structures) or some other process in order to have considered all the different options that may arise during the negotiation.

In any negotiation, it is important to determine the main issues at hand and the current state of the relationship between the parties. Once these opinions have been identified, it is then important to examine *your* interest and objectives, including a fair assessment of your best alternative to negotiated agreement (BATNA) and your worst alternative (WATNA). There also needs to be consideration as to how the other party would see the negotiation, including their desired underlying needs and interests and what drivers might enable agreement. During the preparation, it is also important (particularly if you know the other party) to consider what particular negotiation style they might adopt and what your strategic reaction might be, in order to achieve success.

When working with a negotiation team, use them to develop a variety of different processes and outcome choices (these can be explored by brainstorming, using the expertise around the table in a 'managed' environment). It is also important to understand, before entering negotiations, everything you might need to know (sometimes asking challenging and difficult questions). This makes bad decisions less likely and provides some flexibility when working with the people in the team and dealing with issues as they arise.

Figure 5.1 gives six different criteria that individuals need to consider as part of their preparation.

1. **BATNA** – this is a term often used and sometimes misunderstood. Essentially, what it does is provide a mechanism for those engaged in negotiation to consider alternatives: so if there was no agreement, what would be the best outcome for the parties involved? This will form part of the decision-making process as to whether an agreement on the terms presented is

WORKING WITH POWERFUL PEOPLE IN A DISPUTE CONTEXT

Preparation criteria
Six things to consider

BATNA
- What is our Best Alternative to a Negotiated Agreement?
- How can we develop it?
- Are there BATNAs for some issues?

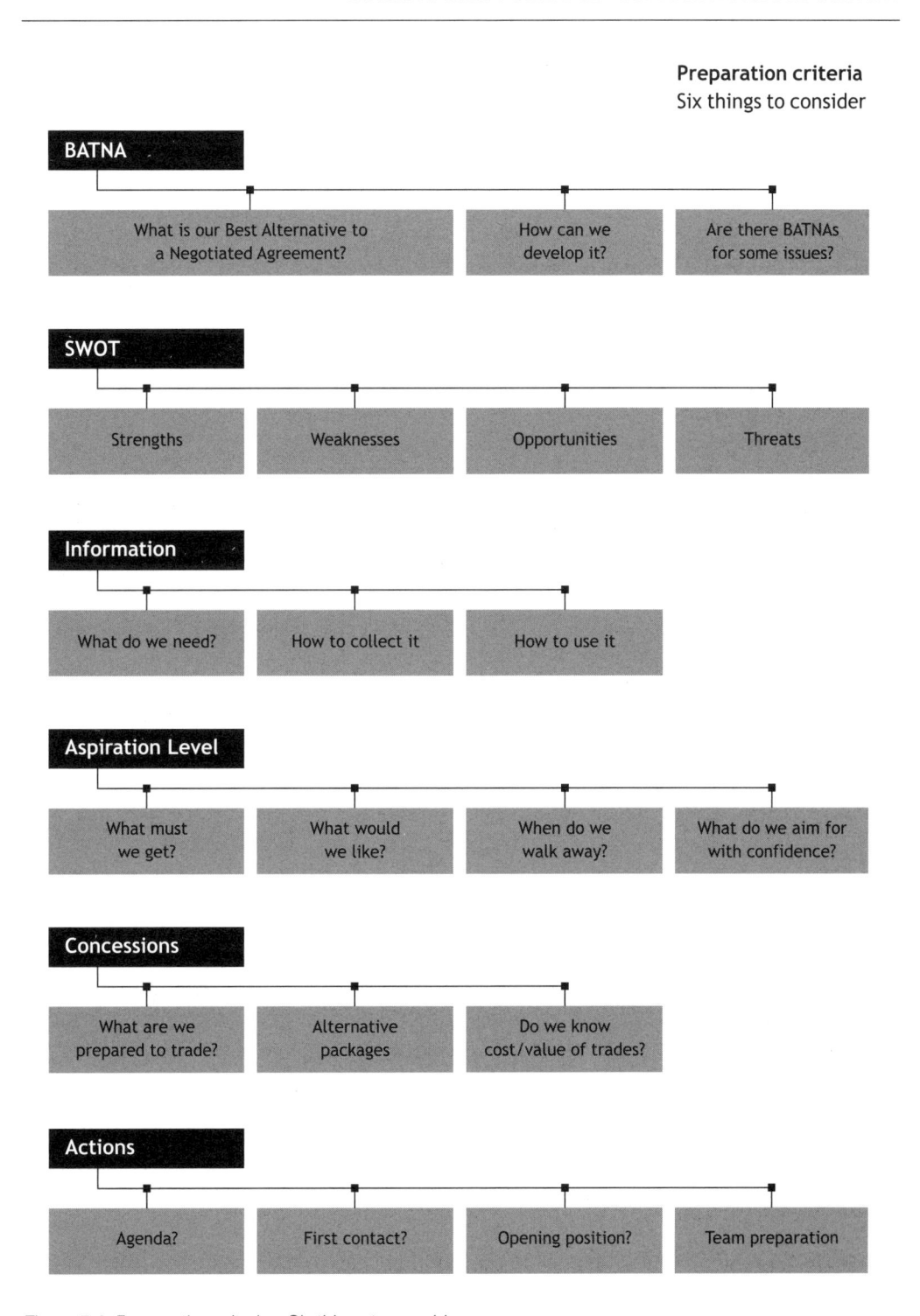

SWOT
- Strengths
- Weaknesses
- Opportunities
- Threats

Information
- What do we need?
- How to collect it
- How to use it

Aspiration Level
- What must we get?
- What would we like?
- When do we walk away?
- What do we aim for with confidence?

Concessions
- What are we prepared to trade?
- Alternative packages
- Do we know cost/value of trades?

Actions
- Agenda?
- First contact?
- Opening position?
- Team preparation

Figure 5.1: Preparation criteria – Six things to consider

worthwhile or should be rejected as there is a better alternative. The more work on a clear and identifiable BATNA in the preparation phase, the better equipped people are at making informed decisions. What should also be considered is the *worst* alternative to a negotiated agreement (WATNA), providing an indication of some of the risks if an agreement cannot be reached.

2. **SWOT** – this is a preparation tool that provides individuals with a clear understanding of their strengths (S), weaknesses (W), opportunities (O), and threats (T) that should always be considered, and this is certainly something that the parties in the case study would have done with the lawyers and other professionals. The mediators would have also worked with the parties in order to establish a true understanding of the strengths and weaknesses of the case as well as providing a robust risk assessment. The mediator would have also reviewed with the parties what opportunities were available and helped uncover any threats to success (settlement). Appendix 2 provides a SWOT analysis template.

3. **Information** – it is important that when parties are preparing for a negotiation, they gather as much information as possible. This would not necessarily be something done in isolation but would be part of the team's preparation. In the case study, during the preparation the mediators would have worked with the parties to get a further understanding and an idea of some of the information available, and this would also be given to the mediators in the form of mediation briefs. Additional preliminary information might have also been given to the mediator through personal contact (such as pre-mediation conversations with each party).

    When preparing for any negotiation, it is essential that you have as much information as possible in order for you to make an informed decision, particularly when dealing with very difficult and complex issues. Emotions can easily get involved in any negotiation, and later in the chapter there will be a discussion of how to work with parties who become emotive. Needless to say, the more emotional an individual becomes, the less likely they are to manage/process information to any degree of satisfaction.

4. **Aspiration level** – it is important to understand what the parties want (which might form part of an agreement package) and also what their bottom line or walk away point is. In any negotiation, it is essential that these have been prepared in advance in order for there to be a true assessment of the offers that will be put forward, and these need to be considered by all parties. Without creating this opportunity, individuals will respond and react on instinct rather than on facts, perhaps achieving a result that is emotionally dissatisfying. In the case study, it is apparent that the parties have worked through the aspiration levels of the client because they were able to bring forward solutions that could drive a settlement, providing a very clear indication of what would and what would not be achievable.

5. **Concessions** – individuals enter into negotiation with the idea of achieving success and wanting everything they have claimed however, if parties stayed in that polarised position, they would achieve very little. Therefore, as part of preparation, individuals should work with

their teams to identify what movement is 'possible'. They would consider: what areas they would be prepared to concede on; what 'tradables' are available; and they would identify the essential 'haves' and 'have nots', in order to reach agreement. The case study provides an example of both parties conceding on several areas, so that some momentum was created to bring parties to a workable agreement.

6. **Actions** – these are generally process points and are things that are often not thought about yet can leave a lasting impression. When working with the negotiation team, there should be some thought and consideration as to who will make an opening presentation on behalf of the individuals, what the statement should contain, and what (if any) signals will be given to the others assembled around the table. In this case study, it was very important that the parties put forward a position that indicated that they had done their homework and that contained a sentiment that they wanted to work together in order to reach an agreement. When working with teams, careful consideration should also be given to the roles of each member of the team, and also some thought as to whether individuals need to be in the main plenary (meeting) room or whether they are providing a support role and should be located in private rooms. The mediators would have contacted the parties before the mediation to get an understanding of who would be attending, their role and what they hoped to achieve. In any negotiation or mediation, it is essential that there be an agreed process, resulting in an agreed agenda, providing a neutral framework that is mutually acceptable.

In the case study, there was a tremendous amount of care given in the preparation to ensure maximum success when the parties came to the table, one being mediator selection. It was this careful consideration about the appropriate mediators used to facilitate the dialogue together with who should be attending the mediation that led to the successful settlement of the mediation. Additionally, in the preparation, mediators had to develop a strategy in order to engage with the parties in a way that would actually help them feel fully comfortable and confident with the process and that they understood where the parties would need assistance.

Individuals in negotiation and mediation know that preparation should be conducted and are acutely aware of the importance of adequate preparation, but often when working with individuals in conflict (and sometimes crisis), this preparation has not been conducted. For example, some senior-level executives were asked about the amount of preparation that they do before an important negotiation, and they responded by saying 'we know it's important but we don't have enough time.' This might not be an acceptable answer, but it is a business reality. Such short-sightedness and poor allocation of time will only result in individuals having to deal with the conflict that has arisen because of the poor preparation. They will then have to engage in lengthy conversations, often with their lawyers (and at some expense). Therefore, individuals should always have time to prepare effectively. If not, they should prepare themselves for the inevitable conflict that arises as a result of the misunderstanding of some of the facts and the damage to the relationships that this will undoubtedly cause.

Dealing with the present – managing emotions

Emotions are a natural part of human interaction and a physical and biological reality, although their existence has often been ignored or discounted, and some even believe that emotions have no place in commercial decision-making. The case study tells the story of a man's life, in which he was once a chief executive and had been removed from his position and subsequently felt what? Did he feel angry, annoyed, upset, hurt or sad? These and many more words might have been valid descriptors of how he felt. What is important is how these feelings (and emotions) were dealt with by the mediators.

In order to give a framework for analysis, and further discussion, a conceptual framework will be used. This framework is based on the work of Fisher and Shapiro and articulated in their book *Building Agreement*.[1] When referring to emotional states, these Harvard professors used a framework of core concerns. These core concerns are: appreciation, affiliation, autonomy, status, and role. When these core concerns are recognised either by the individual who was feeling them or others who are affected by the individual, there will be an opportunity for the individual to feel that their emotions have been heard and recognised. The negotiator or mediator would certainly need to be aware of these core concerns when engaging in a situation where individuals are likely to have a strong emotional response.

Fisher and Shapiro suggest considering the 'core concerns' that have led to this emotional response, rather than simply addressing the emotion. Using the case study as an example of how the mediators were able to do this successfully provides us with an opportunity to see how other methods can be used when faced with similar situations and circumstances.

A closer look at Fisher and Shapiro

Appreciation – this is the understanding of others' thoughts and feelings, and the communication of that understanding. The mediators in the case study were able to do this in a variety of ways. First of all, ensuring that they understood what was important to the individual/s. They did this by 'establishing a strong mediated party dialogue to find out in detail what the former CEO's expectations were of the process.' The mediators were able to communicate this by doing something that was essential in making true progress – they listened. The mediators would have listened for information pertaining to the negotiation but must have truly listened for understanding. It cannot be said enough how important it is for individuals who are in conflict and in some form of emotional state for somebody to sit down and listen to what they have to say. The reflecting back, the questioning, the non-verbal communication provides an opportunity to create a working dialogue. So in order to express appreciation for the other, it starts with what the individual can do in order to engage in effective dialogue.

In the case study, it was important that the chief executive felt some sense of appreciation, not only from the mediators working with him but also from the parties that they were negotiating with. He felt that he had done an excellent job and what was required was an opportunity for him to feel that this work was appreciated.

Five core concerns

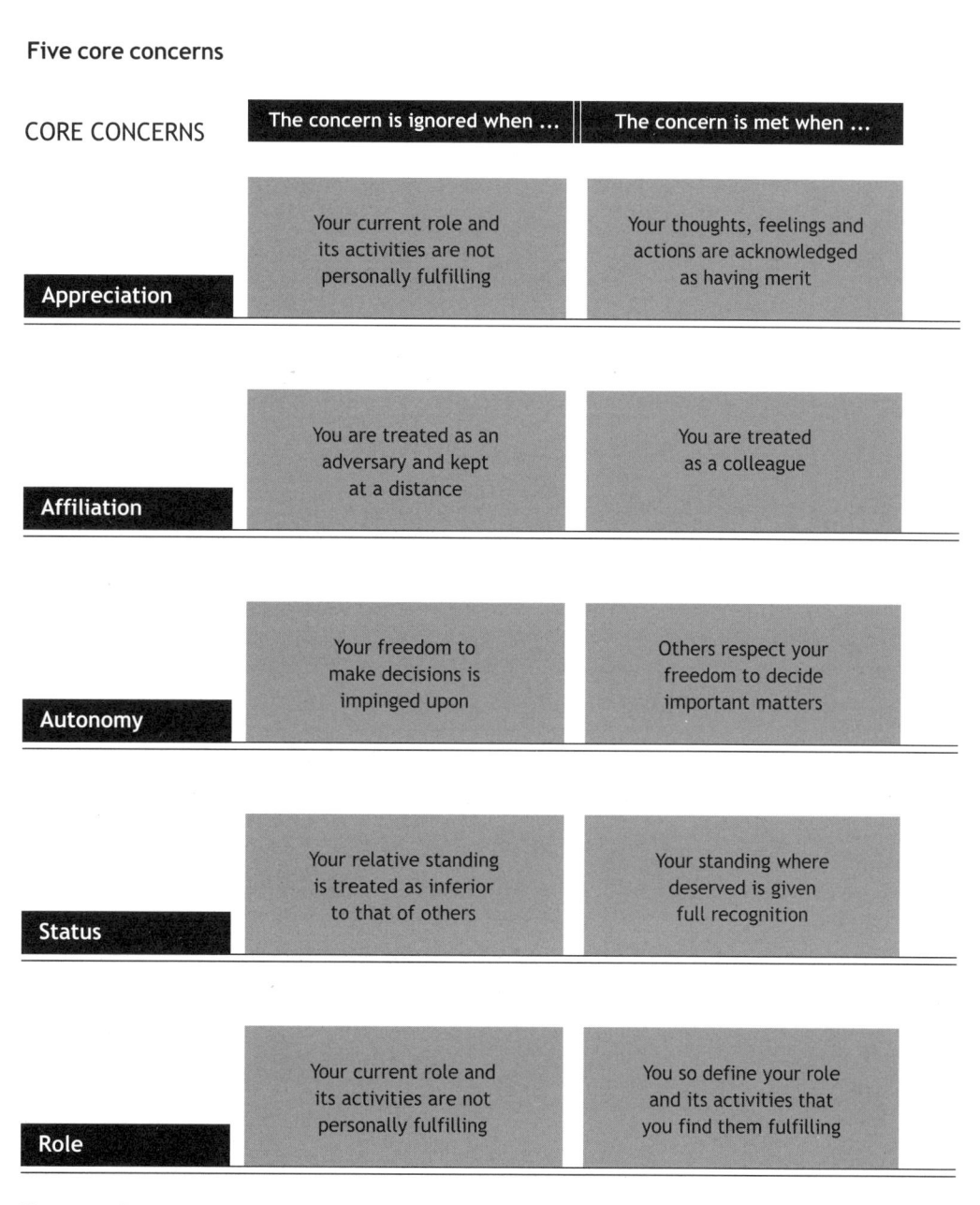

CORE CONCERNS	The concern is ignored when ...	The concern is met when ...
Appreciation	Your current role and its activities are not personally fulfilling	Your thoughts, feelings and actions are acknowledged as having merit
Affiliation	You are treated as an adversary and kept at a distance	You are treated as a colleague
Autonomy	Your freedom to make decisions is impinged upon	Others respect your freedom to decide important matters
Status	Your relative standing is treated as inferior to that of others	Your standing where deserved is given full recognition
Role	Your current role and its activities are not personally fulfilling	You so define your role and its activities that you find them fulfilling

Figure 5.2: Five core concerns

The corpus of management literature is full of research with articulated discussions on the need for active listening which involves the individuals to be truly engaged in conversation. Unfortunately, it happens rarely and if more care was taken to help individuals interact then perhaps conflict would not arrive.

Affiliation – is building a connection with the other party. In the case study, it was essential that the mediators 'build' a connection with both parties in order to reach some sort of agreement. One of the ways in which the mediators did this was by allowing the parties to tell their story in the safe 'mediation' space in which they could 'talk, think and explore...'. Careful balance and consideration of the balance of power always has to be given, particularly when working with multiple parties dealing with many issues over a number of days. These are the same issues and concerns that are a factor in any mediation or successful negotiation, and questions should always be asked about the 'positive' connections being established. You might also consider whether there is some sort of relationship that you have with the party or another member of the team – or one that you can create – to foster effective dialogue. It is a normal part of business for negotiation teams to be established in order to achieve success: it is important that there are the appropriate methods of communication and opportunities for dialogue within these teams in order for conflict to surface, and so that it can be dealt with as and when necessary.

Autonomy – people need to feel that they have the freedom to make decisions. In the case study, the chief executive was originally brought into the company in order to make decisions that were going to be quite ambitious, 'to help modernise the company and take it into new markets and a fresh direction.' The former chief executive in the short term did achieve some cost savings; however, in the long term things did not go in the direction that the board and other members of the organisation felt were appropriate. As a result of the chief executive's decisions, the company lost market share and eventually he was asked to leave.

In the mediation, it was necessary that the mediator recognised that the CEO's autonomy was something that had to be valued rather than discredited. In addition, he had to feel that he could make a decision in the mediation that would provide him with the best outcome. This was initially quite difficult because there were a number of other factors that needed to be dealt with before an agreement could be reached. There were several underlying drivers: the issue of the press being aware of what had happened and the CEO's ability to achieve a reference that would offer him the ability to get another position. However, to reach agreement it was essential that he did not feel pressured into making a decision; rather, he had the ability to make it because he wanted to. This sense of making decisions free from pressure is often ignored and people feel like they have to make decisions under very difficult circumstances. Alternatively, if they have been given the appropriate information and the opportunity to make a choice even if it is a difficult decision, then emotionally they can deal with the decision and move forward.

Status – it is important to recognise and acknowledge status rather than competing with others over who has higher social status, whether it is actual or perceived. In the case study, the former chief executive, by his very appointment, had a prestigious social and commercial status. He was removed in such a way that would have negatively affected his status, how he felt about himself and how he felt others would have perceived him. He was replaced by a 'younger, more energetic individual' and in order for him to reach some sort of agreement in the mediation, there would need to be some acknowledgement first of all that his status could be recovered (even preserved) and that he was respected as an individual. Individuals excel because they have ambition and strive to achieve success so they can be respected by others and achieve the status that mirrors this sense of accomplishment. When working with parties, particularly in conflict, it is very important to acknowledge their status as well as your own. Be wary of competitive feelings and try to use status as a point of similarity or difference to aid mediation.

Additionally, when considering status, we should also be aware of the need to recognise ego. There is a place for ego, but only if appropriate. Ego should be recognised and not challenged: it can help inform the negotiation and assist the parties in reaching agreement, rather than becoming a barrier. In the case study, the mediators working with the former chief executive were able to provide an acknowledgement of his status and its importance. The other side were also able to acknowledge that this status was not taken lightly through what was said about the importance of the issues.

Role – it is important to choose a role that everyone can work on together and that can be expanded whenever possible. In the case study, the former chief executive had the role of making some very difficult decisions. When he first came into the organisation, he had to make changes, cut costs, and try and lead the organisation in what he thought was the right direction. Unfortunately for him, and indeed for the organisation, the company lost market share which cost him his job and 'role'. The mediators had to work with the parties to help establish that while his role was difficult, it was one in which he had tried to achieve success (although this unfortunately ended in failure). Other barriers to 'role' success exist, such as having to carry out additional activities which may distract individuals from performing essential tasks. Internal conflicts arise because people are asked to do more with less. It is important to first identify what the role is and the activities within it, to nominate actions to make it more fulfilling and to alleviate those unhelpful tasks. One of the difficulties in negotiation is that parties often feel that they, and their role, go unacknowledged or unappreciated, that there is little understanding of what their 'role' entails and that they would prefer to be doing something else, given the choice.

Considering the future – breakdown and rebuilding of trust

Trust is something that is expected in transactions and is a very fragile commodity. It can be won and lost with one key stroke, a dismissive word, or an unfortunate exchange. Too often in business, trust is assumed, not necessarily explicitly discussed, and people react badly due to the emergence of distrust, or misunderstanding because of a breakdown in trust.

So what is trust? Trust is the 'expectation by one person, group, or firm of ethical behaviour—that is, morally correct decisions and actions based upon ethical principles of analysis—on the part of the other person, group, or firm in a joint endeavour or economic exchange'. But what does that really mean? Do people just assume trust because of their particular role or profession? 'Trust me, I'm a mediator': what does this statement say about both the person who makes it and the person who relies on it?

In the case study, trust operated in several ways. The ousted chief executive trusted the mediators and the mediation process. He also needed to trust that the former employer would be

Breakdown and rebuilding of trust

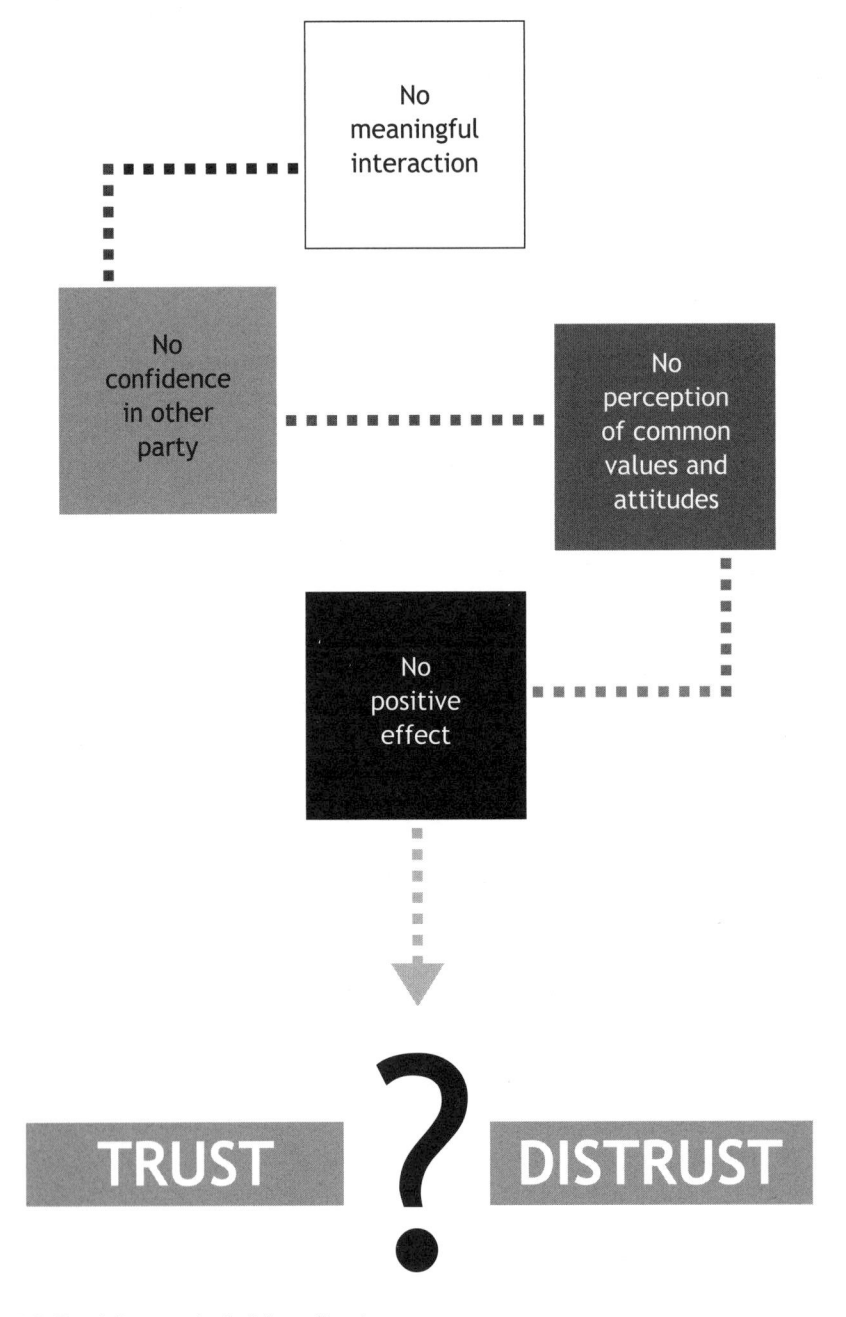

Figure 5.3: Breakdown and rebuilding of trust

doing something that would provide him with a satisfactory resolution. The parties had to trust that the process would work for them and that they could trust the two mediators, who had to work together. The mediators were selected because they had 'a strong reputation in their respective fields' and had a reputation for producing results even in the most complex cases. By engaging with two mediators, the case could be managed more effectively because there were times when the parties would receive attention from both mediators simultaneously. The parties received solid legal advice before entering the mediation, giving the parties a better sense that they could trust the process. The aggrieved party also felt that he could begin to trust the representative from his former employer because of who was at the negotiation table. There was somebody present who was senior enough that the aggrieved party felt that his importance was acknowledged and that he could rely on this person having the appropriate authority to make a decision on behalf of the organisation.

In many ways, before the mediation the former chief executive felt betrayed by what had happened and needed a process in which he could rebuild trust in not only his former employer but any future employer. The mediators worked with both parties to get to a place where they could respect each other and reach a point of eventual agreement. This would never have been achieved without acknowledgement, in some way, of how the parties felt about the lack of trust and the need to rebuild trust, in order to move forward. In a mediation situation, there may not always be an overt discussion of trust issues and the breakdown of trust, but it should always be considered as an underlying concept and barrier to agreement.

Trust has to start with somebody taking an active first step, and those parties that do take the first step will often set the 'pace' and 'anchor' the future interactions. In the case study, the mediators working with both parties were able to establish a trusting dialogue which resulted not only in a settlement, but also in the facilitation of a position where the parties could move forward with their lives. Although this was a monetary claim, additional 'value' can be created by attending to the interests and emotional needs of the parties. The mediation also provided an opportunity to restore trust and respect while renewing the identity of those individuals involved.

In difficult or challenging negotiations it is, therefore, important to take a step back and ask yourself:

- Do I trust the process?
- Do I trust the party that I'm negotiating with?
- Do I trust myself and information that I am relying on?

The answer to this and to many other questions may be the underlying cause of any conflict that might arise. Part of the process of regaining trust is to explore the needs and interests of each party and to establish a process whereby incremental steps of trustworthiness can be displayed and acknowledged. Part of this exploration would require individuals to put their own thoughts and desires aside and instead ask: 'what is important for you and what is it that we need to achieve together in order to reach agreement?' This creates a dialogue and opportunities for conversation, and this sharing of ideas is often a useful 'first step' to resolution. However, this requires someone to take the first step and parties in conflict often feel reluctant to do so. They should consider what American political scientist Robert M. Axelrod called 'tit for two-tats': that is, you should not retaliate immediately when something has been done to you, but instead offer an opportunity for re-engagement. Some feel that this negotiation strategy is risky because it exposes them to potential exploitation. However, it is worth the risk because while most parties are aware of what would happen if they choose to retaliate, they may not know what would happen if they choose to do otherwise.

Conclusion

The resolution to any dispute is never easy, particularly when parties are in high-conflict situations, having to deal with high emotions and complex negotiation teams. However, the one thing that will not be discussed in this chapter is *time*, and this is relevant when considering past, present and future behaviour. Time is something that should always be considered in any negotiation and has a huge impact and influence on how individuals will *approach* negotiation. In any mediation or negotiation, time can make or break settlements, particularly when people feel pressured to come to an agreement. Time (or its absence) will often cause people to make irrational decisions as they become emotional and stressed. Thus, whatever the desired outcome, there should always be consideration of the appropriateness and need for possible interventions (be they breaks or a pause in proceedings), as well as the time that it would take in order to achieve agreement. Allow someone to ask the difficult question: 'do we need to reach agreement today… and at what cost?'

Success can be achieved if you follow some of the steps discussed in this chapter, but what is important is that conflict is dealt with rather than ignored. Conflict does not go away; it just gets bigger and uglier!

Powerful people and disputes: eight points to success

Work with parties privately – before any joint session, and ideally before the mediation day, the mediator should attempt to make contact with the mediating parties, either in person or via telephone. This gives the mediating neutral a chance to weigh up the personalities they will be dealing with, and allows the parties in dispute to put a face and personality to the details they will have about the mediator.

Keep people informed – in a difficult situation such as mediation, every effort should be made to avoid surprises. All parties should be clear on how the mediation will work in practice, and who will be contributing in joint and plenary sessions. It is not necessary to provide details on what each person will be saying.

Be patient – the mediator will be used to exercising patience over a long, focused day in a way that the mediating parties will not. Patience is not just an inbuilt quality; it is also something that can be fostered by circumstances. The mediator can do a lot to encourage patience and goodwill by creating a comfortable environment for everyone to work in!

Develop a culture of respect – this applies to position and process. Everyone has something valuable to contribute to the day's discussions and encouraging respect for the mediation procedures will help to draw out that value effectively.

Build operational rapport – one of the mediator's main hats is that of facilitator between parties that used to enjoy a functional relationship. Some parties leave mediation with their relationship restored; others come away with a resolved ending that promises a separate but respectful future. In every case, the mediator must build a brief, trusting relationship with each party that allows them to explore their situation and, ideally, find a solution.

Think about other people who could contribute positively – in some cases, a figure like a former colleague could contribute positively to the mediation, adding a more personal touch to what might otherwise be a more tense round of discussions. This is especially true if the person is one that the mediating parties respect, or think well of. When mediating disputes with more senior figures, bringing in another person to contribute to the exit negotiations can be an effective marker of respect for the exiting party.

Be aware of what else is going on intellectually – this refers to remaining aware of who else the parties have consulted with, the reasons for the exit, and what each party hopes to achieve from mediation negotiations. Engaging sophisticated lawyers, for example, indicates that the parties both expect to get maximum value in terms of a good settlement. In terms of preserving a good image, all parties stand to benefit from a well-managed exit and therefore have an interest in working towards a solution.

Remember that the exiter is just a person – much of our discussion has focused on preserving dignity and creating respect based on the exiter's power and authority. As our case study demonstrates, these factors are important and make a noticeable difference to how negotiations happen and reach a resolution. The other side to this observation, however, is the broad and perhaps clichéd point that the exiter is also 'just a person'. Like everyone else, they will have foibles, vulnerabilities, strengths, habits, families, hobbies, memories, aspirations. Bearing this in mind will help put negotiations in perspective, and could provide the window of affinity that you need to make a connection that matters.

> Although handling powerful people in disputes can be challenging, it is also very doable. Bearing the learning points in mind, we can see that by keeping a balanced perspective, a person acting as a neutral party for powerful people in conflict can be effective and efficient in achieving outcomes that benefit everyone.

Note

1. Fisher, R, and Shapiro, D (2005) *Building Agreement*. London: Random House.

6
Projected success – how not to let conflict undermine critical projects

Andy Grossman

Introduction

For large-scale or critical projects, the sheer scale of the undertaking provides ample opportunity for conflicts and disputes to occur, deepen and escalate. Each stage of the undertaking is a potential incubator of misunderstanding, circumstantial change, 'grey areas', and unforeseen occurrences whose effects ripple through an industry or project.

The initial shock of encountering conflict is not the only problem one might face. Disrupting a project that can cost millions (or indeed, billions) of pounds, employs thousands and has been planned for many years carries significant implications. One must consider how, for example, a dispute with a project's building contractor might affect the delivery of concurrent commitments (such as those with architects or infrastructure suppliers) and those planned for the future, such as with IT, furnishing and catering contractors, to name but a few. Adding on the financial, time, emotional, focus and reputation costs of solving these disputes through litigation in many cases serves to compound the existing problems associated with dispute.

In this chapter, I shall examine not only how alternative dispute resolution (ADR) can be used as a response to disputes, but also how the integration of its principles into contracts and business practices can help large-scale projects deliver results on time and on budget.

Adapting to a changing world

The uncertain political and financial landscape we currently inhabit magnifies the problems arising from inadequate risk management, and correspondingly the need for robust risk and conflict management procedures. Issues such as developing lasting relationships, creatively finding solutions to problems and delivering value for money are now more than ever at the forefront of business' concerns. Expectations, from the business world and the general public, are at a peak as 'doing more with less' becomes a cultural norm.

The potential for disputes to arise between contractors and clients becomes acute when the issue of finance comes under scrutiny. In 2010, the UK Government, for example, outlined plans to save £1.7 billion by delaying or stopping contracts (initially contracts worth over £1 million had to be referred to the Treasury for approval); reviewing how **Private Finance Initiative** and Public-Private Partnership (PPP) projects can be managed to deliver value for money; and by renegotiating contracts to improve their affordability. In May 2010, the National Audit Office and the Audit Commission jointly issued a publication ('A Review of Collaborative Procurement Across the Public Sector') recommending that public bodies work together more effectively to maximise procurement savings. Finally, the Government issued a moratorium on new consulting, ICT, recruitment, marketing and property spending contracts to make savings of £500 million over six months. All of these actions, designed to save money, highlight how changes in circumstances can force changes to even the most clear, encompassing contractor agreement.

The certainty therefore amidst much uncertainty is that more detailed ADR, dispute prevention and dispute management guidance will become necessary. As with the UK Government's big budget squeeze affecting various suppliers, so too will budgetary issues come under scrutiny on large-scale projects. Funds that were once specifically available, or on a scale that clients and contractors had become used to accessing, may at short notice be diminished or removed entirely. Coping with this new reality will almost certainly lead to the types of misunderstandings and disagreements that, without appropriate management, will lead to disputes.

The other effect of a spending squeeze is a paradigm shift about budgets towards wrap-around service delivery: as far as possible, every last penny should show results that offer value for money. This is not only practical; it touches on areas such as stakeholder engagement and building a positive public image. These factors come into their own when considering future outcomes, with goodwill being a particularly golden gift. A client developing goodwill from a contractor, and vice versa, is often the basis of a mutually rewarding business relationship, which can pay dividends in the long term. Equally, positive public perception of a company can bring many benefits, such as deep brand loyalty from consumers and access to funding from financial institutions. A reputation for anticipating and dealing with potential areas of conflict is therefore extremely valuable, for clients and contractors alike.

On large-scale projects, it is highly likely that clients and contractors will be operating internationally, presenting another compelling argument in support of such projects adopting ADR practices. One of the common reasons for parties pursuing ADR before litigation is cost – the litigation process can be long and very expensive compared with a process like mediation. Consider then how much more complicated, time-consuming and expensive litigation may become between parties from different jurisdictions, nationalities and even cultures. Even when contracts specify a jurisdiction and language of trial should litigation become necessary, there is still great potential for expense and time delays.

An international theatre of business also presents different opportunities for problems to arise. If, for example, a contractor manufactures components in Country A for a project in Country B for cost reasons, the contractor and client in Country B are automatically exposed to risks in Country A. Political unrest, a natural disaster or dramatic economic changes are just three obvious factors that could inhibit production in Country A, affecting the contractor's ability to supply to its client in Country B. For a large-scale project comprising many individual projects, difficulties in one project area are likely to affect other project areas and subsequently the entire undertaking. While the delivery failure may be outside of the contractor's control, it will face the consequences in terms of penalties and possible sanctions. In this situation, there is potential for conflict to arise between the contractor and client, the contractor and other contractors, and the contractor and their suppliers in Country B.

Given the increased and varied potential for disputes in a project with international reach, introducing ADR processes into contracts seems increasingly practical. If done at an early stage, for example, the agreement can take into account specific cultural customs and behaviours that might otherwise give cause for confusion – this also has the benefit of uncovering such attitudes, forestalling moments of misinterpretation. The parties entering into the contract 'own' the process of drafting ADR contract clauses, and can tailor the provisions to suit their particular needs. Similarly, ADR processes such as mediation are voluntary and 'owned' by the parties, giving a private time frame for discussion and reflection in the event of a dispute.

This sense of ownership is closely aligned to the other great selling point of ADR processes – compared with litigation, ADR methods are notably flexible and creative. Consequently, this means that the full range of needs that might be posed by international disputants can be accommodated. It also acknowledges the different problem resolution philosophies and approaches that international parties might bring to a conflict situation. Rather than the more prescriptive approach that litigation might offer, an ADR process developed by the parties in question will be genuinely responsive to their needs; their investment in planning will have a far greater chance of engagement should the clause need to be invoked.

Model clauses

One way of anticipating disputes between contractors and clients is to include an ADR clause or pledge in the body of contract agreements. Essentially, an ADR clause outlines that, in the event of a dispute, the parties in conflict commit to trying ADR methods of resolution before resorting to litigation.

Some people may feel that the intention to try ADR methods is sufficient, and that codifying the intention is in some way a gesture of suspicion, or even an open invitation to bad luck. Experience suggests otherwise. The number of large-scale projects that suffer from client-contractor disputes, and their associated effects, far outweighs the number that do not. Indeed, projects that do not experience this kind of disruption often are those that make use of ADR clauses.

At a glance: Heathrow T5

- Clear communication is a key factor in delivering projects on time and on budget

Following the longest public inquiry in UK planning history, approval was given for the £4.3 billion Terminal 5 project at Heathrow. The undertaking consisted of 16 projects – sizeable projects in their own right – under a single umbrella programme including:

- a primary site the size of Hyde Park, including a main and satellite concourse building to handle in excess of 27 million passengers annually;
- converging roads meeting in parking facilities for bus, coach, taxi and car users;
- the extension of the Piccadilly and Heathrow Express public transport lines;
- rerouting two rivers that at the time bisected the T5 site;
- the building of off-site factories to manufacture adequate reinforced steel structures.

In order to deliver T5 on time and on budget, BAA sought a new way of working with contractors:

1. A novel approach to contracting with the same conditions applying to all key suppliers, irrespective of type. Contractors worked within BAA's framework agreement aimed at facilitating more collaborative working between stakeholders irrespective of company and profession.
2. BAA adopted an innovative approach to risk management with the aim of minimising time and resources spent on disputes with contractors and consultancy companies.
3. BAA sought to manage the design and construction much more rigorously than in previous projects, investing in a comprehensive data management system as well as in promoting off-site manufacturing and pre-fabrication of sections of T5.

The resulting 'T5 Agreement' was ground-breaking in its scope and aims. Its central tenet was to manage cause, not effect: in practice, this meant BAA accepting the vast majority of the (financial) risks of the project, while rewarding innovation, collaboration and productivity. Cost and profit margins were guaranteed to suppliers in exchange for an agreement that contractors would supply services at an industry leading standard through integrated teams. Collaboration was emphasised through common insurance policies and additional bonuses for delivering exceptional performance across stakeholder teams. 'T5 Behaviour' became a living, breathing philosophy, promoting a culture of safety, communication, collaboration and achievement for everyone connected with the project.

BAA kept comprehensive performance monitoring records, and the final data is impressive. The project was completed on time and within its £4.3 billion budget; 9.6 million hours were worked with no time lost to disputes; and at 5.4%, labour turnover of first-tier suppliers stood at one-third of the construction industry average.[1]

As the T5 example demonstrates, clarifying expectations of behaviour and practice from the outset is helpful to all parties involved in delivering a large-scale project. ADR contract clauses form part of that expectation management. Far from inviting bad feeling, a clause that a) recognises that disputes can and often do arise and b) commits the signatories to exploring collaborative, non-litigative solution methods before beginning court proceedings does much to promote realism and respect between the parties.

Drafting ADR contract clauses: a guide

Should you wish to include an ADR contract clause in the drafting of a client-contractor agreement, there are a number of things to consider. The checklist below may be useful in helping you clarify how best to form a contract suited to your particular needs:

Who?

Do you want to identify the decision-makers engaging in the ADR process, e.g. managing director, CEO? This may provide clarity but is not strictly necessary: you can simply refer to 'the parties', leaving decisions on appropriate attendees to the relevant time. Ideally, attendees should be able to come to the mediation with full authority.

What?

Do you want to attempt the ADR process before any adversarial process begins? In England, one cannot oust the jurisdiction of the court, but the court will stay proceedings to allow parties to honour their agreement to mediate. A party's right to seek injunctive or declaratory relief or to avoid a time bar will always be preserved. The prospect of settlement may be higher before the lines of battle have been drawn by the hostile step of commencing court proceedings/arbitration.

How?

Do you want a single-stepped process or a multi-step process? The choice is whether to move straight to mediation or to combine different ADR processes, for example to provide for direct negotiations followed by mediation if the negotiations fail.

When? I)

What time frame do you want to work within? To be effective, it is better to outline a clear process and timetable. This is particularly true if mandatory negotiation or mediation is to be included, so everyone involved knows how much time they have to act before moving to the next stage.

When? II)

Is there a clear, agreed trigger for the ADR process being activated? A trigger could vary from a formal notice of dispute, a letter from a senior manager or even the agreement of an executive group. What grounds will there be for invoking the ADR contract clause? How will you measure whether, or how far, these criteria have been reached?

Which rules?

Will the clause refer to existing procedural rules or will it have its own specific set of rules? Your clause will be more effective if you refer to a known and accepted model mediation procedure. In *Cable & Wireless plc v IBM* [2002] EWHC Ch 2059, Mr Justice Colman said: 'Resort to CEDR (Centre for Effective Dispute Resolution) and participation in its recommended procedure are, in my judgment, engagement of sufficient certainty for a court readily to ascertain whether they have been complied with.'

Creating an 'ADR culture'

The benefits of creating a collaborative, proactive culture between contractor and supplier are evident, with the example of the 'T5 Agreement' illustrating in irrefutable detail what can be achieved with an anticipatory approach.

It is also possible to replicate these structures within a company, creating what might be called an internal ADR culture. How this is implemented will depend to some extent on how the company is organised: there will be different opportunities for a multinational company with many offices in many countries than exist for a company with national reach, or one with high levels of outsourcing. The underlying principles of ADR – anticipating where problems might arise, keeping communication channels open, adopting a grassroots approach to problem solving – can be adopted in a number of forms. One particularly interesting innovation is the training and use of employees as mediators within a company, as the example from E.ON Group illustrates.

**Implementing
ADR contract clauses**
The five-step process

WHO?

WHAT?

HOW?

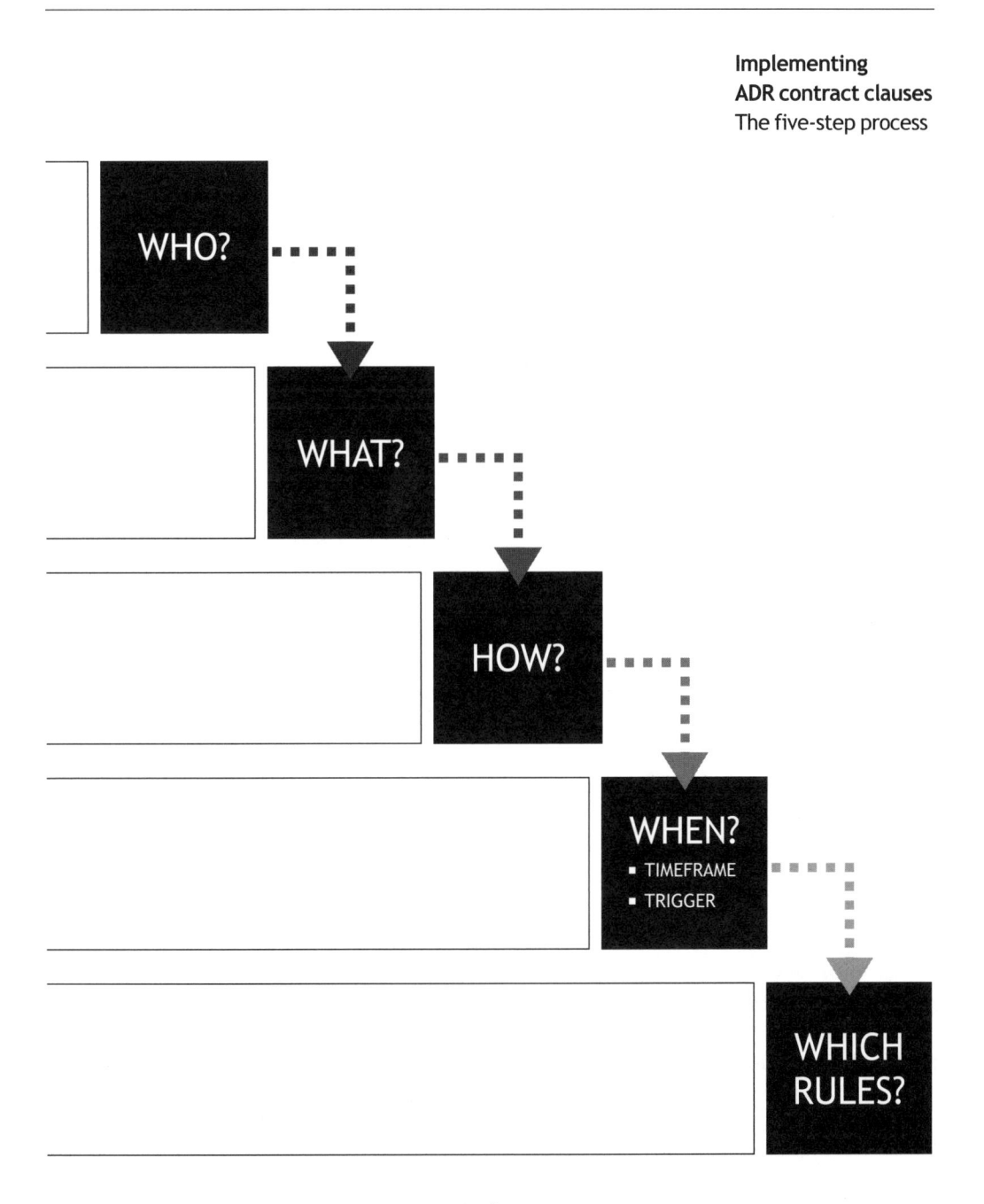

WHEN?
- TIMEFRAME
- TRIGGER

WHICH RULES?

Figure 6.1: Implementing ADR contract clauses – the five-step process

At a glance: E.ON Group

- **Successful 'best practice' trials can influence wider industry attitudes**

With just under €69 billion in sales and close to 88,000 employees, E.ON – headquartered in Germany – is the world's largest investor-owned energy service provider. The company has shown consistent commitment to the introduction and progression of ADR techniques, with mediation being a particular area of focus. Through a comprehensive range of activities dating from 2006, E.ON has introduced ADR principles to all of its individual 13 businesses, and has even gone as far as promoting the benefits of ADR principles as applied to large-scale projects to other industry-leading German firms.

In 2006, the E.ON Group decided to introduce an ADR culture across its individual businesses, as part of a wider aim to develop E.ON's core values in a cohesive, proactive way. The company introduced a range of measures to ensure the use of ADR across the group, showing 'model' corporate behaviour:

- ADR clauses were developed and circulated by the legal team, with the expectation that they would be included in all appropriate contract agreements;
- Conflict management clauses were also developed for use in internal policy documents;
- Information was produced and workshops delivered to appropriate E.ON employees at a number of levels to promote ADR as an option, and to explain how the ADR process worked.

In creating the 'mediation project', the team considered:

a) which processes to use: they opted mainly to use mediation, making it voluntary rather than mandatory;
b) how to resource the project: E.ON recruited employees to become mediators across the group. Within the first year, they had recruited and trained 25 mediators and this number has now risen to 49 across the group of 13 companies. This initiative ensured that while mediations were kept 'in-house', mediators could feel like an external neutral presence by conducting mediations for companies that were not their own.

While a remarkable set of initiatives in itself, E.ON took this one stage further by effectively creating a business mediator's forum; inviting industry-leading companies to round-table discussions on the adoption of institutional ADR practices.

Building mediation into projects

In a number of dispute cases involving large-scale projects, mismatched expectations are a significant factor in the dispute's inception and escalation. Adopting ADR principles, such as including 'mediation clauses' or signing an ADR pledge, provides a straightforward, effective way of keeping lines of dialogue open between parties. This reduces the likelihood of misunderstandings arising in the first instance, and sets in place procedures that promote clarity and insight should confusion occur.

As already suggested, conflict frequently has wider and self-perpetuating consequences beyond its original bounds. In many cases conflict, arising from mismatched expectations and poor communication, is avoidable or at least largely containable through planning. Why then, if it is manageable, are there so many cases of conflict?

The answer lies partially, perhaps, in how people view ADR methods such as mediation. In addition to it being viewed as a somewhat second-tier option in some quarters, there persists an unfortunate view of mediation as a 'distress purchase' when relationships and progress have already deteriorated significantly. While it is true that mediation has a unique ability to unlock disputes which remain impassable by traditional litigation channels, the fact is that mediation, along with other ADR techniques, is exceptionally effective in a preventative capacity. Preventative in this sense is best defined in terms of developing a standard approach, or mindset, integrated comprehensively as part of project strategy rather than bolted on as an afterthought.

While some people look askance at ADR methods, almost everyone, if asked, would respond appreciatively to the benefits of a robust risk management strategy. In reality, a *comprehensive* risk management strategy should include recourse to ADR customarily. Indeed, ADR methods successfully augment traditional risk management strategies by anticipating the 'human factor' and the challenges this might pose to a project. A traditional risk management approach, for example, will account for technical risk potential but is likely to miss those associated with how parties relate to each other and within each group. This strategy approach is lacking; it does not account for the tendency of communication breakdowns to be both cause and effect of project failings.

The CEDR project mediation protocol

Project mediation is designed to help support the successful delivery of a project by identifying and addressing problems before they turn into disputes about payment and delay.

It enables conflict management and dispute resolution to be integrated into the contract as part of a collaborative contracting approach and can be used for almost any project. It may, however, be particularly appropriate for:

- PPPs or long-term contracts
- technically complex contracts
- contracts involving many contractors/sub-contractors/suppliers
- contracts sensitive to a history of poor contract performance and/or adversarial relationships.

The benefits of project mediation include:

- offering a robust conflict management approach with a focus on dispute prevention
- showing that parties are taking collaborative working seriously
- more flexibility, and cost-effectiveness, than other conflict management mechanisms adopted at the outset of a project (such as a dispute resolution board)
- can be budgeted for in advance
- giving the option, should a dispute arise, of pre-empting an order from the court requiring ADR – the parties in this circumstance are able to conduct any ADR processes on their own terms.

As project mediation is integrated into the contract, it will be included as part of the contract procurement documentation. However, if it has not been included, the parties are still able to adopt project mediation.

Project mediation is communication-focused while other non-escalation methods such as dispute boards are traditionally more directed at dealing with legal and contractual issues. Both are complementary non-escalation methods that encourage more effective communication within a technically and contractually complex project environment.

Communication – and the lack, or mismanagement thereof – is a major factor in escalating a brewing conflict situation. A survey carried out in 2010 by CEDR found that for both managers and non-managers, failing to communicate change in working life was the primary cause of workplace conflict. Nearly two-thirds (62%) of all respondents cited this as the main instigator of conflict, ahead of concerns over the economy (51%) and worker apathy (50%). These results confirm that having processes put in place that promote effective, productive communications are imperative to the well-being of a work environment. Managing project and supplier relationships is no exception. Understanding what is available in terms of non-escalation and prevention mechanisms is not only desirable in itself, but also raises awareness of effective communication, which lies at the heart of these mechanisms.

The ADR Pledge

In 1984, the International Institute for Conflict Prevention and Resolution (CPR) initiated its first 'ADR Pledge', a

> 'statement of policy aimed at encouraging greater use of flexible, creative and constructive approaches in resolving business-related disputes. It promotes systematic, early resolution and establishes a flexible framework for helping to resolve complex multi-party disputes'.[2]

The CPR ADR Pledge outlines that:

> 'We recognize that for many disputes there is a less expensive, more effective method of resolution than the traditional lawsuit. Alternative dispute resolution (ADR) procedures involve collaborative techniques which can often spare businesses the high costs of litigation.

In recognition of the foregoing, we subscribe to the following statements of principle on behalf of our company and its domestic subsidiaries:

In the event of a business dispute between our company and another company which has made or will then make a similar statement, we are prepared to explore with that other party resolution of the dispute through negotiation or ADR techniques before pursuing full-scale litigation. If either party believes that the dispute is not suitable for ADR techniques, or if such techniques do not produce results satisfactory to the disputants, either party may proceed with litigation.'

To date, the CPR states that the pledge has over 4,000 signatories from industry and the corporate world. This figure refers to the number of signatories acknowledged by the CPR – there are many, many other companies large and small that routinely include similar pledges and clauses in their contract agreements.

ADR and conflict management techniques are an increasingly popular method of not only solving disputes, but also acknowledging the potential for disputes to arise and moving to anticipate them, thereby ameliorating the widespread consequences of disputes. An article written for *The Sunday Times* in December 2010 claims that the number of business disagreements settled through arbitration or mediation rose by 78% between 2007 and 2009. The article went on to conservatively estimate the claim value of mediation cases alone at £5 billion per year.

At a glance: EDF Energy

- **ADR-focused change management can yield morale, value and efficiency gains**

EDF Energy's policy of training staff to spot and negotiate conflict early is a prime example of how incorporating ADR practices into an organisation's everyday structure can deliver real value for money:

The project
EDF realised that problem solving – in terms of managing positive outcomes and value creation – was a key competitive strength, as well as a core competency to develop. The challenges of future infrastructure projects are as likely to stem from issues such as creating value for money and working collaboratively as they are from the pressure to compete on price. Identifying this led to EDF staff undertaking training in advanced negotiations which aimed to foster dispute resolution skills and value creation.

Part II of the project involved a review of EDF's bidding and tendering capabilities and processes against a maturity model. Part of this evaluation draws on past experience to identify the key success factors in successful major projects and partnerships. One of the overriding skills, highlighted by the review process, is the ability to proactively manage potential for conflict and create value for money through a joined-up approach to problem solving. If neglected, problem-solving procedures hold the potential for lengthy and costly disputes to arise.

Individuals trained at EDF are intended to become champions for proactive application of ADR, within the Rail and Airports infrastructure sectors. The approach is one of building from the grassroots in order to foster a cultural shift in approaches to competence development.

Achievements

Since the initiative's launch, there have been a number of noteworthy successes including:

1. Successful completion of the novation of a 90-year DBFOM [Design, Build, Finance, Operate and Maintain] contract for the change of ownership on the sale of Gatwick Airport.
2. Establishing a skills development framework, to break the dispute on how to move forward on joint trade union negotiations, on collective terms and conditions.
3. Breaking of deadlock on a multiparty complex negotiation to deliver Network Rail's Thameslink upgrade for Farringdon Station (which, at a cost of £5.5 billion, places the deal in the top 10 of rail infrastructure projects).

As EDF's example shows, proactively adopting ADR methods can yield considerable financial, innovation and productivity benefits. This in turn presents key opportunities to deliver value for money without compromising on standards. The ability to deliver services at this level offers competitive advantages, which could prove crucial when tendering for contracts or considering bids.

Summary

- In an increasingly complex, international theatre of commerce, a system of anticipating problems and handling them early can make the difference between a project's success and failure.
- Contract clauses planned in advance can help nip disputes in the bud before they have a chance to derail a large-scale or complex project. The emphasis should be on fostering good relationships rather than 'being negative' or 'assuming the worst'. Change management focused on creating an 'ADR culture' is a logical, worthwhile 'next step' – bringing gains in productivity, innovation and workplace satisfaction.
- When drafting ADR Contract Clauses, consider: *Who, What, How, When, Which?* rules.

- Contract clauses, and other ADR processes, can still be adopted and used successfully as part of a project that is already underway.
- Project mediation is cost-effective, efficient, and relatively simple to establish. It is also flexible enough to adapt to your particular organisational needs.

> **Case study: nipping conflict in the bud with a contract clause**
>
> The following case study provides a classic example of how complex, large-scale projects can invite conflict between parties; it also highlights how using ADR clauses in contracts can save time, money and the frustrations of an escalating conflict.
>
> *The dispute*
>
> Following a comprehensive performance review, a major multinational company department decided to install a new software system to process and store significant volumes of data. The project was offered for tender, and the department received a number of strong bids. After considering each bid carefully, the department selected a supplier and signed a contract that promised software designing, testing, development, implementation, maintenance and consultancy support for the project.
>
> The department also understood that, prior to final acceptance, there would be a trial period in which the software would be tested for suitability. The software was intended to be used by a number of different groups within and connected to the department, each with varying degrees of ICT knowledge and ability. Designing a system to accommodate these user groups, which was also capable of performing sophisticated operations, was an imperative requirement of the department.
>
> The supplier designed the software and the system was trialled by a mixture of testers drawn both from independent backgrounds and from the department which had commissioned the software. Feedback from testers was mixed. The main criticism of the software was about its accessibility, especially from users with limited ICT knowledge who only needed to carry out basic tasks with the software. They reported that even with additional training and support, the software's lack of 'simple' mode made performing straightforward routine tasks lengthy and frustrating. Other testers pointed out flaws in convertibility between the new system and the one currently used by the department – this presented a danger that information could be lost or misplaced. While this design flaw could be, and was, remedied by the supplier, concerns about accessibility remained. The department declared the software to be unsuitable, and informed the supplier of termination of the contract, without payment.

The news was not received well by the supplier. From their perspective, they had delivered a software system that met all of the requirements given by the department. They contended that the software was user-friendly and accessible, and that the consultancy and maintenance support package included in the contract was more than adequate to address any difficulties that new users might initially experience. Additionally, the suppliers did not agree that continuing with the contract was contingent on a successful trial – they said that this was not in the contract agreement, and was not discussed prior to the trial itself. As well as feeling confused and embarrassed, the supplier felt angry at incurring a financial loss with the early termination of the contract. They said that not only would current revenues be affected, but also that shareholders and investors would be less willing to hold the supplier's stock if there were concerns over reputation and solvency raised by the contract's end.

Initial discussions between the department and supplier were fruitless. It became clear that there were three main areas of dispute that seemed irresolvable:

- Whether the department were entitled to terminate the agreement without making any payment;
- Whether payment was contingent upon successful completion of the trial;
- Whether the software provided met the requirements of the brief.

A second dispute, over the provision of consultancy support and software maintenance, soon developed. The supplier had invoiced the department for consultancy and maintenance services while the initial dispute was brewing, which the department challenged on the grounds that these services were terminated along with the software contract. The supplier insisted that these services were subject to a different contract, whose terms were still in effect because the contract had not been cancelled.

On closer inspection, both contracts contained a clause directing the parties to arbitration in the event of a dispute. This had an important brake effect to proceedings, and can reasonably claim to have been a deciding factor in the dispute's eventual satisfactory resolution.

Contract clauses in action – containing contagion

The clause committing each party to arbitration before pursuing litigation anticipated exactly the potential for misunderstanding, and snowballing disagreements, following from an initial contested point. In planning ahead and providing guidance for each party, the clause diminished scope for a knee-jerk litigative response and prompted the parties to consider a resolution process that they may not have considered in the heat of the moment.

The clause's brake effect produced an even more creative solution than arbitration: the department and supplier both agreed to attempt mediation as an initial resolution method. Trying mediation would, if successful, minimise each party's costs, keep 'control' of the dispute with the parties rather than with an external authority like an arbiter or judge, and generate a solution far quicker than comparative resolution processes. The sensitivity of the issues at hand, and the domino effect the dispute was beginning to have on other projects, made the prospect of a quick and private solution especially attractive. The department and supplier agreed that should the mediation fail, they would pursue arbitration before considering other remedy processes.

The advantages offered by mediation, outlined in the previous paragraph, particularly suited the parties involved in this dispute. With large-scale or critical projects, a dispute such as the one we are exploring – which ordinarily would be a sizable dispute in itself – is concentrated in one area of a much bigger project. Therefore, the effects of a dispute are felt within the sub-project and throughout the overarching project. It is perhaps an obvious claim, but if one sub-project is (for whatever reason) unable to deliver the goods or services promised, there can be significant implications for other sub-projects. Because project managers tend to underestimate the time and cost consequences that a dispute can have, the contagion from a dispute in one project area can derail an entire project with relative ease.

Effects of the disputes

In our case study example, the dispute had immediate and gradual effects. Obviously, the cancelled contract left the department without the software it had anticipated having, forcing employees to quickly find a stop-gap solution making good the absent software. In local cases, this took the form of keeping paper-based records. While this was effective in serving its immediate purpose – and displayed a great sense of initiative among the department's staff – this solution completely defeated the integration objective the new software system was intended to facilitate. Information sharing was inhibited and made more expensive as a result of the cost of postage, secure packaging and couriers. In the broader sense, uncertainty over the cost of outcomes such as litigation, compensation and commissioning a new software system precluded accurate budget forecasts, affecting other projects the department had intended to undertake. Senior managers within the department were starting to worry that, if the dispute were made public, attitudes towards the department as a whole would become less favourable.

The impact on the supplier was slightly more nuanced – although still a sub-project of its entire operation, the supplier's business model had an inbuilt degree of anticipation for large projects going awry. The effect of this dispute, however, was acutely felt. Notwithstanding the possible loss of a multimillion-pound payment, senior managers at the supplier company felt used and embittered by the department's actions. The department, however, was a major client and the supplier company had hoped to build a good working relationship with it as part of a long-term business strategy. Delivering the software system would, in the supplier company directors' plans, have led to winning similar contracts with the department, and provided a prestigious springboard for other headline contract bids. The cancelled contract jeopardised this path of growth, and put additional pressure on the company's other revenue-generating projects.

Choosing the right mediator

Owing to the specialised nature of the dispute claims, the parties were both keen to work with a mediator with substantial ICT experience. A mediator with a background in ICT offered the advantage of already being up to speed with issues and practicalities affecting large-scale software implementation, while also appreciating factors such as software accessibility for novice and experienced users. Both the department and the supplier felt confident that the mediator they eventually selected would be able to use their specialist knowledge effectively to facilitate a productive discussion.

Exploring the issues

Once the mediation was underway, exploratory work established that there were additional factual issues in dispute. Discussions with each party revealed that on the issue of accessibility, there had not been clear discussion of what an accessible system would look like in practice. The supplier had worked with an average user competency benchmark that did not take into account some of the limitations actual users were contending with. Equally, the department had not made its user ability spectrum clear to the supplier, and had instead assumed that both department and supplier were working – perhaps through the power of telepathy – with a shared sense of 'access' and 'ability'.

The emergence of this point neatly illustrates why effective communication is so important to any large-scale project. Had the department and supplier discussed the issue of accessibility, a prominent source of confusion and conflict would have been avoided. It is very possible that the assumption of common understanding was a good way of sidestepping the fear of looking foolish, with each party pretending to have more understanding than they actually had. Equally, the confusion might have arisen from an ironic sense of shared understanding; with each party hearing the word 'accessible' and assuming that their individual definition was the one being used. In any case, the mistake was an expensive one – and could have been avoided or minimised with considerable ease.

Further to this, each party had conflicting views on the issue of payment. The department firmly understood that any payments to the supplier would be subject to successful trialling and implementation, and that if these conditions were not met they were entitled to end the agreement without making any payments at all. The suppliers firmly understood that successful trialling did not constitute part of the agreement, that full payment was contingent on successful system implementation, and that payment was due for the work undertaken up until the point of cancellation. When the contracts were looked at more closely, there was in fact no specific outline on what circumstances would be grounds for the department not paying the supplier.

Hearing these viewpoints was helpful in itself, and both parties found considerable value in listening to the other's perspective on events. Understanding the frustrations of both parties was cathartic; responses and actions that had seemed angry and aggressive became instead comprehensibly defensive. In turn, this fresh understanding helped each party to begin to see the other less as an adversary. Lancing the anger boil was another key moment in resolving the conflict, encouraging both parties to turn their focus from frustration and resentment to understanding and cooperation.

Assessing the risks of not settling

The mediator in this case also did valuable work in outlining the risks of following arbitration or litigation. In normal cases, these avenues incur the risk of expense (through arbitration awards or legal fees) and time wasted waiting for a hearing date (not infrequently in years), but the scale of the project and standing of both parties compounded these risks. For the company department particularly, pursuing an expensive and lengthy litigation course could damage its reputation: other departments, customer and even rival companies could argue that this course of action did not provide 'value for money', and that the department was out of touch and 'off-message'. The supplier also carefully considered the impact this type of action might have on its reputation – to shareholders, investors, customers and other firms in the industry – and finances.

In light of the exploratory work made possible with the mediator's help, the department and supplier were willing to negotiate – but only on a positional basis. While the expression of willingness was significant and productive in itself, the positional line each party adopted threatened to create fresh impediments to finding a solution. The positional approach undermined the valuable attitude shifts that had started to take place between the parties, reintroducing an adversarial tone to the discussions.

Discussions had reached a delicate point, and could reasonably end in either success or failure. The mediator sensed that the parties were in danger of allowing an illusory inner narrative to influence both their willingness and ability to have open, forward-looking discussions about the issue. With this in mind, the mediator introduced the idea of 'reality testing' to the discussion. The key decision makers of each party were asked to think deeply about the best and worst scenario outcomes for their side, and were then encouraged to consider how and in what ways these outcomes were practical, likely and fact-based. Testing these ideas against known facts – freshly established and acknowledged earlier in the mediation – was invaluable in shaping a new, credible vision for what each party hoped to achieve from the discussions.

'It makes commercial sense to settle'

Reality testing and evaluating proved to be the key that unlocked the gates to collaborative, cooperative discussion between the parties. Invited to realise that there was much to be gained from engaging with the mediation process rather than trading in fears and fantasy, progress was swift. The company department and supplier were able to see the commercial sense in the settlement:

- the cost to each party of the mediation was £2,825, representing a huge saving on the cost of litigation or arbitration;
- the entire mediation process, from referral to the mediation, took three months – a significantly quicker resolution process than that offered by the courts;
- the principle of confidentiality kept the dispute and its details private, thus maintaining the public and industry reputation of each party;
- the process procured an agreement through collaboration, allowing both parties to agree to the course of action while being spared the ignominy of being seen as conceding to the other.

The settlement itself was written up at the mediation meeting, and signed on the day by the parties. Achieving this outcome was significant considering the scale of the project at risk and the number of people affected. Although there had been extra costs incurred by remedying the software's shortcomings and in the time lost while the dispute was ongoing, mediating the dispute and establishing a conflict management framework for the future prevented legal escalation and its associated costs.

Notes

1. All data Baker Mallett (2008).
2. Taken from 'CPR's ADR Pledge' http://cpradr.org/About/ADRPledge.aspx, retrieved 9/10/12.

7
The world outside – managing conflict with external stakeholders and clients

Gregory Hunt and Andy Rogers

Introduction

We all make assumptions all the time, and the subject of conflict is no exception: the typical immediate response to words like 'conflict', 'dispute' and 'crisis' is one of discomfort. This is an entirely valid and reasonable response, but it is also perhaps self-fulfilling in many cases. Fear of conflict and its consequences causes people and organisations to go into an elaborate form of denial, as if by pretending that conflict does not and will not exist for an organisation, that conflict won't ever be an issue for it.

Sadly, this is not the case. In fact, refusing to think seriously about conflict can leave an organisation more open to conflict and its negative effects. When conflict hits – and it invariably will, in one form or another – organisations that have had their heads in the sand will be less well equipped to respond to the situation. Furthermore, these organisations will potentially be missing opportunities created by crisis. As counter-intuitive as it may seem, a well-handled crisis offers a chance for an organisation to show its substance, to change or reinforce public opinions, to gain feedback and learn lessons. Doing this successfully, however, requires an organisation to accept that conflict can and will touch them, and to put response plans in place for when it does.

Reputation, reputation, reputation

Reputation is an important consideration for any organisation, especially when considering the impact of conflicts and disputes. Recent research carried out by the Centre for Effective Dispute Resolution (CEDR) and the Chartered Institute of Public Relations (CIPR) highlights in detail how important reputation is to organisations. A survey of 160 public relations officers revealed that not only was preserving relationships the first priority of organisations in conflict, it was also imperative to be seen as preserving relationships and getting settlements rather than winning.

'We asked respondents to reflect on their experience of organisational disputes in which they had been personally involved or consulted. Sixty-five per cent of respondents reported personal experience of their own client or organisation being involved in a dispute which became public. And they reported that, not only did the public exposure of the existence of the dispute generally (79%) have a negative impact on the organisation's reputation, but 50% of the time further damage was then done by the public exposure of the conduct of that dispute.'

Centre for Effective Dispute Resolution, 2008

Respondents suggested that an organisation's dispute experience might be an indicator of:

- Low management quality: e.g. 'Disputes of any kind, once they come into the public domain create the impression of incompetence and that the organisation is not in control. This erodes confidence and trust'.
- Lack of management focus: e.g. 'Senior executive disputes attract the most attention from nearly all stakeholders - they're the ones who are supposed to provide leadership which is lost during conflict'.
- Poor employee relations: e.g. 'The more disputes, the more evidence of an undesirable employer'. 'People are generally less understanding when you are perceived to mistreat your staff'.
- Weak brand management: e.g. 'Lack of synergy with company slogans and claims creates doubt and suspicion; sense of being unethical affects brand values and loyalty'.
- Concerns about underlying business performance: e.g. 'All of these impact on businesses' reputation to do business – which can manifest itself in problems with the share price and investor willingness, productivity, product desirability, fitness as an employer and even as an operating business'.

The negative connotations of poor dispute handling are serious. Once a dispute enters the public arena, people begin to divide their attention between the dispute itself *and* how the organisations involved conduct themselves in that situation. This backs up the idea that exposure of disputes with external organisations has a doubled and compounding effect, and that proper handling is an essential element of damage limitation and rehabilitation.

Two approaches to stakeholder conflict

Managing conflict with external parties has two main aspects – prevention and handling. These aspects are not mutually exclusive: indeed, they work best as complementary strategies. Anticipation leads to better handling, and better handling in turn leads to a shift in how intense monitoring and anticipation of problems needs to be.

THE WORLD OUTSIDE – MANAGING CONFLICT WITH EXTERNAL STAKEHOLDERS AND CLIENTS

Preventing conflict

Preventing conflict – either from escalating or from occurring altogether – is the Holy Grail for most organisations' PR and communication departments. Conflict is costly, and spending time thinking of ways to minimise or avoid it is often the course that makes business sense. It is far easier to budget for engaging a PR consultancy, or producing a 'crisis management handbook', than it is to anticipate the long-term financial impact of poor conflict handling: lost revenue, falling consumer confidence, and a tainted brand.

The other side of preventing conflict is prediction. Rather than consulting a crystal ball or reading runes, predicting conflict is very much within the realm of good organisational self-awareness. This means considering who your external audiences are, how you communicate with them, and how they might share information with each other. It also means applying the 'what if?' principle to your organisation's actions and stakeholders. Will all of your stakeholders respond in the same way to a decision, or for the same reasons? What are the implications of a decision now and in the future, or if circumstances were to change?

Handling conflict

'Handling conflict' is itself a double-sided entity. Handling conflict arising from a crisis is the kind of handling no business ever wants to be faced with, as it is a high-stakes, high-pressure gauntlet to run. Often organisations fear that conflict caused by (and often causing) a crisis is something they have little control over, but this is not strictly true. While situations can develop in unforeseen ways, and do so very quickly, organisations can wrest back a degree of control by being well prepared – this means taking the comprehensive crisis conflict management strategy (devised with 'prevention' in mind) and implementing it.

Handling conflict can, and is more likely to be, of an altogether more run-of-the-mill variety – responding to complaints from multiple customers, for example, is inevitable for any organisation. If crisis conflict is a klaxon, consumer complaint conflict is more like a buzzing light switch: long term, low frequency, and relatively easy to accommodate. Thoughtful planning of systems like independently run consumer redress schemes and procedures is an effective way of anticipating and handling these kinds of conflict, and can bring benefits through improved feedback and the goodwill of satisfied customers.

Who are my audiences?

One of the challenges of handling conflict with external parties is its public nature: unlike internal board conflicts, for example, an organisation in conflict with an outside body has significantly fewer means of keeping the conflict and its details under wraps.

This causes obvious and 'hidden' problems. Clearly, conflicts and disputes played out in a public theatre benefit less from privacy: actions and decisions have immediate and far-reaching impact across different stakeholders and audiences. Accordingly, crafting an appropriate message is fraught with pitfalls. Communication with one or more target audiences, for example, is also an address to other audiences who, while perhaps not directly affected by the communication, are still interested observers. If a message is communicated poorly – a multinational company disputing its tax liabilities with a specific national government, for example – consumers all over the world may take away the message 'Company X doesn't pay taxes! I won't buy *their* products anymore, I'll just be paying for the CEO's yacht!' This is clearly bad for the bottom line, and it could take years for the company to win back those consumers. But think also of the time, effort and resources that Company X might devote to repairing its reputation – legal action to prove that it is right, overpaying tax to show good faith, taking out full-page newspaper advertisements to woo back customers…

Preventing stakeholder conflict

Relationships with external stakeholders can be like having running water in your home: when it's working, it's not something you think about. Yet like running water, when something goes wrong in a stakeholder relationship, it can make life difficult and eventually impossible. A conflict with a supplier over an unpaid invoice, or with a customer who refuses to pay you, for example, can spill over into other areas of your business and cause real damage to your bottom line.

Broadly speaking, there are three types of external stakeholder disputes that an organisation can be drawn into:

Invested stakeholders: those who have a very close concern for the well-being of the organisation but that are technically outside it. *Shareholders* (or trustees) are probably the most obvious example of these. Much has been made recently of the Activist Shareholders who protest when they feel an organisation is not listening to them. Shareholders as a group and their specific features are dealt with in more detail in Chapter 8 of this book. Other invested stakeholders could be seen as a body directly involved; on a management level, this might be a strategic partner cooperating on a new product or on another level a trade union that represents a significant proportion of the workforce.

Commercial partners: these are the 'bread and butter' of any commercial organisation; the *customers* that you sell to and the *suppliers* that you buy from. These are key relationships that the organisation needs to focus on and its administrators need to be aware of. There are interesting dimensions of scale here: organisations that target the consumer market, like a supermarket, can have hundreds of thousands of consumers, whereas a professional services organisation that targets a particular business sector, such as a management consultancy, may just have a handful, although both may be as successful as the other in their own ways. Whilst both will have different media for communicating with their 'consumers' (the supermarket may advertise nationally and the management consultancy may do everything via face-to-face meetings and a website), they will both have relationships with their clients and the opportunity for interaction with them. It is always important to get this communication right to help relationships have the right tone – having a strong relationship can be invaluable if issues arise or events go wrong as they can make the difference between a conflict avoided, a conflict that is managed well and an outright dispute which may damage one or all sides.

Interested (but not closely invested) external parties: this may sound less specific, but there are very identifiable types of stakeholder that come into this category. There are public stakeholders interested in your organisation (or potentially interested in your organisation if something goes wrong). Chief of these is *government*, both the executive, monitoring how the country performs, and the legislative, looking after the interests of its constituents and willing to ask questions and make changes if there are issues to be addressed. Many organisations will also come under some form of *regulator*, and unsurprisingly the larger the organisation, the closer that working relationship may be. When relationships with these stakeholders go wrong, the outcome can occasionally result in painful penalties. Also to be considered in this group are the *communities* in which your organisation is physically based. These can be wide and varied including the families of your employees, businesses with which you work on a casual basis (the Sandwich Shop across the street, for example) and even the local weekly newspaper. Many people in the local community, some of them unknown to you, will have an opinion on your organisation, and whilst their goodwill might not be essential for the organisation's survival, the absence of it can make life very difficult. An interesting factor about all these stakeholders is that they do not have to be ever-present in working life, yet when the opportunity to communicate with them arises, it is important to get it right or (as we will see in our case study) the consequences can be disastrous.

Working in a vacuum?

Whilst it may be a truism, the key to any relationship is communication. If there is regular communication between your organisation and a key stakeholder, it is harder for conflict to develop unchecked. However, in a vacuum where your organisation has not communicated with a supplier or key customer in months, it is easy for misconceptions to develop or misunderstandings to be blown out of proportion. In this way, it is possible for conflict to develop from what initially might be perceived as a 'small difference'.

Imagine a client-supplier relationship that is characterised by minimal, perfunctory communication. The client asks for a delivery of 'the blue widgets'. They don't mention why they want them but when the widgets come off the production line they are more purple than blue, but they get sent to the client anyway, and no one checks that the client is happy. The client isn't happy but doesn't tell the supplier – and so the pre-conditions for conflict are set. If the same thing happens a second time, only then does the client tell you that they cannot make blue versions of their product with purple widgets, and they intend to source their widgets from elsewhere or, potentially more damaging, sue you for their losses. A situation like this can sound far-fetched, but at CEDR we see this has happened far too frequently when parties bring their disputes to our dispute resolution service.

Business communication scenarios

Business relations (i.e. provider-customer) have an additional constraint upon them: we naturally behave in a different way in business than we might in our everyday or home lives. Whilst in many provider-customer relationships one would rightly expect that as part of the level of service provided there would be a respectful tone used in communication and even deference shown in how the 'paying customer' is treated, such a tone and deference would not be expected in a non-commercial relationship. Yet this way of communicating, whilst it might be acceptable and desirable when there are no issues to be addressed by either side, can be highly problematic when difficulties emerge, or when things simply go wrong. Most people would not speak to a customer they were annoyed with in the same way they would address a family member that had vexed them.

Problem scenarios that might lead to conflict (for example, between a supplier and a customer):

1. *Where both sides are culpable in a mistake*

   - The customer may take the provider to task for the error (which they feel is their right).
   - The provider will respond that the customer is also in the wrong – but in a forthright way that the customer may not be used to hearing from them.
   - The customer responds in an outraged way – which in turn antagonises the provider, and thus provokes an unreasonable escalation leading to dispute.

2. *Where one side is in the wrong*

   - If it is the provider that has committed the offence then the customer may reprimand them; however, if the customer is used to more of a subservient relationship with the provider, then to the provider at least the harshness of the reprimand can seem unwarranted and thus foster resentment.
   - When the customer is in the wrong (as mentioned above), they are not used to being criticised by the provider and this can create difficulties. Furthermore, an unwillingness to admit any wrong or even any feeling of guilt might exacerbate the situation.
   - It is possible for conflict to emerge from either of these scenarios.

3. *Where something untoward, outside of anyone's control takes place*

   - One might think that in a situation where neither customer nor provider were to blame for something going wrong it would be less problematic. However, where the lines of communication are influenced by the constraints of certain business relations, difficulties can still arise.
   - The customer might over or under-react to the situation, which in turn might result in an inappropriately scaled reaction from the provider. At one extreme, the provider might throw too many resources at solving the problem (incurring disproportionate expenses in the process), and at the other extreme might do too little to address the issue.

- The provider might also instigate an over or under-reaction to a situation. If the provider does not act or communicate sufficiently (and they might feel uncomfortable differing from the norms of the business relationship), then the customer might not realise the problem until too late. Potentially, there is less of a drawback for the customer if the provider is over-active – although as mentioned above, being left out of pocket by an over-spend on resource is an unwanted consequence.
- Thus conflict can emerge even when no one is to blame if the business relationship is not robust enough to adapt to the communication needs of both organisation and stakeholder.

However, rarely is a stakeholder just one person. Frequently, there can be a main external contact that owns the relationship but there will also be secondary contacts. Each may have a different outlook albeit moderated by their own 'organisational culture'. Keeping the role of individuals in mind, it is worth considering their personal make-up and the impact that might have on conflict and how to avoid it.

Dynamics affecting communication with stakeholders

Social factors: personality types

When you add personality into the mix, the realisation must come about how difficult relationships can be in business and how important it is to recognise the triggers for conflict. Thirty years ago, psychologists David Merrill and Roger Reid published 'Personal Styles and Effective Performance'. The work identified four different social styles of interaction: *Analytical, Amiable, Driving*, and *Expressive*. The model then offers the refinement of suggesting that most people have a primary social style and then a secondary style which can frequently moderate an individual's behaviour. This model has become influential in how the Western business world looks at business dynamics, and how potential business targets might respond to different sales approaches. However, we believe that the Merrill-Reid Model can also be an interesting medium to help us reflect on how personality might create opportunities for conflict to arise.

At the heart of this model is a piece of common sense: people are different and should be treated differently. This particular theory, however, takes us past that to say that different types of personality will react differently to other people's personalities, and whereas sometimes this will have a beneficial impact, at other times, if left unmanaged, it may result in conflict. In this respect, the Merrill-Reid Model has useful lessons for conflict in work or team dynamics in the same way that the Thomas-Kilmann Conflict Mode Instrument[1] does. The interesting feature of Merrill-Reid in terms of preventing conflict is that whilst Thomas-Kilmann tells us how people will react when a conflict situation emerges (as an advantage or hindrance), the former shows us the relationship and communication ingredients that can bring the conflict to a boil.

Key to both of these models is learning to alter your instinctive approach, which can be naturally difficult and may initially seem counter-intuitive. We tend to think most people are just like us

The Merrill-Reid Model of social styles

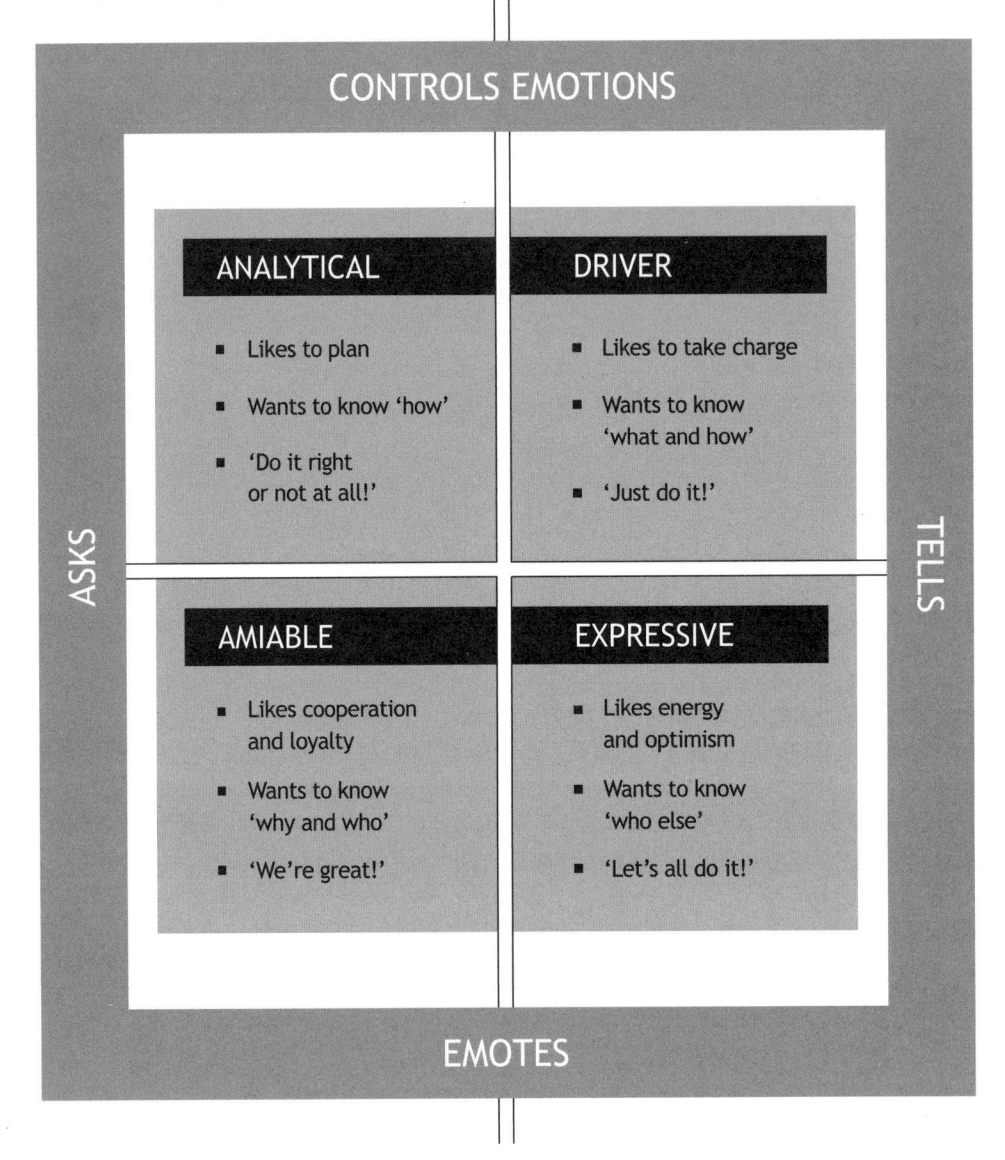

```
                    CONTROLS EMOTIONS

        ┌─────────────────────┬─────────────────────┐
        │   ANALYTICAL        │   DRIVER            │
        │                     │                     │
        │ ▪ Likes to plan     │ ▪ Likes to take     │
        │                     │   charge            │
        │ ▪ Wants to know     │ ▪ Wants to know     │
        │   'how'             │   'what and how'    │
        │ ▪ 'Do it right      │ ▪ 'Just do it!'     │
        │   or not at all!'   │                     │
 ASKS   ├─────────────────────┼─────────────────────┤ TELLS
        │   AMIABLE           │   EXPRESSIVE        │
        │                     │                     │
        │ ▪ Likes cooperation │ ▪ Likes energy      │
        │   and loyalty       │   and optimism      │
        │ ▪ Wants to know     │ ▪ Wants to know     │
        │   'why and who'     │   'who else'        │
        │ ▪ 'We're great!'    │ ▪ 'Let's all do it!'│
        └─────────────────────┴─────────────────────┘

                         EMOTES
```

Figure 7.1: The Merrill-Reid Model of social styles

(until we find that they are not) and assume that if we are being courteous, we should treat them in the same way we would like to be treated. This is certainly a good rule of thumb, but it is not always the case. If personality styles happen to match, it can be a happy coincidence, but when they do not it can lead to aggravation. In order to keep relations with key stakeholders on the best footing, one can first consider their and your personality types, and second adjust our own approach accordingly to best match the situation.

It therefore follows that we should look in a little more detail at this model and its four main social styles. To this end, we have looked at the work done by Padgett's SmallBizPros Marketing Manual (published online, last revised March 2009, www.smallbizpros.com).

Driver (Aggressive-Intellectual)

Overview: The Driver tends to have a more aggressive outlook in their business life but also has the capacity for an intellectual rather than emotive approach. They tend to be fast-paced, results-oriented and to the point.

Some possible characteristics:

- A desire to control
- Assertive appearance
- A sense of impatience
- Working in an organised space

How conflict can arise with Driver types:

- Competence is highly valued and correspondingly signs of incompetence are very difficult for a Driver to tolerate.
- In their list of priorities, business comes way before social interaction. Too much chatting with no focus on work objectives is likely to be very frustrating for a Driver.
- Delivering work on time is important and delays are irritating. Time is viewed as a valuable commodity and meetings that go nowhere will be proportionately more annoying for a Driver.
- As achieving objectives is key, things that get in the way of this can be annoying, such as too much focus on less important activities or details.
- Drivers respond well to upfront communication, they may not mind conflict and even meet it head on, but they will be frustrated by those that try to avoid talking directly and may even doubt their integrity.

Expressive (Aggressive-Emotional)

Overview: Expressive types are often creative, impulsive and full of energy, and often more interested in the big picture than they are in the details. They can seem very outgoing in business and emotive in working relationships.

Some possible characteristics:

- Preferring spontaneity over organisation or process
- A desire to dominate the conversation (and perhaps to discuss non-business-related issues)
- A willingness to look at new ideas and take part in a creative process
- A strong sense of pride

How conflict can arise with Expressive types:

- Expressive personalities like excitement – they like to hear about imperatives. If they are told 'well, you can take it or leave it' – they may well leave it.
- Too much focus on detail will be frustrating for an Expressive. They would rather focus on key points rather than having minutiae explained.
- Expressive types are more inclined to respond to someone who is obviously emotionally invested in what they are doing. Someone who seems bored will be an anathema to them. Fun and creativity are motivating and the lack of it is discouraging.
- Denigrating the status of an Expressive in the workplace, even unintentionally, will be felt deeply and cause resentment.

Amiable (Passive-Emotional)

Overview: the Amiable type is likely to take a more passive approach in their work and sometimes display an emotional approach in personal dealings. They can be perceived as keen to please others and therefore sometimes slow to make decisions.

Some possible characteristics:

- Avoids conflict
- Generally shows a positive, amenable attitude
- Unsure about new developments
- Uncomfortable with pressure

How conflict can arise with Amiable types:

- The worst thing for an Amiable is to have someone be aggressive towards them. They can feel uncomfortable and even threatened in high-pressure situations.
- There is a dislike of over-formality which they may pull away from, as their more natural inclination is for warm, personal and even friendly relationships.
- Amiable types can feel more comfortable when decision-making is a shared process – they do not necessarily want to be left to work out issues on their own.
- An amiable person will tend to prefer a story about people than pure facts and figures.

Analytical (Passive-Intellectual)

Overview: Analytical types display a methodical way of working and can be motivated by an interest in detail, sometimes leading to working at a different pace than others. They tend to be more intellectual than emotional in their personal dealings.

Some possible characteristics:

- Display a calm demeanour
- Work in a highly organised space

- Very time conscious (often early for meetings)
- Can come across often as being quite formal

How conflict can arise with Analytical types:

- Analytical personalities come to decisions carefully, therefore they dislike decision-making that does not seem well thought through, that contains too little detail or when it happens too quickly.
- More time than might seem necessary to others may need to be spent fully convincing an Analytical type of a particular new development or process.
- Accordingly, being too insistent to get a decision made will typically go down badly. A 'hard-sell' approach is likely to irritate them.
- Being informal in a business context is likely to erode credibility, with the potential to show lack of respect for processes.

Analytical personalities are interested in a high level of detail; only dealing with issues superficially is likely to be very frustrating.

Environmental factors: communicating internationally

Increasing levels of cross-border commerce also increases the complexity of the communications between stakeholder groups and a company. It is entirely possible, for example, that a company secretary may be part of a company whose client base is international, headquartered in Europe, with suppliers in the Far East and board members based in North America. Asynchronous communication through email, time differences and different cultural approaches make this set-up vulnerable to misunderstanding and conflict, but the most immediate difficulty can be that of language. When groups do not share a language they feel comfortable communicating in, an interpreter may become a necessary part of discussions: this brings its own set of advantages and things to be wary of.

> **The international dimensions in relations: language barriers and using interpreters with stakeholders**
>
> *by Danny McFadden, Managing Director CEDR Asia Pacific*
>
> Few would argue that not sharing a language or using interpreters in any communication between an organisation and stakeholder is not easy, and in business relations there are extra dimensions to be considered. This is especially true when things go wrong and a commercial mediator comes in to mediate: at its core, this is a facilitated negotiation, which means parties introduce the third-party neutral to help them move towards settlement, often from a deadlocked or highly emotional situation. Communication is already highly sensitive and the further introduction

of any new party/actor of any kind to mediation has to be handled with great care, regardless of whether their role is to be passive or active.

Interpreters are in effect fourth parties to any conversation, negotiation or mediation, and not only are they new parties, they will be conduits of that most important element of mediation – communication. So a two-party discussion where one party brings an interpreter will result in a 'triangular' communication tree during the mediation. Most mediators will have been trained and gained experience in the use of sophisticated communication skills, but not necessarily how to handle or manage the inclusion of an interpreter.

There are many threshold issues that need to be decided in setting up a negotiation, such as the choice of chair or mediator, venue, participation list and timetable. However, when parties do not share the same mother tongue and need an interpreter, additional issues need to be discussed including the choice of a 'pivot' language, type of interpretation, the interpreter and how the interpreter will fit into the mediation process.

The interpreter/extra actor at the table will be handed a lot of 'power' to influence the dialogue and even potentially the outcome of the session. Simply meeting the interpreter on the morning of the meeting, for example, is not a good idea because just as the chair or mediator needs to build rapport and trust with all parties, they also need to fully exercise their relationship skills with the interpreter. In a best-case scenario, all mediators should try to meet with the parties beforehand to begin the process of building trust and working out process issues. Ideally, the interpreter should be included in these meetings to give them an understanding of the subject matter, build initial rapport with the mediator, and learn about the facilitated discussion process they will be helping bring to life.

We should also be mindful of the problems that can arise with interpreters during negotiations; for instance, how to deal with cases of interpreters being too passive and/or getting too involved with the conversation. This, for example, can disrupt the flow of open communication between the speaker and the mediator which in turn can then distort the communication with the party on the other side. There is always the danger that the interpreter can inadvertently become part of the problem rather than the solution, which is something to be avoided at all costs.

Handling conflict with stakeholders

There are of course an infinite number of ways for events to conspire against a beleaguered organisation, but there are a small number of 'typical disputes' that seem to cover the salient points of most conflict scenarios. An in-depth discussion of stakeholder conflicts is provided in Chapter 8, but here we look at some of the tips and schemes that might be particularly appropriate conflict-handling tools.

THE WORLD OUTSIDE – MANAGING CONFLICT WITH EXTERNAL STAKEHOLDERS AND CLIENTS

1. **The supply of goods and services**

    This itself can be further divided into: a) business customers; b) suppliers and partners; c) professional negligence. There is also a distinction between d) one-off complaints and e) regular consumer complaints.

a) **Business customers** are the obvious recipients of goods and services, and are a major party in an organisation's external disputes. Dealing with consumer disputes effectively is vital to the continued success of an organisation: if consumers are unhappy and stop using your goods and services, your organisation's profit and growth will be negatively affected.

'Business customers' in this sense refers to corporate customers – for example, a computer hardware manufacturer purchasing microchips from another hardware manufacturer specialising in microchip manufacture. These types of conflict are always worth trying to resolve out of court, purely for business reasons – it makes little sense to further damage a working relationship at great cost, inconvenience and upset.

Case point
A dispute arose between Party A and Party B, both German companies, concerning their contractual relations and future development thereof. Party A was a manufacturer of shoes, ski boots and similar products. Party B had been distributing these products for approximately ten years on the basis of merely verbal understandings. Party B had also been involved informally in the development of certain products. The dispute arose between the companies because of the fact that Party A anticipated their wish to terminate or at least change the terms of the relationship with Party B. Party B subsequently filed a lawsuit against Party A before a Californian court. In total, the value of the dispute was US$800,000.

Despite the lawsuit being filed, the parties never gave up *direct* contact because of the fact that they needed reciprocal support. There was, therefore, a substantial interest for both parties in maintaining good relations and finding an acceptable way out of the crisis. For this reason, the parties agreed to attempt to solve their dispute using mediation, which they were able to do while agreeing a new distribution agreement.

b) **Suppliers and partners** are also crucial to the success of an organisation, whether their product directly reaches consumers or if the end consumer is the organisation itself.

Often disputes between organisations and their suppliers and partners refer back to the supply contract; with performance breaches, delivery delays, issues over price and quality, and debt recovery all frequently cited as sources of conflict. Questions of product liability, outsourcing and franchising are also fertile ground for misunderstandings, and disputes, to arise.

Case point
A manufacturer was given a one-year licence by an entertainment company to sell spin-off merchandise from a television series. When the licence expired, the entertainment company

refused to renew the licence. The manufacturer allegedly continued to produce and sell the merchandise without a licence for a number of years.

Proceedings were issued for breach of copyright and passing off. The manufacturer counter-claimed for failure to renew the licence. In addition, the manufacturer claimed that some of their own merchandise, registered at the UK Design Registry of the Patent Office, predated the creation of the entertainment company's merchandise. They therefore claimed for breach of their own copyright against the licensor.

Proceedings had been issued for an injunction and damages and an application was pending in the Design Registry for cancellation of the design. The dispute had been running for several years without a trial date being set; and mediation was suggested as a way of ending the dispute quickly.

During the mediation, it became clear that the entertainment company wanted to bring an end to the dispute and avoid any adverse publicity. The manufacturer wanted to ensure their business remained financially viable, as they had established a reputation in the trade.

Turning points occurred when a number of options were developed to bring the dispute to an end. Once each party realised that the other was negotiating seriously, contrary to their prior expectations, each side was prepared to make a concession in order to reach an agreement.

Alternative Dispute Resolution (ADR) processes can be very helpful in these disputes, especially as a way of preserving relationships that have become strained by a dispute. Although contract clauses are an ideal anticipatory dispute handling method, it is never too late to institute one: it might be practical in the wake of a dispute to include a clause referring parties to mediation or arbitration. In a similar vein, it is never too late to try ADR – courts will often grant a stay of proceedings to allow parties to mediate or arbitrate, and should the dispute end up litigated, an earnest attempt at ADR tends to have an ameliorating effect on cost sanctions.

c) **Professional negligence** is a particularly acute kind of goods and services dispute, largely because of the deep impact these actions can have on consumers. There are two main kinds of professional negligence to consider – the familiar 'personal' professional negligence in areas such as injury and healthcare provision, and the less obvious 'corporate' professional negligence focused more typically on legal and financial carelessness.

Case point
A disabled patient alleged serious physical assault, including severe bruising, by a member of staff whilst in a care institution. All allegations were denied by the carer. Proceedings had been issued and were stayed by order of the court to allow mediation to take place.

It became clear from a number of telephone conversations that the parties did not need to rehearse the merits of their case to each other, as this had been done recently before the court in a painful way. The telephone calls together with the cooperative approaches of the parties meant that the mediation did not start with the usual opening presentations from each side.

At the mediation, the parties were brought together to sign the mediation agreements, and the mediator gave a short introduction to the process, confirming the safe atmosphere of the mediation. The day continued by way of separate private meetings (caucuses).

The caucus sessions were concentrated initially on the wording of a letter of apology, which became quite a sensitive matter. A significant factor in obtaining the former patient's acceptance of the letter was the fact that it was handed over personally by a representative from the institution. This had the effect of bringing the parties together, both literally and psychologically, breaking tensions and enabling a settlement to be reached shortly afterwards.

Monetary compensation was agreed, although the focal issue of the mediation was to satisfy the patient's emotional need to bring closure to the dispute. The care institution also benefited from the mediation's outcome – they achieved a 'line in the sand' for their staff, and had an opportunity to respond to the patient's serious allegations.

In this particular case, mediation was well suited to the dispute because feelings were as much at stake as facts and finance, but facilitated discussion is also worth considering in other professional negligence cases. Many professional negligence disputes seem to have a strong basis in misunderstanding or misinterpretation – an organisation thinks they have clear understanding of a contract or task, but in practice something gets lost in translation. In disputes caused by folly rather than malice, it is a great pity to see relationships deteriorate to the point of irretrievability when they could be repaired.

d) **One-off complaints** about a product or service can be difficult to foresee, but it is possible to respond quickly and effectively. In fact, a successful response can often mitigate the effects of the original dispute, and create goodwill credits for the organisation. The reverse is also true, where an inadequate, slow, or misjudged response can create and reinforce a negative view of the organisation.

Case point
In 1994, technology giant Intel launched its new Pentium chip to much acclaim, but soon discovered a bug affecting the chip's maths co-processor. It chose not to make the problem public as the company believed that only users performing the most complex calculations would encounter the problem. A user did discover the problem, however, and publicised it online. Intel maintained that it would not replace any chips unless the customer could prove that they were personally carrying out the calculations that would be affected by the error.

Intel's stance on the chips clashed with its global 'Intel Inside' advertising campaign, which sought to promote the company's products among home PC and small business users. Although these consumer constituencies were not directly affected by the faulty chips, they were unimpressed by Intel's response to those who were. Not only had Intel lost the chance to create goodwill by handling the chip fault issue generously, it had allowed a perception that 'Intel chips are faulty' to take hold among other target markets and demographics. Although Intel eventually did offer to replace the faulty chips on demand, there had been nearly two months of bad publicity, developing criticism and lost sales. Andy Grove, who was chief executive at the time, commented:

'Our previous policy was to talk with users to determine whether their needs required replacement of the processor. To some people, this policy seemed arrogant and uncaring.

We apologise. We were motivated by a belief that replacement was simply unnecessary for most people. We still feel that way, but we are changing our policy because we want there to be no doubt that we stand behind this product.'

e) **Consumer complaints** are the 'buzzing light-switch' mentioned earlier in the chapter: a steady trickle of consumer complaints will always be with an organisation even if it has the definitive market-leading, made-of-solid-gold-and-makes-a-great-cup-of-tea product in its field.

The key factor in managing this kind of dispute is having a robust handling process in place, such as an independent ADR-based scheme or process. Schemes in particular are ideal for handling large volumes of complaints, allowing consumers and organisations to benefit from economies of scale and a clear, well-publicised process.

Consumer complaints are an increasingly prominent area of disputes for companies: in the past decade, the internet has completely changed the way consumers shop, introducing issues such as handling cross-border trade on a large scale. Consumers can and often do cross international borders online, sometimes unwittingly, while looking for their perfect purchase.

There are particular implications for cross-border trade within the European Union: the 2009 European Commission report, *Cross-Border Consumer E-Commerce*, found that the market was 'estimated to be worth 106 billion Euros in 2006'; and one-third of EU citizens indicate that they would consider buying a product or a service from another member state via the internet because it is cheaper or better[2]. The same report also found that around 60% of cross-border internet purchases in the EU could not be completed by consumers because the trader did not ship the product to their country, or did not offer suitable means of cross-border payment.

Consumers without legal advice can find it difficult to know where to go for help in resolving disputes, and this can be even more fraught and tense when dealing with matters in a different language. Indeed, should something go wrong with a purchase, the costs of going to court alone, even without instructing a lawyer overseas, frequently tallies higher than the value of the purchased item. ADR is by far usually the cheaper option when it comes to commercial disputes, but with a consumer purchase of hundreds rather than thousands of pounds, there can be a problem with proportionality – you don't want a disproportionate cost for ADR which could cost even more than the amount in dispute or the resolution achieved.

ADR redress schemes, often run by dedicated independent ADR providers, industry groups or occasionally governments or other organisations, typically exist to help achieve a faster and cheaper resolution of disputes. To this end, it is not unusual for the cost of ADR to be partially (and occasionally completely) underwritten by the scheme owner (covered by a membership cost to the retailer, for instance) with the claiming consumer just paying a nominal fee or no fee at all. Also, to keep schemes affordable, the form that the ADR process takes may be a customised version of what a lawyer might expect to find in a mainstream commercial dispute. For example, mediation might take place by telephone or adjudication may take place with only the submission of forms and papers and no personal interaction. It is also fairly rare to find consumers legally represented in these high-volume low-value disputes.

The main ADR processes likely to be encountered by the consumer are mediation, conciliation, ombudsmen (often free but not always the speediest process), arbitration and adjudication. *Which?* (the Consumers' Association) has said that using an 'ombudsman'-like service, such as The Communications & Internet Services Adjudication Scheme (CISAS), in the first instance can be useful to consumers because they are usually free, and as they investigate the claim directly, the onus does not rest solely with the consumer. Also, as any decision is only binding if it is accepted by the consumer, the consumer retains the possibility of recourse to the courts.

There has traditionally been a problem in the corresponding levels of quality and usability of the provision of consumer redress schemes. The European Commission can help consumers make sense of these schemes, while fulfilling (for consumers) the European Directive on Consumer Rights, covering rights of redress, and the European Mediation Directive, which obliges member states to make access to ADR available for those in cross-border disputes.

Case point
Renewable energy technology is a new and growing area for service installers and consumers alike, and as a result, disputes are inevitable. To handle consumer disputes, many firms selling or leasing small-scale renewable or low carbon heat or power generation units have agreed to comply with the Renewable Energy Assurance Ltd. (REAL) Consumer Code.

REAL's arbitration scheme deals with alleged breaches of contract and/or negligence between consumers and REAL members, as an alternative to litigation. Prior to arbitration there is a less formal telephone-based mediation option for REAL members and consumers. Initial feedback shows that the incidences of arbitration and litigation as an alternative decrease due to the success of the telephone mediation service. Offering two ADR routes to consumers is a particularly effective way of ensuring that the dispute resolution scheme is accessible, ensuring that all kinds of possible disputes are covered by at least one ADR scheme. The scheme system is self-regulatory, as it links effective complaint resolution with feedback from REAL members and their consumers to improve quality.

2. **Regulatory disputes**

    These can be broadly categorised as involving the government in some way, either directly or through regulatory bodies such as the Office of Communications (Ofcom), the Office of Gas and Electricity Markets (Ofgem), and the Health and Safety Executive (HSE).

Case point
A dispute arose between a regulator and a professional leadership organisation over the content of the renewal of the organisation's Royal Charter, and the revamping of its historic legislation. From one point of view, the Charter and legislation was seen as an opportunity, while from another point of view the potential for the organisation and particularly its members to lose out was also a possibility.

The dispute had already been the subject of an acrimonious court case won by the leadership organisation – the Society's Council had reached an impasse and there was pressure for agreement to keep the Charter and legislation progressing.

One of the most important benefits of mediation in this case was that it provided time and space for all involved parties to air their concerns and diverging points of view.

The mediators approached the Charter in a line-by-line fashion in order for even the smallest dispute over the wording to be addressed. Following an evidence session from officials, the parties were able to agree to a new Charter, which was later sealed.

Taming the tiger: effective resolution of tax disputes
by Graham Massie, CEDR Director

The idea of negotiating with the taxman may sound like one of those things that is never going to happen in the real world, but in fact the resolution of tax issues is currently one of the most innovative, and potentially fastest growing areas of business life in which there could be very significant opportunities for the company secretary to promote effective dispute resolution and early settlement of disputes.

It should go without saying that neither Her Majesty's Revenue and Customs (HMRC) nor, indeed, any other national tax authority, are going to be cutting deals, or turning a blind eye if they suspect that any illegal tax evasion or fraud is going on. And they aren't likely to be interested in splitting the difference if they think they're right on a point of law. Their job is to uphold Parliament's law, and if their lawyers tell them they have a strong case then their 'bottom line' for a settlement is the full amount that they believe the tribunal or courts would determine as due. Conversely, if they think they have a weak or non-worthwhile case, they will concede rather than pursue the taxpayer. All of this is spelt out very clearly in HMRC's Litigation and Settlement Strategy document, available on their website.

However, not every tax dispute is quite so black and white. There are cases where the law may be clear, and the facts undisputed, but nevertheless there is scope for reasonable professional people to come to different conclusions as to how much tax may be due. For example, what is the 'fair' price for transfers of goods and services between the UK subsidiary of a global multinational and another subsidiary in a lower tax jurisdiction? In early 2010, AstraZeneca negotiated a settlement with HMRC of just such a dispute which was reported at the time as having lasted for 15 years.

And what about one of the most famous tax-related debates of all time? Is a Jaffa Cake a cake or a biscuit? A lot hangs on this, because under the law at the time, no VAT was chargeable on cakes, even if they were covered in chocolate, but a chocolate biscuit did attract VAT. Sadly, this one was decided by a tribunal (it's a cake) rather than by negotiation, but if the same case cropped up nowadays it would probably be handled through what HMRC call 'collaborative dispute resolution' (CDR).

CDR is simply a process of trying to resolve disputes and differences as quickly and efficiently as possible. Some examples of approved HMRC approaches include:

- Applying an 'Openness and Early Dialogue' approach which sets out the specific areas of contention and avoids unnecessary wrangling or positioning.
- Early discussion of a particular issue in order to make sure that both sides fully understand the relevant facts and the law that might apply to those facts.
- Jointly agreeing a timetable with key milestones and target dates for:
    - Establishing facts
    - Providing information / documentation
    - Reviewing documentation
    - Reaching decisions
    - Testing conclusions
- Discussing, sharing and testing of technical arguments to assess relative strengths and weaknesses in analyses.
- Establishing a decision tree (i.e. agreeing the key questions that need to be answered in order to resolve a dispute).
- Exploring possible alternative interpretations of the facts/relevant law that might give a different outcome from those initially proposed by each side.
- Engaging an independent neutral to serve as a mediator, or to chair meetings.

In order to build up its capabilities for this approach, HMRC have had a group of around 25 officials fully trained as mediators accredited by CEDR. Alongside this group, advisers from many of the leading law and accounting firms have received similar training, meaning that there are now professionals on both sides of the tax fence who are fully trained in effective dialogue and dispute resolution approaches.

And this mindset does not just apply to the large corporate cases. A vast number of tax issues for small and medium-sized enterprises, and even some individuals, get tied up in lengthy correspondence between tax-payer and inspector, sometimes with the writers talking at cross-purposes, being distrustful of each other's motives and generally keeping their cards close to their chest rather than engaging in open dialogue. Indeed, this is one reason why the backlog of tax cases going to the tribunal is growing inexorably, with about 10,000 cases being referred each year and less than half that number being resolved. So now HMRC is deploying its newly accredited mediators to act as facilitators, being called into small and medium enterprise (SME) cases that have got stuck to see if they can unblock the logjam, either by clarifying communications or getting parties, including the tax inspector, to focus on the key issues.

All of this is still a work in progress, but HMRC have seen considerable early success in pilot programmes with both their large corporate and SME groups, and the CDR approach, including the use of internal HMRC facilitators and external mediators, is now being rolled out across the taxpayer community.

> Perhaps, however, the most exciting opportunity for the company secretary is that there are lessons here which can be applied in other contexts. The CDR mindset of establishing the facts and identifying the key points of difference in the early stages of a dispute is a very valuable discipline, as is the emphasis on understanding the basis of your opponent's argument (ask why they think that, instead of simply focusing on what you think of their view). The use of a decision tree, or at least the approach of asking oneself what are the key questions to be answered if we are to resolve this dispute, is also a very valuable, and sadly still under-utilised technique. And finally, the external neutral can help a lot – even if, as in the case of the smaller HMRC disputes, they have just been sent from head office.

3. Governance

This involves an organisation and its shareholders. This is discussed in greater depth in the next chapter; however, we can touch on the subject here. Much of the work of preventing and handling conflicts rooted in governance issues lies in realising that the continuing health of the company is (likely to be) a shared interest, making attritional point scoring and personal attacks a damaging waste of time and energy. Once this fact is acknowledged, it is possible to guide the parties to the negotiating table and start looking for 'win-win' pathways out of the situation.

Case point
Two parties formed several land development companies, of which they were both shareholders. One of the companies moved forward with a project and the other company went out of business. Upon the failure of the second company, one of the principals wished to sell their shares in the other company. The parties then disputed not only the value of the shares but also whether the principal was in fact a shareholder of the ongoing company.

The parties should have been able to resolve the dispute if they had talked to one another effectively. Mediation offered the forum to do this. During the mediation, the parties had to face for the first time the commercial reality of the cost of continuing to trial both in regards to the financial consequences and in terms of what it would personally mean to give evidence during the proceedings.

During the course of the mediation, the joint session was able to expose the fact that the continuing company could face a significant threat to its viability and might be forced into receivership pending the outcome of the litigation. This development would not only have had the obvious negative impact on the company's ability to successfully maintain its ongoing operations, but could also have had a detrimental impact on the remaining principal's own finances if personally guaranteed debts of the operation were called as a result of the receivership. This exposure was instrumental in reality testing the downside risks for that party and led to a good faith effort on their part towards the eventual settlement.

4. **Environment**

   These disputes largely involve issues such as planning, and draw in communities, government and shareholders as stakeholders. For the breadth of stakeholders this can draw in, and the ethical arguments associated with environmental issues, handling these disputes intelligently is a prime concern.

   Case point
   British Waterways, the public corporation that maintains the UK inland waterway network, operates both as a landlord and as a competitive vendor in the moorings market for pleasure craft using the waterways. In 2003, the British Marine Federation, the trade association for the boating industry of which British Waterways is a member, raised concerns that British Waterways' operations in the mooring market amounted to a breach of competition law. Over a three-year period, British Waterways internally reformed many of its practices in its moorings operations, but tensions over the issue continued to increase between the organisations.
   In late 2005, discussions between the organisations broke down and the parties decided to attempt mediation to reach a resolution. Particular features included:

   - British Waterways and British Marine's primary business concern is the same industry and therefore they do not have the option of walking away from their business relationship;
   - British Marine was no longer willing to continue simple informal discussions to resolve their issues;
   - If litigation were chosen as an option, it would be time-consuming, costly and would detract from both organisations' abilities to support the UK marine leisure industry.

Working together with a CEDR Solve mediator, over a two-day period, the parties were able to construct an agreement in principle that allowed them to maintain a working relationship enabling them to work together to ensure that British Waterways' mooring operations would exemplify the ideal of free trade.
   This case is even more unusual in that both parties were happy, even keen, to make the fact that they had mediated the dispute public (many organisations cite the confidentiality and privacy surrounding mediation as a strong factor in their decision to mediate). We cannot be sure, but it would be reasonable to suggest that making the mediation public was valuable to each party – perhaps in showing that they had approached the situation in such a way that put the needs of the industry above their own individual interests. As the direct opposite of the Intel case, the parties in this instance created an impression that they were responsive to wider stakeholder interests, and responsible enough to factor those interests into the settlement process.

Summary

- Conflict is an opportunity, and if managed well it can actually be a source of good PR for companies.

- Reputation management is a) holistic and b) shown in every action you take.
- Managing company reputation when it comes to conflict has two prongs: prevention and handling. In practice, these prongs can include having and enacting a crisis plan, monitoring what consumers think of your products and organisation and even introducing an ADR redress scheme to manage disputes.
- Stakeholder communication can be affected by environmental (e.g. using an interpreter for parties who don't share a language) and social (e.g. personality type) factors.
- In any stakeholder communication, awareness of audience is key: who you are addressing directly may not represent the full spectrum of who is listening to your message.

Case study: inviting 'the world outside' in to a dispute

The dispute

The dispute we will be looking at in detail centres on the valuation and sale of a partially completed development site. Two valuations were given on the same property to the vendor and purchaser, and this fact was uncovered by the purchaser as they ran into financial difficulties. The very public fallout from this discovery drew in wider stakeholders such as local and national government, local communities, company shareholders and investors, charities, and even faith leaders. Settling the dispute quickly and effectively became a priority, as the messy way the primary parties handled matters had begun to affect public attitudes towards the companies, and their profit margins.

Background

A supermarket chain sought to sell a portfolio of investment development sites, with one site in particular catching the eye of another commercial entity (known as 'X Limited'). X Limited found the size, location and long-term potential of the development site especially exciting, and were keen to make sure that when bidding for the site opened, they were in pole position to bid successfully.

- The prospect of a sale was, however, controversial. When news of the intended sale broke, various stakeholder groups raised concerns about what the site's future could mean for them:
- Local residents, who were unhappy when the supermarket bought the site, were concerned by the uncertainty surrounding the sale and possible new owners. It was not clear how the new owners would develop the site, how long development would take, or what the impact would be on the community.
- Local government officials took an interest for a number of reasons. As well as having to invest more time and money in considering planning proposals, officials

were concerned that if the new owners were to 'land bank' rather than actively develop the site, the council would miss central government targets for attracting investment and development. Missing these targets would have financial implications in the form of lost subsidies and other forms of central government assistance.
- Central government departments took an interest because of implications for revenue-raising avenues: not only would the nature of the new development affect their ability to raise tax, it would also receive financial incentives under European Union development schemes.
- Wildlife charities expressed ongoing concerns that developing the area would be immediately and permanently disruptive to the local environment and ecosystems.
- Shareholders received news of the intended sale with interest, and an eye on profit. Shareholders of the supermarket chain were divided: while some thought that streamlining the land portfolio was a sensible way of generating revenue, others were anxious about the message the sale sent to the markets. They said that the wider programme of sales counted as deleveraging, and that this raised issues around the company's solvency and long-term strategy.
- X Limited operated as a general partnership and did not have shareholders. It did have external investors, however, and they took an interest in X Limited's new acquisition and how it tallied with the company's long-term growth and development strategies.

A valuer had already provided the supermarket chain with a guide price for the development site, advising that an optimistic sale price would be in the region of £5 million. This valuation had not been made public, and was known only to a select group of people at the supermarket. The same valuer was approached by X Limited to provide a valuation on the site, having no knowledge of the earlier valuation. The valuer gave X Limited an estimate of £7 million, which X Limited found to be expensive: trusting in the judgement of the valuer, however, X Limited made the supermarket an offer in this region.

Acting on the valuer's advice, X Limited acquired the site for £7 million. Reactions were as mixed as had been anticipated: X Limited's shareholders and employees were pleased that the company had completed an auspicious, forward-looking deal, and the strong sale price did much to allay the disquiet felt by many of the supermarket's shareholders. Local residents were still unhappy at the prospect of development, but the local council department seemed to be increasingly reassured by X Limited's plans, thanks to extra effort on the part of the company to show how their plans for development would revitalise the locality and attract secondary investment from other companies. X Limited also went to a lot of trouble to highlight their green credentials, particularly their close work with environmental charities and consultancies, in a bid to win round the wildlife charities who still had concerns about how development would affect the local environment. While there was still a considerable level of concern and opposition to X Limited's future in the locality, the company had worked hard to set up lines of communication with each stakeholder group, and looked forward to slowly winning around a 'critical mass' of its unfriendly audiences.

A series of disruptive events led to X Limited experiencing trading difficulties, successive quarters of flat sales, and eventually it was forced to cease trading, owing significant debts. The company's plans for the development site had never materialised – covering the cost of the purchase ate up the company's ever-shrinking pot of income, leaving no spare cash to maintain let alone develop the land. To make matters worse, X Limited's general partnership structure left its controllers, F and P, personally liable for the company's debts – F and P were themselves forced into personal bankruptcy following the company's collapse.

It later became clear that the valuer had not acted fairly or impartially in their dealings with X Limited. The valuer knew that the supermarket needed to achieve a sale price of £7 million to cover financing on the land, and had therefore knowingly misled X Limited in the purchase of the development site. The valuer deliberately inflated their estimate of the site's value because they wanted the prestige of brokering a deal involving the supermarket – the strong publicity opportunities and industry kudos a successful deal would provide made 'bending the rules' an attractive option. It seemed that the potential publicity wins outweighed the potential negative consequences from acting from personal interest rather than in the interests of the client, X Limited.

An intricate case

The subsequent litigation was complex, taking in a number of issues. Following the bankruptcies, F and P discovered the prior dealings the valuer had had with the supermarket, and were furious at the thought of being deliberately misled by the valuer because of conflicting interests. F and P exchanged heated letters with the valuer highlighting these views, and had even begun to voice suspicion that the supermarket had also acted deliberately to, in their words, 'deceive and defraud' them, when they had acted in good faith in the purchase. There were also arguments over whether F and P were personally entitled to rely on the valuation given to X Limited – the valuer claimed that the valuation on the site was given to X Limited only, and that F and P should have obtained a second valuation with respect to their personal interest in the transaction.

Besides the issues of cost and trust, reputation also quickly proved to be an important issue. Stakeholders in the dispute found that the nature and value of the case drew public attention to the outcome, and that interest was further stoked by the way that each stakeholder responded to each step of the dispute.

- The supermarket found itself pulled into the forefront of the dispute, as popular opinion decided that it must have colluded with the valuer to achieve a higher sale price for the development site. Although this was not true (the supermarket had accepted the valuer's site valuation as an honest one), the underlying message that began to stick was that the unscrupulous supermarket had ripped off X Limited, that it habitually ripped off anyone connected to its business, and that it took the attitude of 'we're too big to be caught out, so everyone else will have to fall in line'. Local consumers were put off by this attitude and started to take their custom to competitors to 'punish' the supermarket. Worryingly, the publicity surrounding the sale prompted people to start inferring that the supermarket was having financial difficulties (and that the sale was part of a budgetary rescue plan), which encouraged shareholders and investors to begin looking at the company's accounts and actions more closely.
- The valuers were utterly humiliated by the case – their credibility was shattered, and companies who had worked with them were threatening legal action because of the fear that they too had been 'stitched up'. The actions of one person – who was trying to improve the profile of the business – had instead caused the whole company to face suspicion and accusation.
- X Limited and its controllers had to manage a precarious relationship with the situation, as there were obvious opportunities and pitfalls connected with the dispute. Public opinion was sympathetic to X Limited on the basis of 'fairness', and because the representation of the case allowed people to confirm their worst thoughts about the supermarket. F and P's personal bankruptcy story also elicited sympathy, as the effect of the mis-valuation and subsequent dispute had clear consequences for F and P's families. However, there was also a risk that the general mood of cynicism around the companies' behaviour – 'everyone's out to make a quick buck' – would attach itself to X Limited, and F and P. F and P were faced with the dilemma of how to act in a way that kept a productive focus on the dispute without being seen as opportunistic, greedy, or personally incompetent.
- The local council began to attract attention also because of their role in granting planning permission and because they had a clear stake in how the dispute progressed. Their decision to encourage the site's sale, and enthusiasm for X Limited's ill-fated plans, reflected poorly on their fact-finding and diligence as many people voiced that the council should have spotted that something was amiss. They were also faced with the possibility that the site would remain undeveloped for the foreseeable future, leading to lower tax income, increased fly-tipping, and general environmental degradation. Settling the dispute became a priority for the council, even though their connection to the situation was less direct than the disputants and valuer.

These starting positions share, besides investment in settling the dispute, a strong need to anticipate how the public responds to the dispute. So vital was positive public engagement, each of the four 'direct' stakeholders decided their next steps with a strong view to gaining and keeping public support. As well as using traditional communication lines such as issuing press releases, granting interviews and establishing a customer care line, the direct stakeholders also opened up digital lines of communication, and sought active, inventive ways of portraying the messages needed to create good publicity. Some of these methods included:

- Separate donations to a local environmental charity by the valuers and the supermarket
- Television interviews given by a representative of the supermarket
- Establishing Twitter pages and a consumer hotline to provide up-to-date information on the dispute, and to collect comments from the public.

These methods enjoyed mixed success. In particular, providing information online proved to be a double-edged sword. The supermarket's Twitter feed, for example, began unsuccessfully – responding to individual queries with stock answers was intended to show engagement but instead resulted in frustration. Users felt that receiving cookie cutter responses neatly encapsulated the supermarket's attitude – an unconcerned and uncaring company whose words didn't match their actions. It reinforced the growing narrative that there was no dialogue to be had with the supermarket, which was a dangerous idea to allow to take hold.

When the supermarket realised the impact of the cookie cutter quotes, they decided to change tactic. Comments were responded to personally, with more helpful replies and a 'human face' behind the words. This proved successful because it showed the organisation as engaging with other stakeholders on an individual level, which not only responded to the needs of each specific questioner but also sent a message that the organisation was committed to addressing its audiences fully.

As these issues played out in the public arena, they were also tested in the courts over a long stretch of time, and the appeal court struck out much of the original claim. The amount in dispute had increased substantially, standing at £11 million – this amount did not include costs, which added a further large sum to the value of the claim. The dispute's other ripples included:

- Lost profits across the board as consumers chose to take their business elsewhere, affecting the supermarket and the valuer.
- Suppliers to the supermarket and valuer suffered great swings of uncertainty, as it was not clear that their services would be needed in the future at the same level as before.
- Shareholders and investors were feeling heightened tension amid conflicting reports on each company's immediate and long-term stability.
- F and P came under increasing financial and personal strain, finding the attention from the dispute intrusive and stressful.

- A general increase in the level of scrutiny directed at how assets were valued, sold, and the organisations involved.

Not all of these effects are, in isolation, bad things – proper investigation of the details of a big ticket sale, for example, is generally to be applauded as correct diligence – but the particular dispute circumstances amplified the negative impact of each effect.

Mediation was agreed to by the valuer and F and P as the primary disputants, and the supermarket also asked to be included in the process. At this point, everyone accepted that the protracted dispute was seriously affecting each party's present-day activities, and threatened to jeopardise the future. The suggestion to mediate came from the local community's vicar – a local resident, consumer, taxpayer, and faith leader – who could see that the issues being raised by the dispute and its drawn-out path would not be solved by litigation.

Reaching a settlement

The mediation involved three parties: F and P, the valuer, and the supermarket were all represented on the day of mediation. Each party came with a hope of reaching settlement, chastened by how the reputational fall-out had dwarfed everyone's expectations.

Mediation also offered a secondary appeal for the parties – it had the potential to repair the damaged reputations of the organisations involved. This was possible on two levels. Firstly, taking ownership of the solution-finding process meant that the parties could show, in practice, that they were serious about ending the dispute and that they had the necessary communication skills to achieve such an outcome. Secondly, the holistic view taken by mediation promised an opportunity to openly discuss the mistakes made by each party, to acknowledge them, and to find a way of redress. This was especially important for F and P, who felt that they had lost their business as a direct result of the valuer's actions.

Representatives for the supermarket attended the mediation: even though the dispute started off as one between the valuer and F and P, circumstance drew the supermarket in. They wanted primarily to correct the public belief that they had deliberately overvalued the development site, and win back the custom they had lost because of the dispute. Buoyed by the reception given to the spokesman on the television interview, some in the company felt that a successful mediation could help turn heightened public interest in the company into commercial success.

Initially, the parties spent a lot of time debating the legal merits of their respective cases, and going over this ground quickly threatened deadlock. The mediator, however, refocused the discussion on commercial and reputation issues: she reminded everyone of the straightforward truth that the dispute was hurting everyone, and that finding a solution that made commercial sense was the aim of the process. She also made a point of reality testing against the likely responses of different stakeholders – 'what if', 'what might' and 'how could' became mainstays of the discussion.

Resolution

Over two days, the three parties explored the different faces of the dispute and ultimately came to a settlement. This came in two parts: financial recompense was made from the valuer to F and P, with a smaller amount granted to the supermarket, and joint statements were prepared acknowledging errors, expressing apology, and outlining the steps that would be taken to put things right. The development site, an asset of X Limited, was not considered as part of the settlement because of the company's insolvency.

Most of the stakeholders were satisfied with this outcome:

- F and P were able to understand fully what had happened between them, the valuer and the supermarket; this helped them to psychologically gain closure on the situation and focus on the future. The financial award also helped to discharge a large portion of their debts owed through the personal bankruptcy process.
- The valuers were seen to take the situation seriously – they took the chance to apologise sincerely and explain how they had learned from the experience. Taking this action honestly did not repair the company's reputation overnight, but laid important foundations for future rehabilitation.
- The supermarket also laid the groundwork for a promising future – faced with a difficult situation, the company responded in a timely and effective way. Although public opinion was initially hostile, the mix of efficient social media engagement, the leadership shown by the company's representatives, and being consistently 'on-message' combined to create a positive impression of the supermarket.
- The local council were relieved to see a settlement because it meant that there was, finally, an outcome for the development site. Despite preferred partners X Limited falling out of the development race, the council came away from the situation with a much stronger understanding of public attitudes to development and the consultation process. In turn, the new acquirers of the development site were asked to submit detailed plans and impact assessments, which were then put to the public at a series of open consultation forums.
- Supermarket shareholders were pleased with the settlement because it provided clarity and certainty – the confident attitude shown by the disputant parties diffused into the wider corporate atmosphere, and gave the corporate community confidence in the supermarket's long-term stable prospects.
- Residents benefited from the resolution directly and indirectly: as a result of the process, the council made sure that local residents were fully consulted when

future development plans were under consideration. Opening this channel of dialogue between residents and the council proved to be mutually beneficial, with both groups benefiting from hearing and understanding the other's point of view. The cultural change at local government level to one of active listening made relations with the public far smoother, and resulted in a reduction in the volume of complaints made to other council departments. In an attitudes survey carried out six months after the dispute, over two-thirds of local residents reported that they were 'very satisfied' with the council's complaint and feedback handling process – an increase of almost half.
- Consumers who used the supermarket also benefited from a cultural change at the organisation: the supermarket saw that active listening was a valuable brand enhancement tool as well as an easy way to improve its service offering. Following the dispute, the supermarket launched two new, actively publicised schemes for consumer feedback and consumer complaints handling. These schemes differentiated the supermarket from its competitors, and led to a sustained increase in footfall, sales and customer satisfaction. Even though the dispute threatened to greatly damage the supermarket, judicious use of PR techniques and active listening helped transform what could have been a disaster into a golden opportunity for growth.
- Representatives from environmental charities were disappointed that development on the site would still go ahead under the aegis of a different company: the prevailing feeling was that development of any nature would threaten the local environment. However, this stakeholder group did make gains from how the dispute was resolved. The public response to the dispute meant that when mediation took place, environmental concerns were more prominently featured on the discussion agenda because of the support shown for the issue as the dispute played out.

Notes

1. Thomas-Kilmann Conflict Mode Instrument found at: http://www.kilmanndiagnostics.com/developing-forced-choice-measure-conflict-handling-behavior-mode-instrument.
2. http://ec.europa.eu/consumers/strategy/docs/com_staff_wp2009_en.pdf retrieved 19/12/12 p. 2.

8
The potential for conflict over ownership – who is in control?

Andy Rogers and Gemma Oke

Introduction

The purpose of this chapter is to examine where conflict may arise over ownership and what characteristics these conflicts might display, rather than look at the different models of ownership for organisations and the corresponding regulations that govern them. With this in mind, it can be said that conflict between an organisation and its shareholders, investors or trustees (or between the owners themselves) can frequently be boiled down to one issue: who exercises ultimate control.

Basic logic would dictate that ownership of a company (or partial ownership) would translate to a greater say in the management or operation of the organisation. However, in business there are various checks and balances, and – as we will see – rival claimants to the title of principal controller of an organisation.

Following their study of 200 of the largest non-financial companies in the USA in 1932, Berle and Means, in their book *The Modern Corporation and Private Property* (Transaction Publications), stated that:

> 'The economic power in the hands of the few persons who control a giant corporation is a tremendous force which can harm or benefit a multitude of individuals, affect whole districts, shift the currents of trade, bring ruin to one community and prosperity to another. The organisations which they control have passed far beyond the realm of private enterprise – they have become more nearly social institutions.'

Although this remark was made over 80 years ago, the dynamic it identifies between those who control companies and those who patronise them still holds true today. The implicit messages that have emerged about organisations in the 20th century is that the larger the organisation, the more stakeholders it may have and crucially, that shareholders' views should be regarded and not simply ignored. Thus the formal owners of an organisation have found themselves, if not competing for influence, at least sensitive to the needs and demands of the organisation's workforce, the communities in which they live and the customers they serve. When the intentions of owners are viewed to contradict those of the other less formal stakeholders, an environment where conflict can emerge is created. Notable examples of this come from the field of mergers and acquisitions – two notable examples in the last decade being the takeover of Cadbury by the food giant Kraft Foods (now Modelez International) in 2010, and the purchase of the controlling shareholding of Manchester United by US businessman Malcolm Glazer in 2005. With hindsight, we can say that initial difficulties surrounding these takeovers have softened with time, but the lesson remains that there is high value in being sensitive and responsive to potential conflict.

**The company secretary -
A web of influences**

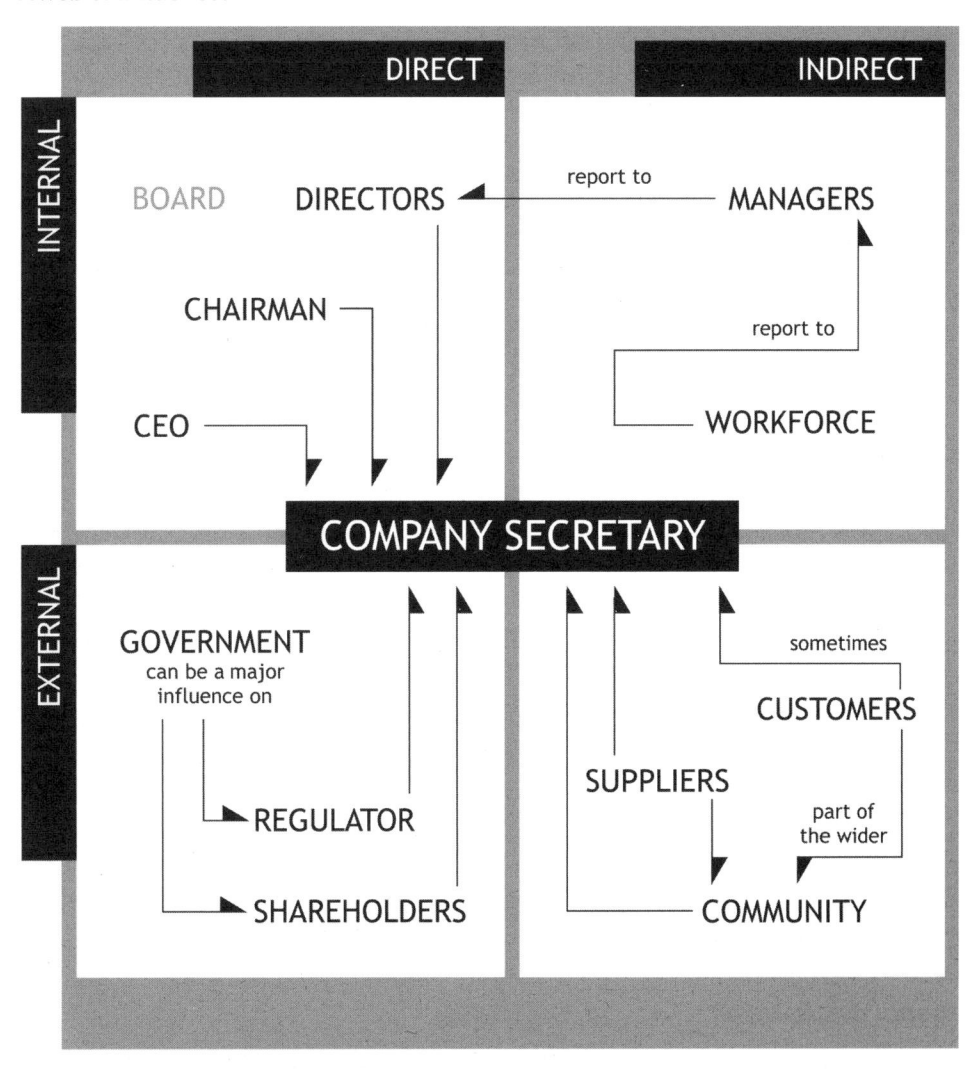

Figure 8.1: The company secretary – A web of influences

Owners: managing the managers or relinquishing responsibility?

Writing in their influential paper 'Theory of the firm: Managerial behaviour, agency costs and ownership structure' in 1976, Michael Jensen and William Meckling described the dynamic between the owners of a company and the management as the 'agency problem'. An agent is essentially contracted by a second person to perform a task on that person's behalf – and for our purposes this is a view which can be extended to the manager-shareholder relationship. Jensen and Meckling recognise that the relationship has the potential to be fraught because agents, however professional, always have the ability to put their own interests in advance of the owners'. Expressly, they say this can mean that executive directors might be more likely to exploit their own needs or circumstances over the long-term interests of the owners or even the organisation itself. This is a breach of the fiduciary duties that may be conferred on an executive director, and certainly creates a damaging conflict of interest.

> 'This has been identified as an issue in the relationship between ownership and control and the conflict between owners and managers is seen as an example of the "agency problem".'
> David Needle, *Business In Context* (5th Edn, 2004)

The theory of agency problems suggests that because conflicts arise from two parties to a contract, they are virtually limitless in nature. More recent research (of which there has been much in the last three decades) has categorised four main areas where conflict can arise: morality, risk, earnings and time. There would also appear to be an issue with scale, as the larger an organisation is, the greater the potential for some of the agency conflicts to exist and escalate.

Moral hazard conflict

This theory element maintains that managers of an organisation will direct and invest in a business in a way that best suits their abilities – rather than putting the actual needs of the business first. This action, as argued by Andrei Shleifer and Robert Vishny ('Management entrenchment', *Journal of Financial Economics* **25**, 1989), strengthens the individual manager increasing their status and importance but also ultimately delivers less value for the shareholder than an investment that benefited the whole business.

Earnings retention conflict

As the name might suggest, this element refers to whether profits should be held within the organisation, for its own benefit or paid to shareholders as a return for their investment. It has been argued that this is one of the biggest potential drawbacks for shareholders: the opportunity cost of receiving an immediate return is the potential to achieve higher returns in the future.

Managerial risk aversion

Eugene Fama ('Agency problems and the theory of the firm', *Journal of Political Economy* **88**, 1980) argues that managers, with only one source of living (their employment), are less likely to speculate on investing in less certain initiatives for the company, despite potentially high returns, than investors who typically hold shareholdings in more than one company. It has been observed that this occurrence is even more likely in organisations that do not use an executive bonus or reward structure. Implementing bold organisational initiatives, or drastically changing a company's direction, raises the chance of conflict between those shareholders or board members advocating change and risk-adverse managers tasked with putting those changes into effect.

Time horizon conflict

This conflict theory supposes that managers are unconcerned with the finances or share price of the organisation beyond their period of employment. This means that executives will tend to favour short-term investments/business decisions that will see returns whilst they are with the company, rather than long-term cash flow. In particular, this has led to questions about attitude to long-term research and development by organisations.

More information on agency problems can be found in the chapter 'Agency Theory, Incomplete Contracting and Ownership Structure' by Clacher, Hillier and McColgan, published in *Corporate Governance, A Synthesis of Theory, Research and Practice*, Eds Baker and Anderson (John Wiley & Sons, 2010).

Two levels of dialogue

In relationships with shareholders, the Centre for Effective Dispute Resolution (CEDR) has observed there are explicit and implicit levels of dialogue and communication. Explicit communication refers to the duty of an organisation to its shareholders, and what an organisation *must do* to inform its shareholders. The second implicit dialogue can probably best be quantified as the *tone and openness* of its communication, and what it additionally tells shareholders that it is not compelled to do by way of information sharing or the way it is revealed.

Essential information

The explicit is obviously the way in which a company honours its commitments to shareholders and includes the payment of dividends and the communication of its financial performance and accounting. Investors need this information to make informed judgements about existing investments as well as potential new investments. The accountability of companies to investors has been encouraged around the world to create a climate where investment can flourish with confidence. This obviously includes companies having independently audited and published accounts that are capable of bearing public scrutiny.

Finance and accounting play central roles in corporate governance, which may be defined as:

> 'The system of checks and balances both internal and external to companies, which ensures that companies discharge their accountability to all their stakeholders and act in a responsible way in all areas of their business activity.'
>
> Jill Solomon, *Corporate Governance and Accountability* (John Wiley & Sons, 2007)

There are links with business ethics and responsibility (both financial and corporate social responsibility), and these clearly play a central role in providing checks and balances.

Tone and openness

Quantifying tone and transparency in the communication between an organisation and its owners or investors is not straightforward, yet it can be instrumental in building a strong and loyal relationship between the two. Without wanting to become too intangible, tone can be explained as involving the building of closeness and friendship through the amount of information given and the way and style in which it is delivered. Later in this chapter we will touch on investor relations, which is a discipline designed to manage information flow to shareholders effectively.

The flip side is a lack of openness and a poor tone of communication, which can ruin relations between organisations and investors, and of course beyond to other stakeholders. Whilst this theory of communication in corporate governance is a sound one, the process has on occasion been shown to be imperfect. Auditing processes have on rare occasions been shown not to be truly independent. Financial reports can be presented in such a way as to hide information. Worse was evidenced in the case of Enron in 2001, where the auditor Arthur Andersen was also a consultant acting on the company's behalf. Following Enron's collapse, Arthur Andersen's conflict of interest – and therefore complicity – in the scandal was discovered. Writing in 2004, Andrew Cornford's paper entitled 'Internationally Agreed Principles For Corporate Governance And The Enron Case' said that

> 'The evidence available to us suggests that Andersen did not fulfil its professional responsibilities in connection with its audits of Enron's financial statements, or its obligation to bring to the attention of Enron's Board (or the Audit and Compliance Committee) concerns about Enron's internal contracts over the related-party transactions.'[1]

In such circumstances where a shareholder feels deceived, or worse financially cheated, the relationship between company and shareholder and even the entire investment community must be regarded to a large extent as being beyond repair.

Types of shareholders and examples of disputes

The different structures of ownership may present their own challenges and dilemmas when it comes to conflict. It will be useful to look at what the characteristics of each may be and how they relate to the issue of control.

1. Owners with vested relationships

a) Partners

Typically, the members of a formal partnership will be largely active in the running of the organisation, just as business partners will frequently be both equally active in the business, and any conflict that emerges will be part of their day-to-day management. Many of these everyday conflicts have been dealt with elsewhere in this book so what we will concentrate on is disputes over ownership. Partnership disputes make up a steady proportion of the cases that CEDR Solve is asked to provide dispute resolution for, and frequently this relates to problems over ownership, control and struggling relationships.

There are of course silent partners and here, when communications break down or simply cease and assumptions diverge from the current reality, there is genuine potential for difficult and crippling conflict to emerge. These disputes, when they arise, can lead to a breakdown in confidence and irrevocable damage to relationships. In our experience, involving a third-party neutral can help to rebuild this relationship, and in some cases even strengthen it by helping to clarify processes and systems for future working practices. If the relationship is not salvageable, a neutral third party can help facilitate a clean division of ownership.

> **Case study: partners**
>
> In 2007, Liverpool Football Club was purchased by two American businessmen, George Gillett and Tom Hicks, who each owned different sports teams in the USA. The two had not collaborated with each other in this way previously.
>
> By 2010, the club was put up for sale by Gillett and Hicks. This followed years of apparent disagreements between Gillett and Hicks themselves and also between them as owners with the managers of the club. Additionally, there was a lack of support from the fans, many of whom had become very disenchanted with the deal and direction of the club. What is of interest for us in this chapter is what went wrong in the ownership relationship.
>
> An article published in *The Independent* newspaper on 14 October 2010 summarised the differences between the two owners:
>
> **'Odd Couple' who agreed about everything. Except coach, finance, stadium...**
>
> Signs of disagreement between the Americans over how to run Liverpool were evident almost from the start.
>
> It became clear that Tom Hicks' and George Gillett's ownership of Liverpool was heading for serious trouble during a meeting in a Marseilles hotel room on the afternoon of Tuesday 11 December 2007...

...They were already exploring the sale or part sale of the club, and they had wildly different views about how Liverpool should be managed and developed.

Those differences were at the heart of most of the problems that beset Liverpool from late 2007 until now. They fell out, bitterly, about the manager(s), the new stadium, the funding of the club, whether to sell a chunk of the club or not, and for what price.

These problems only really began to manifest themselves from late 2007 onwards, after that fateful meeting in Marseilles, and anyone who claims anything emphatically to the contrary is likely to be looking through revisionist specs...

...Hicks and Gillett were at loggerheads over the Stanley Park (Stadium) project, Gillett inclined to push forward with the design on the table (if money could be found) and Hicks insistent on bringing in his own planners, architects, ideas – and ultimately costs. The stadium plans, palsied and without funding, festered, so the opportunity of a brand new ground with naming rights and other income drifted.

Hicks and Gillett fell out about managers too; Hicks began the courting of Jürgen Klinsmann in late 2007, something he revealed in January 2008 to the horror of many pro-Rafael Benitez fans. In what now looks like a PR-driven decision, Hicks then fell four-square behind everything Benitez did for two years, while Gillett, although supportive of the Spaniard, believed Benitez should not have an entirely free rein, and worked best under the supervision of a 'moderating' executive, namely Parry.

Hicks was the driving force behind Benitez's extended five-year contract last year, and when Parry left at the end of the 2008-09 season (when Liverpool finished second in the Premier League), Gillett became increasingly bitter about what he perceived as Benitez's failings.

If the owners were at war over this, then they had always had major differences. Gillett realised as early as late 2007 that buying Liverpool had probably been an error. Hicks agreed only partially and thought the pair would still find a third investor to give them a lot of money for a bit of the club. Hicks ludicrously valued Liverpool at around £1bn and wanted the club's former suitors, Dubai International Capital (DIC), to pay around £150m for a 15 per cent stake.

DIC's representative Amanda Staveley met Hicks in Yorkshire as early as October 2007 to discuss that deal; DIC rejected it but returned with an offer of about £500m in early 2008 for the whole club. If Hicks and Gillett had accepted then, they would have walked away with an overall profit.

Instead, Hicks said no, and made it clear he did not approve of Gillett trying to sell his own stake separately. So 2008 passed too with no stadium and no investment, then Christian Purslow arrived as managing director in 2009 to seek solutions to both, as did – at the behest of a desperate Royal Bank of Scotland – Martin Broughton in April 2010. New ownership is the result...

> How can outsiders tell what went wrong with this relationship? Leaving aside the issue that the owners in reality did not have enough funding for what they wanted to achieve, a number of other elements are discernible. It was clear that both men, who were experienced sports club owners, made assumptions about how the other would work and chose to believe that they would share similar approaches on the best courses of action for Liverpool. Added to this is the fact that they did not know each other's personal working styles and as two senior respective figures probably had insufficient recent experience of collaborating with a peer. It is also possible to infer that after the partnership was formed, insufficient energy was put into maintaining clear communications between the two owners: accordingly, when one put forward an opinion or proposed a course of action, the other was often genuinely surprised and therefore less willing to look at the opportunities for consensus. In this situation, significant positive steps towards understanding could have been achieved for the owners and Liverpool FC fans across the globe with the intervention of a neutral third-party facilitator.
>
> 'Was this also a shotgun marriage of financial, if not footballing, convenience? Watching Foster Gillett (George's son and representative) refusing to speak a word to the Hicks boys (at a press conference) should have told us that the families may both have been from the same country but geographically and culturally they were thousands of miles apart.'
>
> Brian Reade, *An Epic Swindle*[2]

b) Family Business

The majority of businesses in the world are family owned and managed, and almost half of all publicly listed companies around the world have a majority shareholding block that is accounted for by one family. The reason is simple: the strength of the family unit makes family businesses a tried and tested model that works. From traditional merchants in far-flung places to some of the largest businesses in the world, family businesses abound. Examples include Samsung in Korea, Tata in India and Ford in the USA, where the descendants of Henry Ford still own 40% of shares in the company. What makes family firms different from other businesses? Family enterprises are unique because the family and its future remains at the very core of the firm's raison d'etre and its governance. The most important forces in the business are not individuals but a set of people linked by close relationships, and the nature of those relationships is likely to have an impact on how the company is run and the decisions it makes.

Family businesses, like all enterprises, work best when everyone understands their roles, communication is possible and issues are dealt with in a respectful fashion. However, just like people, families are frequently not perfect and the difficulties of close relationships can spill over into business. Jealousy between siblings, for example, can come to apply to different levels of status in the business or perceived favouritism from an elder. The bias of a parent, who still identifies some of the failings of youth in the younger generation, can prevail and make the individual resistant to allow changes or relinquish control. This can foster resentment of sons or daughters, who do not feel that their achievements have been recognised within the family firm.

Case study: family business

The dispute concerned management and ownership of a successful family textile manufacturer involving three generations. The textile factory, which had been acquired by the grandparents five decades before, had slowly been built into a steady but successful business. Following the death of the grandfather, the dynamics of management changed within the business although the grandmother, who was not present in the business, nominally kept overall control. Over a period of years, there was a bitter fall-out between family members looking at how to restructure or break up the business. The desire to restructure was probably because there was recognition from the younger generation that they would not be able to use their grandmother as the ultimate arbiter of disagreements in the future.

What is distinctive in this instance is that because of the family relationships, litigation had not been pursued as an option. This is not to say that feelings were not every bit as bitter as can be encountered between parties in litigation: in fact, the family dimensions of the dispute may well have exacerbated the matter.

There were a few main issues for the family managers which threatened to bring the business to a near standstill. At the centre of the dispute were issues over the manufacturer's service contracts, the day-to-day management of the site and who might in the future be in overall control.

Whilst stalemate might have been reached on site, there were a number of particular features which in this instance enabled the family to do something about its situation. Importantly, the main legal representative for the textile manufacturer understood the concept of alternative dispute resolution and was very keen to mediate. The representative was also very active in convincing the family not to use litigation to answer their disagreements.

Through the influence of the legal representative, the principal members of the family involved in the dispute had actually come together to prepare a joint statement on what the problems were. Although this may not sound like an important achievement for a running business, the reality was that for this family, at this point, anything that could be produced jointly represented a partial success.

The grandmother was only partially aware of how very bad the relations had become within the family when the reasons for the mediation were given to her. She realised on one hand why excuses to avoid family gatherings had been given and on the other hand why certain business initiatives had failed or been postponed. Her anxiety at the family's fall-out was therefore heightened and a personal determination was formed to, if at all possible, see all issues aired and fully resolved.

The mediation took place on site at the textile factory for logistical reasons. The mediator conducted private sessions with all the constituent family members individually: this readied the different factions for the first face-to-face dialogue they had all had in months, and gave the mediator an opportunity to stress to the family the desirability that they get together later in the day in order that everyone should be heard.

There were then follow-up private meetings with family members and the mediator, and it was only after these sessions had built sufficient consensus for the forthcoming negotiation that a joint session with the whole family took place early in the afternoon.

The mediator gave special attention to the family issues before moving to work on a pragmatic way forward with everyone collaborating to find a sound business solution. This approach meant that all the more personal issues had been largely discharged by the time the business negotiation was underway and therefore a settlement agreement was being discussed. The mediation lasted for 12 hours and did successfully conclude – and the family members, whilst not currently the best of friends, were all able to start communicating and agree a plan for the future.

What this mediation clearly shows is that the mediator has the ability to act intuitively. In this instance, the intuition was to create a space for the principals to take ownership and responsibility – both for what had happened but also for the solution.

In order for the mediation to work, there was a clear need for preparation and full understanding of the business and ways of restructuring from both the mediator and of course the family. This was an objective that the mediator made clear in advance of the session.

This case was undoubtedly helped by having a legal adviser with a clear view and positive attitude who enabled the mediator to get the lawyer to work with different 'teams' to resolve issues.

The mediator also found that the use of coaching techniques greatly assisted the family members to move on in their personal lives, leave grievances behind and focus on what would be most beneficial for the family as a whole and the business, and not just themselves.

2. Non-owner ownerships

Trustees, governors and representative directorships

It is possible to have 'owners' of an organisation who do not hold equity in it. Many organisations, often providing a public service, work on a non-profit basis (for example, charities or membership bodies that are also limited companies) and those that work with them often do so on a not-for-profit basis, which extends to the trustees and directors on the board. The directors of publicly listed companies execute their duties on behalf of the shareholders (and on occasion a directorship can represent a particular shareholding) and the trustees or directors of other types of organisations likewise do so on behalf of other stakeholders (most typically the general public). Examples of this latter model could be charities or a government agency such as the British Broadcasting Corporation.

Therefore you can have a situation where an organisation's board of trustees is a group of individuals who can strongly identify with who they regard as the effective owners of that organisation. This level of identification by directors with stakeholders is naturally desirable in ensuring they feel fully engaged in their role, but it does also have implications for the issue of ownership. This has implications of Fiduciary Duty, commonly between a trustee and beneficiaries of the trust, where the trustees put their own interests to one side and agree to manage a company for beneficiaries of the trust. Furthermore, where the 'ownership' might be a defined group or the general public, having trustees that they feel are acting on their behalf gives them a greater confidence in voicing any concerns. A complication is that because these trustees or directors have a more informed knowledge of the working of the organisation, and the people they represent, any disputes over control are likely to be more complex and detailed, and to become so quite quickly.

This can be compounded by the circumstances that when someone willingly gives their time freely – as trustees frequently do – investing notably of themselves in an enterprise, they can feel even greater ownership, which again can give conflicts the potential to become even further embedded. This adds a further, more personal dimension to disputes involving trustees or other kinds of governing representatives.

Case study: trustees

A land trust that owned a sizeable tract of land was run by a board of trustees, all of whom were elected, unpaid volunteers. The trust was over 100 years old and in that time the value of the land had risen considerably. Some of the land was given over for common use by the community, and some was commercially rented.

As a consequence, the trust was moderately wealthy but not run as such, with only a handful of full-time employees. The land held by the trust was seen as valuable for preserving the local countryside and beauty of the area and being a trustee was seen as an admirable and desirable position.

The board of the trust, the majority of whom lived locally, met several times a year, although the only truly active positions on the board were the chair and the treasurer, both well-respected, long-standing members of the board. The treasurer was seen to work especially hard for the land trust and was responsible for overseeing many of the elements of the finance, as would be expected.

In addition to renting a small piece of land himself, the treasurer's sister rented a larger piece of land, on which she had run an animal sanctuary for a number of years. This was known to the other members of the board but was not seen as a conflict of interest.

The sister was a 'larger than life' character who had run the animal sanctuary as her own domain, and thanks to a large bequest, began substantial material improvements to the sanctuary and the land on which it stood. In doing this she sought no official permission from the trust.

When the work was completed, the sister held a launch event for the animal sanctuary which national TV television attended. On live TV, she stated that the sanctuary was closely linked to the prestigious trust and this launch was a major initiative of the partnership.

When members of the trust saw the TV programme an emergency meeting of the trust was called. The contentious issues discussed were:

- How had the work done to the animal sanctuary affected the condition of the land and its rental value? Was the work reversible, or more permanent? Would restoration be expensive, lengthy or cause difficulties for the local community?
- What had the treasurer known about the work? Had he given permission and why had permission not been sought from the whole board? What had the trust's employees been told and had they been complicit?
- One of the most emotive issues was that the sister had incorrectly presented this as a joint initiative with the trust. Most members of the trust board wanted to evict her but were worried about what that would do to the reputation of the trust. This issue had become even more sensitive in the wake of the sister's public linking of the trust and the animal sanctuary.

The result of this meeting was that there was a majority vote of no confidence in the treasurer, whose position was that he had done nothing wrong, and any wrongdoing was from the over-enthusiasm of his animal-loving sister. He therefore refused to resign.

The chairman, supported by the trust's legal adviser, proposed a mediation between the trust and the treasurer and his sister. Two of the most vocal opponents of the treasurer on the board joined the chairman to represent the trust.

Prior to the mediation, the mediator spent time talking to the legal advisers on both sides to ensure that all the legal issues regarding the trust and the lease of the land were surfaced prior to the mediation, and where possible, consensus was built.

At the mediation, which at the parties' request took place in London, the mediator spent considerable time with both sides to enable them to both feel heard. This exercise of 'feeling heard' was repeated in a joint meeting between both sides. Sentiments were 'raw' on both sides but both sides knowing that they had put their case across enabled them to focus on ways in which the matter could be resolved.

> After a full day of meetings, the agreement produced contained the following elements:
>
> - The treasurer (who no longer wished to work with the other trustees) would not stand for re-election at the end of his term. In the remaining 12 months, the chairman undertook to work with the treasurer more closely to ensure there could be no suspicion of impropriety.
> - At the treasurer's departure, he would be publicly thanked for his long service to the trust.
> - An independent estimate would be made of any essential work that would be needed to reinstate the quality of the land that the sanctuary was on. This work would be undertaken when the land was vacated.
> - The sister agreed to end her lease after five years (by which time the sanctuary would need further improvements) and in that time would look for a suitable new site for the sanctuary.

3. More remote 'owner' relationships

Many shareholders are truly 'silent partners' and do not attend meetings, vote in the annual general meeting or generally communicate with the organisation, even though they might own a significant percentage of a company. Providing good corporate governance is exercised, there need not be conflict arising between shareholder and organisation. When considering the potential for conflict, there are three interesting exceptions: institutional investors, the active investors (who work more closely with their investment) and the shareholder activists (which is not a cohesive group in terms of a common background but rather solely determined by their behaviour). It is these three groups that we will examine for conceivable control and ownership disputes.

a) *Institutional investors*

The institutional investors as a group are composed of mutual and pension funds and other bodies such as insurers. Institutional investors through their equity holdings have the ability to wield much power and influence in the corporate governance arena. In many mature stock markets, these investors make up the majority of large-scale share owners – indeed, such is the size of this field that it functions as a sector of business in its own right. Institutional investors in the UK are represented by a number of professional bodies that provide guidance on issues and offer proxy voting services, such as the Association of British Insurers and the National Association of Pension Funds.

Due to their size and experience, institutional investors expect a high standard of corporate governance from companies in which they hold stock. In response to this expectation, most large publicly listed companies will have an investor relations function and the more sizeable the organisation, the more sophisticated the function. Investor relations add value to this 'organisation-owner' relationship by providing a professional channel for information in both directions which can strengthen and bond the relationship. Indeed, the mere fact of having a dedicated communication channel function speaks eloquently about how seriously a company views the contribution of its institutional investors, and may itself provide reassurance that investor views are being relayed to the company secretary and board.

Added to this equation is who is at the other end of the channel: if investor relations representatives are liaising with an experienced and professional fund manager, the chances are that there will be a smooth day-to-day relationship and conflict can often be avoided. This is not to say that in certain circumstances paths and interests cannot diverge and disputes emerge. However, when they do, they are more likely to be dealt with promptly and the dispute will not tend to be exposed in the media, which as the previous chapter illustrated, can make a substantial difference to how quickly and effectively a dispute can be solved.

Case study: institutional investors

In this instance, we thought it would be useful to look at two examples of relationships between organisations and their institutional investors, one positive and one negative, as reported on the same day, 13 February 2013, in the print edition of the *Financial Times* newspaper.

First, the example of conflict:

OPPOSITION GROWS TO DELL BUYOUT DEAL

T Rowe Price, the second-largest outside shareholder in Dell, on Tuesday added its voice to the growing chorus of opposition to the proposed $24.4bn buyout of the PC maker.

It follows the protest last week from Southeastern Asset Management, the largest outside investor, and a number of smaller investors, and points to hardening in opposition to the $13.65 a share offered for the company by founder Michael Dell and private equity firm Silver Lake Partners.

'We believe the proposed buyout does not reflect the value of Dell, and we do not intend to support the offer as put forward,' said Brian Rogers, chief investment officer of T Rowe Price, in a statement.

Also on Tuesday, Southeastern revealed in a regulatory filing that it had engaged D.F. King & Co, a proxy solicitation firm, specialising in proxy contests and takeover battles, in a further sign that it would fight tooth and nail to defeat the leveraged buyout.

Dell's stock edged up further on Tuesday to reach $13.78, suggesting that Wall Street expects Mr Dell and Silver Lake to be forced to pay a slightly higher price to win backing for their deal. However, the shares still stand far below the $23.72 that Southeastern claims the company would be worth in a break-up.

T Rowe Price owns around 4.4 per cent of Dell's shares, worth nearly $1.1bn. Along with Southeastern, with a stake of 8.4 per cent, its opposition shows that an influential minority of Dell's investors has already rejected the premium that the proposed buyout represents to the company's recent beaten-down share price.

Dell last week put the premium to shareholders at 37 per cent, based on its average share price of the previous three months. However, some investors are angry that the price is still far below the $18 a share at which the shares were changing hands a year ago…

…The early skirmish that has broken out over the buyout price has set the stage for a heated campaign ahead of a shareholder vote on the plan…

And the positive example:

CLIENTS WARY DESPITE BARCLAYS' VOWS

Antony Jenkins' long-awaited restructuring plan on Tuesday received plaudits from investors and staff. But the Barclays chief executive's mantra to restore the lender's battered reputation and turn it into the 'go-to bank for all stakeholders' has yet to convince clients.

The bank's shares surged almost 9 per cent to a two-year high of 327.35p as investors praised the plan to cut costs and increase the dividend.

Dominic Rossi, chief investment officer at Fidelity Worldwide, a top 10 Barclays shareholder said: 'What's got the market reasonably excited was the specificity around the cost base. To be told that costs in 2015 will be £16.8bn… is likely to mean earnings expectations are revised upwards.'

Another top 10 shareholder said: 'The bank is trying to get the message across that it is profitable and sustainable by making big cuts to poor performing parts of the business and parts that have been considered out of control and unethical.'

Shareholders were also pleased with Mr Jenkins' pledge to lift the current dividend payout ratio of 19 per cent to 30 per cent in 2015. One investor said this 'is redressing the problem in the past that most of the profits were going to the bankers in bonuses'…

Whilst we may never know what private conversations (if any) have been conducted, through these two examples it is possible to see two important principles at work. Firstly, these reports demonstrate how conflict can arise over different and sometimes unlikely topics. They also allow us to imagine how it might be possible to ameliorate those conflicts if communication is conducted successfully.

b) Active investors (investment banks and venture capitalists)

Protecting and indeed maximising an investment is a natural instinct for an investor. The most sophisticated at maximising their investments are probably the investment banks and venture capitalists. Generally, these investors are excellent at creating and managing strong relationships which can occasionally detract from the fact that an active investor will always, at some point, be looking for the most profitable exit from that investment.

Many businesses at some point of their existence are willing to accept investment to help build their business and the relationship with the right active investor can seem like an ideal solution. At this point, sharing a percentage of ownership and even welcoming a new director onto the board, with useful experience, can appear far from being an issue. However, conditions can change, the economy weakens, the market becomes crowded, technology more advanced and new personalities come into the equation. In these circumstances, opinions can diverge and new solutions are needed. Therefore what, in a different situation, was a harmonious relationship can become fraught and contesting.

An example of this could be where the founder of an organisation (and the team they build around them) may have a certain philosophy around why they wish to serve a certain market and at a particular price point. If the active investor sees, after several years, a new opportunity or a dissipating market, they may urge or insist (depending on equity) on a new focus for the business. If this focus contradicts a core philosophy, then conflict may emerge and the relationship deteriorates.

Whilst disputes with active investors are possible – CEDR has helped to resolve a number of them – it should be noted that they are relatively unlikely. The reason for the scarcity of conflict is because investors are doing their job well and helping the company. This is obviously not altruism; the active investor is helping to protect their own interests in seeing the company successfully overcome difficulties it may face. Any conflict of interest is offset by the coincidental interest of making the company successful, stable and profitable.

Case study: active investors

A new technology company, working in what was a widely anticipated field, attracted successful venture capitalist (VC) investment (the VC agreed levels of funding in return for a 50% stake).

Due to the amount of attention that the area of work attracted, this start-up company was hit by a 'patent troll' lawsuit. The concept of a 'patent troll' is where another patent holder (sometimes an organisation or individual with no way of making income through regular trading) puts forward a claim against a related product or patent.

For the VC, who would in effect have to fund the legal defence, it was cheaper to just settle the claim than to fight it in court. This can unfortunately be true even when the claim is weak and the defence particularly strong. After this happened once and the VC settled the claim, a second one arrived. In this instance, the CEO said the company would fight the claim to deter future 'patent trolls' and because it was 'the right thing to do'.

It also emerged that there was a connection with this new 'troll' for the CEO which acted as a 'red rag to a bull'. Apparently, the CEO had previous experience of what he regarded as 'dishonest' behaviour by the same team behind the troll claim. For him, the patent troll's claim represented moral and ethical issues beyond the financial 'bottom line' the VC was concentrating on.

The VC had introduced a director onto the board of the company and at the next board meeting the CEO revealed that the decision had been taken to fight the claim. The director cautioned against this but the CEO could not be dissuaded. The VC director then reported back to their superiors at the VC and the message came back very clearly that fighting the claim would be wrong because (a) it was a distraction from launching the technology, (b) it would cost the VC more to go to court and (c) there would be more claims anyway because this area of technology was a crowded space.

The VC director reported this back to the CEO who responded that this was not the sort of organisation to 'back down and roll over', and the VC should be proud of this. There was a heightened disagreement between the CEO and VC. The VC was in a position where it was having to re-examine the safety and wisdom of its investment, in particular because of the unwillingness of the CEO to listen to their advice. The company therefore found itself not only in conflict with the 'patent troll' but also the VC.

In this instance, a personal connection of the parties, who was a trained neutral, was brought in to chair a series of neutral meetings between the CEO, the VC director, and the director's superior. The neutral was able to help both sides to voice their concerns and address these apprehensions, whilst managing any emotions that might derail the discussions. The conversations were an opportunity for both sides to examine the totality of their relationship and explore issues other than 'patent trolls' related to the future of the company. By the end of this flexible process, in addition to consensus on how to respond to the current and any future claims, there was agreement on a new timetable for key stages of the company's development.

c) Shareholder activists

There are distinctions that can be made between shareholder activists and interested investors, who read the company's annual report, vote when requested and attend the annual general meeting even asking appropriate questions. The activist is more likely to publicly question the contents of the annual report, campaign with other shareholders for tactical voting, or may come up with their own proposals at the AGM and seek support for them. The catalyst for creating an activist shareholder would seem to be dissatisfaction with the organisation.

So how does the process of dissatisfaction turn the interest investor to activism? Broadly, the process would appear to turn on the issue of the shareholder not feeling that their concerns have been heard. That is not to say that shareholders should not have concerns of their own and want to vocalise them, or that organisations should always accommodate them, but rather when there is an attempt to voice them there should be mutual recognition. Feeling unrecognised is what allows a spiral of dissatisfaction to turn into activism, and then frequently into open dissent or conflict.

Institutional investors – because they are often engaged with proactive investor relations teams – are generally less likely to become activist shareholders, because there is already the mechanism for a dialogue in place and so it is easier for concerns to be voiced and recognised. It is the lack of a mechanism which can spell trouble and often lead individual shareholders to feel ignored. This sense of powerlessness may encourage them to reach out for others who feel the same way and start campaigning for their objectives to be realised.

The most notable recent example of 'mass' shareholder activism has been over executive salary, or 'fat cat pay' as it was dubbed by some of the press in the UK between 2000–2010, where shareholders felt aggrieved that pay rises were given to executives of companies that were seen as failing or facing significant challenges. In these cases, the media reported that shareholders worked together to vote against pay increases (in the UK, regulations permit that shareholders should have an advisory vote on this issue).

There is an interesting subset to the 'ignored' individuals, and that is the wealthy independent shareholder. This individual frequently has the means and knowledge to start campaigning on their own and can carry with them a level of respect which means their opinion will be listened to. There is possibly no greater exemplar of this type than the tycoon Warren Buffett and his holding company Berkshire Hathaway. That is not to say that Mr Buffett gets into proportionally more disputes than other major investors, but that when he does the world takes notice, as in the instance of his dispute over the preferred share repurchase by Goldman Sachs in 2011. Mr Buffett secured a deal with Goldman Sachs Group that saw the investment bank buy back $5 billion worth of preferred stock, which Berkshire Hathaway purchased in 2008 to shore up confidence in the bank amid the tight conditions of the 'credit crunch'. The influential investor's contribution to the bank acted as an informal stamp of approval, and in a 2011 statement a Goldman Sachs spokesperson said that:

> 'Berkshire Hathaway's 2008 investment in Goldman Sachs was a major vote of confidence in our firm and we are very appreciative of it.'

Case study: shareholder activists

David Einhorn is a well-known American investor, who made his fortune as a hedge fund manager, and undertakes his investments through his company Greenlight Capital. He has been openly critical of the governance of a number of companies, including some in which he holds investment interests. At the time of writing, Mr Einhorn's investment in the technology company Apple has provoked just such a situation, and it is as yet uncertain whether or not this dispute will be played out in a courtroom. On 8 February 2013, BBC News reported online:

APPLE SUED BY DAVID EINHORN OVER CASH PILE

An activist shareholder is suing computer giant Apple, demanding that it share out more of its $137bn (£87bn) cash pile to its investors.

…US hedge fund manager, David Einhorn, who is behind the unusual move, told the television channel CNBC that Apple had a 'Depression-era' mentality, which gave it a tendency to hoard cash and play safe. Apple called the move 'misguided'…

…Mr Einhorn, who owns Green Light Capital, told CNBC: 'It has sort of a mentality of a depression. In other words, people who have gone through traumas… and Apple has gone through a couple of traumas in its history, they sometimes feel like they can never have enough cash.'

He has also been speaking to the Reuters news agency, which he told he had had meetings with Apple's senior management on the subject of sharing out the cash pile. Mr Einhorn said he had recently contacted Apple's chief executive, Tim Cook after failing to interest the company's chief financial officer, Peter Oppenheimer, in the matter.

Mr Einhorn's proposals for releasing funds to shareholders involve 'preferred' stock – which pays a fixed dividend over time. Apple is planning to eliminate these at its shareholder meeting later this month. Preferred shares rank higher than ordinary shares when it comes to paying out a company's assets.

Mr Einhorn has a history of activism. In 2011, he urged Microsoft Corp to get rid of its chief executive Steve Ballmer, accusing him of being 'stuck in the past'.

Five days after this, on 13 February 2013, the story had moved on somewhat, with the print edition of the *Financial Times* reporting the following:

APPLE CLAIMS EINHORN HOLDING INVESTORS HOSTAGE

Apple alleges that activist investor David Einhorn is attempting to hold other shareholders 'hostage' to a proposal that does not serve the 'public interest', in its response to a legal challenge by the Greenlight Capital chief executive.

> Mr Einhorn's lawsuit, filed in Manhattan last week, challenges Apple's 'bundled' vote on a corporate governance change, set for its annual meeting later this month. The effect of it would be that Apple could not issue a new class of high-yielding stock, as he has argued it should without putting it to a shareholder vote.
>
> The Apple filing to the court on Wednesday follows remarks from Tim Cook, chief executive, on Tuesday, describing the Greenlight lawsuit as a 'silly sideshow' and waste of time.
>
> 'Shareholders should not be held hostage to [Mr Einhorn's] attempts to coerce Apple into an agreement that serves plaintiffs' financial interests,' Apple said in the filing, adding: 'The proposed injunction would harm the public interest.'
>
> In his declaration to the court, Peter Oppenheimer, Apple's finance chief, said that in a conference call with himself and Mr Cook on February 6, 2013, Mr Einhorn had described the requirement for shareholder approval as a 'roadblock that was not needed'…

Here is a situation where a relationship has deteriorated to the point that its disagreement over governance had resulted effectively in dialogue through law suits. In this conversation, there are two strong opponents: on the one hand, the experienced and opinionated investor and on the other, a leading company with near-dominance in some sectors of its markets. Both sides are used to being listened to, respected and probably getting their 'way' in their dealings with others. Possibly the need to adapt their positions therefore does not occur very often and it is an area where help in doing so would be beneficial.

Added to this situation, we have the problem that the language used in this dispute, as reported by the media, is having the effect of heating up and personalising the conflict between Mr Einhorn and Apple.

At this stage, we do not know how the conflict will play out. Possibly after having staked their claims in the courts, both sides will restart a more private dialogue. This would be an ideal occasion to use a neutral to chair discussions between the sides, someone who would be able to focus them on how to work better together and avoid the expense and difficulty of litigation.

Summary

What we have seen is that the concept of ownership, as it relates to control of an organisation, can potentially generate a variety of conflicts. However, these conflicts can be managed successfully and early on if there are good, clear communication channels which will allow relationships to continue functioning effectively. Where there is a full-blown dispute, it has also hopefully been demonstrated that there are ways and means to resolve these without resorting to litigation, through the use of independent and neutral individuals and processes. Neutrals can not only help with current issues, they can also assist parties in implementing systems and processes to alleviate potential causes of future conflict.

> ### *Key points to remember*
>
> The 'agency problem' is inherent to any exploration of ownership concerns in an organisational context, and the larger the organisation, the greater the potential for agency conflicts over:
>
> - moral hazards
> - retention of earnings
> - managerial risk aversion, and
> - time horizons
>
> to arise. Allied to this, we should be aware that not only do influencing parties pay attention to the content and style of what an organisation says, they are also likely to be well attuned to what is *not* said, or what is revealed beyond the bounds of essential reporting.
>
> Typical shareholder disputes might involve:
>
> - direct owners with close relationships, such as business partners
> - direct owners who are also members of the same family
> - trustees, governors and representative directors who feel they have personal ownership of an organisation
> - remote owner relationships, such as institutional investors (e.g. pension funds)
> - active investors, such as investment banks or venture capitalists
> - activist shareholders – wealthy individuals or savvy consortiums of shareholders who seek to influence the board and the commercial direction of the organisation.

Notes

1. Andrew Cornford: 'Internationally Agreed Principles For Corporate Governance And The Enron Case', United Nations Conference on Trade and Development, G-24 Discussion Paper Series No. 30, New York, June 2004, p. 30.
2. Brian Reade, *An Epic Swindle* (Quercus, London 2011).

Appendix 1

The conflict management strategy matrix

	Perception		Using the strategies		Coping with others' use of the strategies	
	Self-perception	Possible perception of others	Use it	Avoid it	Try to…	Explore…
Avoid	Focused, busy, scared, uninterested	Scared, distracted, disinterested	Damage of confrontation would outweigh benefits of resolution	Quick action required, issue of importance and time-limited	Be persistent but gentle	When would be a good time to address this?
Accommodate	Understanding, supportive, weak, accommodating, bullied/pushed	Weak, lacking in creativity, lazy, incompetent	Giving up something in the hope of getting something in return. Unfamiliar issues, position of weakness	Issue of importance, belief that the other party is wrong	Demonstrate that you trust them to acknowledge what is best for them	Their needs and concerns
Compromise	Efficient, cooperative, bored (others are slow to agree)	Quick, unprincipled, lazy, quick-fix junkie	Consensus cannot be reached. Temporary solution required. Avoid protracted conflict.	Complex issue that needs problem-solving approach	Explain concerns that need resolving before agreement	Their motives and time-constraints
Compete	Strong, assertive, misunderstood, criticised	Strong, obstinate, aggressive. Don't understand this person	Dealing with routine matters. Implementation of unpopular course of action	Complex issue and sufficient time to make decision. Parties have equal power – deadlock.	Be assertive. Choose words carefully	Their motives and give your own
Collaborate	Creative, cooperative, unsupported, dumped on, unappreciated	Creative, over-complicated, meddling	Complex problems, long-range planning, strategies/issues relating to organisation's objectives and policies	Quick decision required, simple task, others unconcerned about outcome	Acknowledge their motives. Set clear boundaries	Their time-frame and clarify your own

Appendix 2

SWOT analysis template

Strengths, Weaknesses, Opportunities and Threats Matrix

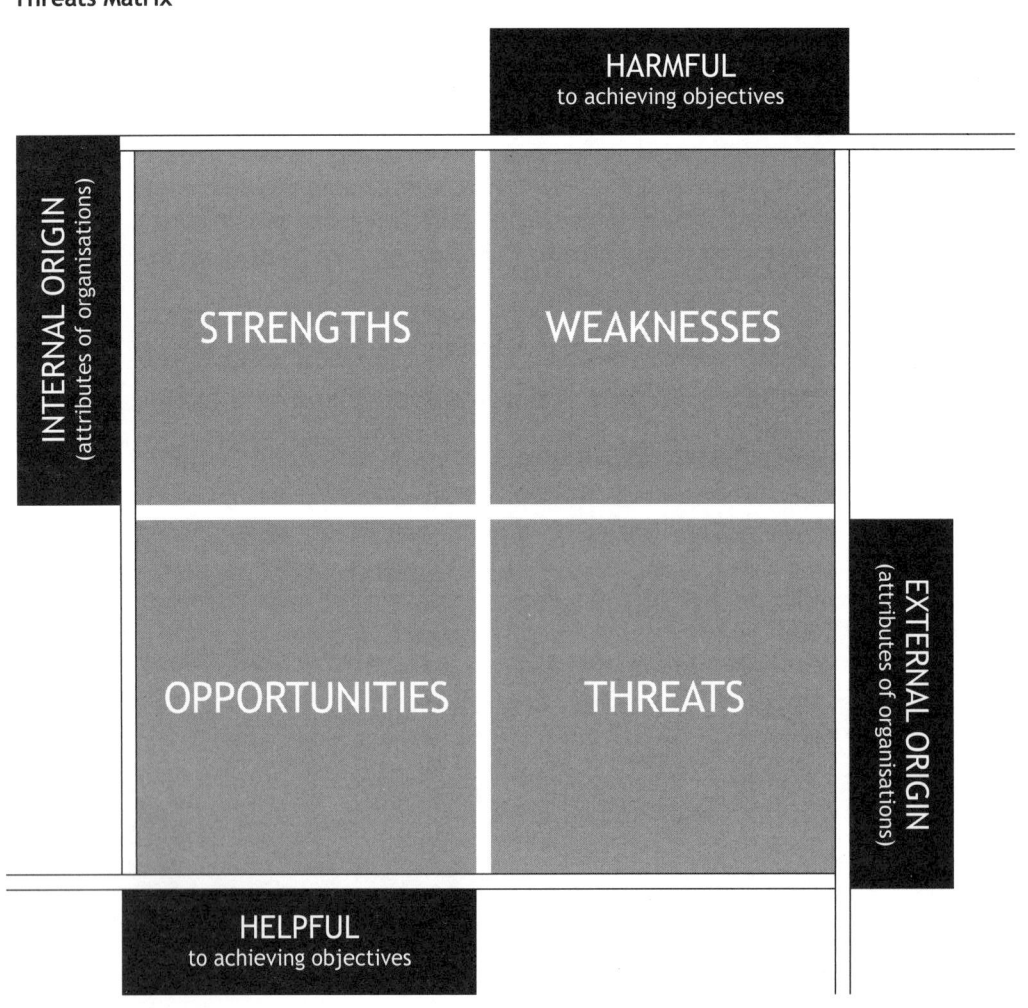

	HELPFUL to achieving objectives	**HARMFUL** to achieving objectives
INTERNAL ORIGIN (attributes of organisations)	STRENGTHS	WEAKNESSES
EXTERNAL ORIGIN (attributes of organisations)	OPPORTUNITIES	THREATS

Bibliography

Primary research

CEDR and ICSA 'Good Conflict Management' survey, 2012
CEDR, C. I. (2008). *'Conflicting Priorities: reputation matters'*
CEDR (2010) 'Tough Times, Tough Talk' survey, (see Web directory for link)
Fulbright & Jaworski (2005) 'Litigation Trends Survey'
BDO Stoy Hayward (2003) 'Commercial Disputes Survey'
Roffey Park 'Management Agenda 2004' survey

Printed resources

The CEDR Mediator Handbook (5th Edition), 2010
The Firefly guide to crisis management, Concise OED, 11th Edition (Revised), ed. Catherine Soanes and Angus Stevenson (OUP 2008, 2009)
Toolkit 4: Resolving Corporate Governance Disputes, 'Volume 1: Rationale', Global Corporate Governance Forum/IFC (ed. James Spellman) (Maryland, 2011)
Abramson, H (2004) *Mediation representation: Advocating in a Problem-Solving Process* (Notre Dame: NITA)
Bazerman, D and Malhotra, M (2007) *Negotiation Genius: How to Overcome Obstacles and Achieve Brilliant Results at the Bargaining Table and Beyond* (New York: Bantam Dell)
Berle, Adolph A and Means, GC (1991) *The Modern Corporation and Private Property* (2nd Revised edition) (New Jersey: Transaction Publications)
Brown, Henry and Marriott, Arthur (2011) *ADR: Principles and Practice* 3rd Edition (London: Sweet & Maxwell)
Carroll, Eileen and Mackie, Karl (2006) *International Mediation – The Art of Business Diplomacy* (2nd Edition) (Wiltshire: Tottel Publishing)
Cialdini, Robert B (2007) *Influence: the Psychology of Persuasion* (New York: Collins Business (HarperCollins))

BIBLIOGRAPHY

Clacher, Hillier and McColgan, (2010) 'Agency Theory, Incomplete Contracting and Ownership Structure' published in *Corporate Governance, A Synthesis of Theory, Research and Practice*, Eds Baker and Anderson (John Wiley & Sons)

Eisenhart, KM, Jean L Kahwajy, and Bourgeois, LJ (1997) 'How management teams can have a good fight', Harvard Business Review

Fama, Eugene (1980) 'Agency problems and the theory of the firm', *Journal of Political Economy* 88

Finkelstein, S (2003) *Why smart executives fail*, reprint edition (London: Portfolio Penguin)

Fisher, R and Shapiro, D (2005) *Building Agreement* (London: Random House)

Fisher, Roger and Shapiro, Daniel (2006) *Beyond Reason: Using Emotions as you Negotiate* (London: Random House)

Fisher, R, Ury, W, and Patton, B (2012). *Getting to Yes: Negotiating Agreement Without Giving In* (New York: Random House)

Gladwell, Malcolm (2006) *Blink: The Power of Thinking Without Thinking* (London: Penguin)

Grossman, Andy (2009) *Good Practice Guide: Mediation* (London: RIBA Publishing)

Harridge-March, S (2006) Can the building of trust overcome consumer perceived risk online? *Marketing Intelligence and Planning*, 746–761

Hayashi, A (2001) 'When to Trust Your Gut'. In *Harvard Business Review on Decision Making* (pp. 169–187). Cambridge, MA: Harvard Business School Press.

Heffernan, Margaret (2011) *Wilful Blindness: why we ignore the obvious at our peril* (London: Simon and Schuster)

Hyde, Gillian and Trickey, Geoff (2009) *A Decade of the Dark Side: fighting our demons at work* (Tunbridge Wells: Psychological Consultancy Limited)

Jensen, Michael and Meckling, William (1976) *'Theory of the firm: Managerial behaviour, agency costs and ownership structure'* (*Journal of Financial Economics, 3*, pp. 305–360)

Larson, C, and LaFasto, F. (1989) *TeamWork: What Must Go Right/What Can Go Wrong* (Newbury Park: Sage Publications)

Lewicki, R (2006) Trust, Trust Development, and Trust Repair. In M Deutch, and P Coleman, *The Handbook of Conflict Resolution* (pp. 86–107) (San Fransisco, CA: Jossey-Bass)

Massie, Graham (2007) 'Conflicting Priorities – best practice in conflict management' in *Managing Business Risk* (4th Edition) ed. Jonathan Reuvid (London: Kogan Page and Contributors)

Merrill, David WRH (1981) *Personal Styles and Effective Performance* (London: CRC Press)

Mnookin, R (2000) *Beyond Winning: Negotiating to Create Value in Deals and Disputes* (Cambridge: Belknap Press)

Needle, David (2004) Business In Context [holder 5th Edn]

Reade, Brian (2011) An Epic Swindle (London: Quercus)

Seligman, Martin EP (2003) *Authentic Happiness* (London: Nicholas Brealey Publishing)

Shell, GR (1999) *Bargaining for Advantage* (New York: Penguin Books)

Shleifer, Andrei and Vishny, Robert (1989) 'Management entrenchment', *Journal of Financial Economics* 25

Solomon, J (2007) *Corporate Governance and Accountability* (John Wiley & Sons)
Ury, W (2007) *Getting Past No: Negotiating With Difficult People* (New York: Random House)

Newspaper editions

Financial Times 13 February 2013
BBC News Online 8 February 2013
Reuters Online Edition, 18 March 2011 (http://www.reuters.com/article/2011/03/18/us-goldman-berkshire-idUSTRE72H6IY20110318)
The Independent 14 October 2010

Academic papers

Bornstein, RF, Leone, DR and Galley, DJ (1987) 'The generalizability of subliminal mere exposure effects: Influence of stimuli perceived without awareness on social behaviour', 53 *Journal of Personality and Social Psychology* 1070

Cornford, A (2004) *Internationally Agreed Principles For Corporate Governance And The Enron Case*, United Nations Conference on Trade and Development, G-24 Discussion Paper Series No. 30, New York, June 2004, p. 30

Dalgleish, T (2007) 'The emotional brain', in *Nature Reviews Neuroscience, v5 issue 7*, July 2007 (print ed.), Nature publishing group (http://www-psych.stanford.edu/~knutson/ans/dalgleish04.pdf) retrieved 13 January 2013

Web directory

Conflict Prevention & Resolution (CPR), 'CPR's ADR Pledge': www.cpradr.org
CEDR: 'Tough Times, Tough Talk' survey, 2010: http://www.cedr.com/docslib/Tough_Talk_Tough_Times.pdf
European Commission: Commission Staff Working Document: Report on cross-border e-commerce in the EU February 2009: http://ec.europa.eu/consumers/strategy/docs/com_staff_wp2009_en.pdf retrieved 19 December 2012
European Corporate Governance institute: http://www.ecgi.org/codes/documents/cadbury.pdf
HMRC: http://www.hmrc.gov.uk
Kluwer Mediation Blog: http://kluwermediationblog.com/2012/06/16/confrontation-or-conciliation-does-science-have-the-answer
National Audit Office and Audit Commission *A review of collaborative procurement across the public sector*, May 2010 retrieved 17 October 2012: http://www.nao.org.uk/publications/0910/collaborative_procurement.aspx
New Scientist: Helen Phillips, 'Introduction: the Human Brain' taken from *New Scientist*, September 2006: http://www.newscientist.com/article/dn9969-introduction-the-human-brain.html?full=true retrieved 15 January 2013
Padgett Business Service: Padgett's SmallBizPros Marketing Manual (Published online, last revised March 2009, www.smallbizpros.com)
Department of Psychology, Stanford University: http://www-psych.stanford.edu/~knutson/ans/dalgleish04.pdf

Index

Active listening 22, 44
    skills spectrum 45
Adapting to a changing world 103–105
ADR clause in conduct 115–120
    assessing risks of not settling 119–120
    choosing right mediator 118
    commercial sense to settle 120
    containing contagion 116–117
    dispute 115–116
    effects of disputes 117–118
    exploring issues 118–119
ADR Pledge 112–114
    building mediation into projects 111
    cost 104
    creating culture of 108
    drafting clauses 107–108
        how 107
        what 107
        when 108
        which rules 108
        who 107
    EDF Energy 113–114
    E.ON Group 110
    flexibility 105
    implementing contract clauses 109
    model clauses 105
Avoiding boardroom warfare 35–57

Board disputes
    remedying 35–57
Board members
    disputes between 12
Board of directors
    breakdown of relationships 16
    company secretary, and 16–17
    early stage intervention 15–16
    fall-outs 16
    involvement in employment and workplace
        disputes 15–17
    market impact of disputes 18
    personal disputes 18–20
    tensions 16
    types of disputes 16
Boardroom warfare 35–37
    active listening 44
    administrative processes 37–38
    adopting collaborative tone 43–44
    allow 'feelings' conversation to take place 45
    asking open questions 45
    be aware of peacemakers 40
    clarity of purpose of meetings/discussions 43
    common clauses 38–39
    consider how to handle personality issues 43
    embrace idea of dispute resolution 39
    exploration 44

INDEX

Boardroom warfare *continued*
    faith in ADR processes and techniques 41
    formal corporate governance disputes policy 40
    IFC/GCGF checklist 38
    key process and skills for dealing with 41
    monitor successes and areas for development 41
    opening meeting 43
    organisational tools for resolving 39
    people 37
    preparation 42
    problem solving 46
    process 37
    reasons for 37
    record agreement and agree follow-up 47
    remedying: checklist 47–48
    setting agenda 43
    think about process 43
    toolkit for individuals 41
    tools for handling 56
    tools for resolving 39
    understand content of dispute 42
    understand interests rather than focusing on positions 44
    'what if' game 39
Boardrooms
    incubator of conflict 35–36
    potential for dispute 35
Brain in conflict situations 60–61
Broken trust among trustees 28–34
    background information 28
    deciding way forward 33–34
    dispute 28–29
    handling dispute 29–30
    issues to consider 30–31
    meeting board of trustees 32–33
    meeting with each side 31–32
    mission drift 30
    political awareness 31
    reporting back to chief executive 33
    wider audience 31
Business communication scenarios 126–127
    both sides culpable in mistake 126
    one side in the wrong 126
    something untoward, outside anyone's control 126–127
Business disputes
    possible consequences 2
Business structures
    emotional turbulence, and 66

Centre for Effective Dispute Resolution (CEDR)
    Good Conflict Management survey 10–13
    role 1
CEDR mediation phase model 42
CEDR project mediation protocol 111–112
CEO, managing exit 83–89
    access to information 86
    age 85
    dispute 83–84
    expectations of power 85
    expectations of respect 85
    how to act sensitively 86
    identity 84–85
    learning points 88–89
    managing factors 87–88
    outcome of mediation 88
    special considerations 84
    who to mediate 86
Chief executive 20–21
Common sense 1–13
Company secretary
    access to information, and 73
    advice for 5
    board disputes, and 16–17
    board procedures, and 59
    confidentiality 15
    conflicting priorities 1–13
    corporate diplomat, as 14–15
    corporate ethics, custodian of 17
    enhancing role 27–28
    executive coaches, and 72
    external neutrals, and 72–73
    interpersonal levels of support 59
    interventions by 20
    key role 14–15
    key skills 22–24

management of turbulent emotions 68
ministers without portfolio 17
natural negotiator, as 19
negotiator, as 21–22
process, and 72
quasi-legal role 19
relationships, and 72
remuneration disputes, and 20–22
response 72–73
role 58
role in managing emotions 59
sidebar conversations 72
support 14
trusted and neutral adviser, as 18
types 15
web of influences 152
who is 58
Conflict
 attitudes to 11
 cost of 2–3
 universal condition 1–2
Conflict management
 focus 8
 options 9
Conflict management skills 24–26
 confidentiality 24–25
 difficult conversations 24–25
 emotions, dealing with 25–26
 explaining 25
 exploring issues 25
 identifying 25
 timing 24–25
Conflict management strategy matrix 172–173
Conflict, science of 59
Conflict styles 68
 accommodating 69
 adapting 70
 avoiding 69
 collaborating 69
 competing 69
 compromising 69
Consumer complaints 136–137
Corporate ethics
 company secretary, and 17

Crisis situations 26–28
Critical projects 103–120

Damaged relationships 3
Difference of opinion 13
Disciplinary matters
 disputes on 19
Dispute resolution
 contract clause 8
Disputes
 records 10–11
Distraction cost 4
Dynamics affecting communication with
  stakeholders 127–132
 amiable (passive-emotional) 130
 analytical (passive-intellectual) 130–131
 communicating internationally 131–132
 driver (aggressive-intellectual) 129
 environmental factors 131–132
 expressive (aggressive-emotional) 129–130
 personality types 127
 social factors 127

Early stage intervention
 costs, and 15–16
Earnings retention conflict 153
EDF Energy
 ADR focused change management
  113–114
Emotion
 behaviour impacts 63
 difficult reactions 64
 evolution vs employment 64
 meaning 60
 negative 63
 neurological effects 62
 physical impacts 62
 positive 62–63
 recognition of experience 64
 reflection on symptoms 64
 response in measured way 65
 thinking impacts 62–63
Emotional contagion 61
Emotional intelligence 70

INDEX

Emotional turbulence
    business structures, and 66
    importance of 70
    meaning 70
Emotions, dealing with 25–26
Exposure, effect of 61
External stakeholders and clients 121–150 *see also* Stakeholder conflict

Faith in ADR processes and techniques 41
Familiarity principle 61
Family boardroom fall-out 48–56
    balancing retribution versus risk 54–55
    beginning restoration of family relationship 52–53
    betrayal, dealing with 52–53
    breakdown of family relationships 51
    dispute 48–49
    distribution to board's focus on improving business 50
    divergent interests 50
    elements of dispute needing addressing 50
    impact of dispute on company 49
    letting people tell their story 52
    loss of status and control 50–51
    managing tough negotiation on both sides 53–54
    mediation, benefit of 51–52
    paralysed decision-making 49
    poor staff morale 49
    reputation 50
    sense of professional identity 50
    wanting justice/retribution 51
Family business 158–160
Fight, flight, freeze 65
Fisher and Shapiro 94–97
    affiliation 96
    appreciation 94
    autonomy 96
    Building Agreement 94–97
    five core concerns 95
    role 97
    status 96–97
Formal corporate governance disputes policy 40

Governing bodies of company
    interaction among 36
Grievance matters
    disputes on 19

Handling high emotions 74–81
    analysis 75
    approach to problematic relationships 79
    dispute 74–75
    ex-directors 77–78
    mediator's tactics 79–80
    problems facing mediator 78–79
    resolution 80–81
    suppliers 75–76
Hogan Development Scale 70–71
Heathrow T5 106–107
Hierarchy of needs 67
High emotion
    handling see Handling high emotions

ICSA
    Good Conflict Management survey 10–13
Institutional investors 163–165
Interpersonal rapport 22

James-Lange theory 60

Key skills 22–24

Lack of communication 13
Language of disputes 9–10
Leadership crisis 26
Limbic system 61
Lost productivity 4

Managerial risk aversion 153–154
Managing emotional turbulence 58–82
Market impact of disputes 18
Mediation 6
    benefits 6,7
    building into projects 111
    core management techniques, as 8
    design of systems 8
    key features 7

negotiation process 7
savings 7
Merrill-Reid Model of social styles 128
Mind into matter 62
Moral hazard conflict 153

Navigation 24
Needs triangle 66
Negotiation skills 22
Negotiations
    company secretary, and 21–22

Objectivity 22
Ownership, conflict over 151–171
    active investors 166–167
    agency problem 153
    disputes, examples of 155–170
    essential information 154–155
    family business 158–160
    governors 160–163
    institutional investors 163–165
    investment banks 166
    more remote 'owner' relationships 163
    non-owner ownerships 160
    openness 155
    owners with vested relationships 156
    partners 156–158
    potential for 151–171
    representative directorships 160–163
    shareholder activities 167–170
    tone 155
    trustees 160–163
    two levels of dialogue 154
    types of shareholders 155–170
    venture capitalists 166

Partners 156–158
Pay
    disputes on 20–22
Peacemakers
    awareness of 40
Performance
    disputes on 19
Powerful people 83–102

dealing with present 94
dispute context 83–102
disputes, and
    eight points to success 100–102
    managing emotions 94
    preparation 90–93 *see also* Preparation
Preparation 90–93
    actions 93
    aspiration level 92
    BATNA 90–91
    concessions 92–93
    criteria 91
    information 92
    SWOT 92
Proactive conflict management 27
Problem-solving 24, 46
    consider risks of not reaching agreement 46–47
    generate options before evaluating 46
    manage negotiations actively 46
    pull back when stuck 46
Procedures
    perpetuating disputes 19
Professional negligence 134–135
Project mediation 111–112
Projected success 103–120
Protocols of disputes 9–10
Psychology of organisational conflict 58–82

Questioning 22

Reconciling science and society 64–65
Regulatory disputes 137–138
Remuneration
    chief executive 20–21
    disputes on 20–22
Remuneration committees 21
Reputation 121–122

Sensibility 1–13
Shared needs 66
Shareholder activists 167–170
Stakeholder conflict 121–150
    audiences 123–124

Stakeholder conflict *continued*
   business customers 133
   commercial partners 124–125
   consumer complaints 136–137
   dynamics affecting communication with stakeholders 127–132
   environment 141
   governance 140
   handling 123, 132
   interested external parties 125
   invested stakeholders 124
   inviting 'the world outside' into a dispute 142–149
      intrinsic case 144–147
      reaching a settlement 147–148
      resolution 148–149
   one-off complaints 135–136
   preventing 123, 124–125
   professional negligence 134–135
   regulatory disputes 137–138
   reputation, and 121
   suppliers and partners 133–134
   supply of goods and services 133
   two approaches to 122
   working in a vacuum 125
Summarising 24
SWOT analysis template 174

Tarnished reputations 3
Tax disputes
   effective resolution of 138–140
Thomas-Kilmann Emotional Intelligence Questionnaire 70
Third-party neutrals
   use of 6
Time horizon conflict 154
Trust 97–100
   active first step 99
   breakdown 97–100
   meaning 97
   rebuilding 97–100

Well-managed conflict
   effects 4–5